Volume 17

Advances in
Librarianship

Volume 17

Advances in
Librarianship

Edited by

Irene P. Godden

University Libraries
Colorado State University
Fort Collins, Colorado

ACADEMIC PRESS, INC.
A Division of Harcourt Brace & Company
San Diego New York Boston London Sydney Tokyo Toronto

Academic Press, Inc.
525 B Street, Suite 1900, San Diego, California 92101-4495

United Kingdom Edition published by
Academic Press Limited
24–28 Oval Road, London NW1 7DX

International Standard Serial Number: 0065-2849

International Standard Book Number: 0-12-024617-1

PRINTED IN THE UNITED STATES OF AMERICA
93 94 95 96 97 98   BC   9 8 7 6 5 4 3 2 1

Contents

Contributors   ix
Preface   xi

Information Specialists and the Cooperative Workplace: Challenges and Opportunities
Terence K. Huwe

    I. Introduction   1
   II. Reference as an Information Alliance   3
  III. Collaboration: Guidance for Alliance Building   5
  IV. Viewpoints on Information in Organizations   10
   V. Rethinking the Information Alliance   14
  VI. Information Alliances in Two Settings   18
 VII. Summary and Conclusions   26
     References   27

Ownership versus Access: Shifting Perspectives for Libraries
Joel S. Rutstein, Anna L. DeMiller, and Elizabeth A. Fuseler

    I. Introduction: The "New Paradigm"   33
   II. The Changing Pattern of Collection Development   34
  III. Scholarship, Information Dissemination, and Publishing   40
  IV. Impact of Copyright Law on the Electronic Environment   44
   V. Impact of the Electronic Environment on Libraries   47
  VI. Conclusion   56
     References   58

Access to Electronic Information: Exploring the Options
William Gray Potter

    I. Introduction   61
   II. Background   61

III. Developments in Computer Systems   62
IV. Types of Databases   63
V. Alternatives for Access to Electronic Databases   65
VI. Selecting the Best Method of Access   66
VII. The University of Georgia   70
VIII. Conclusion   75
References   76

Research Libraries: Past, Present, and Future
Norman D. Stevens

I. Introduction   79
II. A Definition   82
III. The Past   83
IV. The Present   87
V. The Future   94
VI. A Final Comment   106
References   107

The Online Catalog: From Technical Services to Access Service
Barbara A. Norgard, Michael G. Berger, Michael Buckland, and Christian Plaunt

I. Introduction   111
II. Problems   113
III. Users   120
IV. Solutions   123
V. Conclusions   136
References   139

Electronic Journals: A Formidable Challenge for Libraries
Margo Sassé and B. Jean Winkler

I. Introduction   149
II. Definitions   150
III. History   153
IV. Current State of Scholarly Electronic Journals   155
V. Bibliographic and Patron Access   158
VI. Issues and Concerns   162
VII. Projects in Progress   167
VIII. Future   168

IX. Library Trends   170
     References   170

Output Measures for Evaluating the Performance of Community College Learning Resources Programs: A California Case Study
Tobin de Leon Clarke and Elmer U. Clawson

   I. Introduction   175
  II. Standards and Guidelines for Evaluating the Performance of
      Community College Libraries and Learning Resource Centers
      in California: A Historical Perspective   179
 III. Developing Output Measures for California Community
      Colleges: The Present Study   184
  IV. Analysis of the Data   188
   V. Discussion of the Data   193
  VI. Summary and Conclusions   197
      Appendix: A Brief Description of the Twelve
      Output Measures   198
      References   201

New Patterns for Scholarly and Business Communication in Denmark
Helge Clausen

   I. Introduction   203
  II. The Library and Information Sector in Denmark   205
 III. A Delphi Study   212
  IV. Information and Communication in Denmark in
      the 1990s   215
   V. Conclusion   222
      References   223

The International Federation of Library Associations and Institutions and the United States: What Happens Next?
Nancy R. John

   I. Introduction   225
  II. What is the IFLA?   226
 III. U.S. Involvement in IFLA   230
  IV. The International Scene Today   235
   V. The Future   236

VI. Conclusion   242
    Appendix: United States Objectives for Participation
    within IFLA   243
    References   245

Index   247

Contributors

Numbers in parentheses indicate the pages on which the authors' contributions begin.

Michael G. Berger (111), School of Library and Information Sciences, University of California, Berkeley, Berkeley, California 94720

Michael Buckland (111), School of Library and Information Sciences, University of California, Berkeley, Berkeley, California 94720

Tobin de Leon Clarke (175), San Joaquin Delta Community College, Stockton, California 95207

Helge Clausen (203), State and University Library, DK-8000 Århus, Århus, Denmark

Elmer U. Clawson (175), School of Education, University of the Pacific, Stockton, California 95207

Anna L. DeMiller (33), University Libraries, Colorado State University, Fort Collins, Colorado 80523

Elizabeth A. Fuseler (33), University Libraries, Colorado State University, Fort Collins, Colorado 80523

Terence K. Huwe (1), Institute of Industrial Relations Library, University of California, Berkeley, Berkeley, California 94720

Nancy R. John (225), University Library, University of Illinois at Chicago, Chicago, Illinois 60680

Barbara A. Norgard (111), School of Library and Information Sciences, University of California, Berkeley, Berkeley, California 94720

Christian Plaunt (111), School of Library and Information Sciences, University of California, Berkeley, Berkeley, California 94720

William Gray Potter (61), University Libraries, University of Georgia, Athens, Georgia 30602

Joel S. Rutstein (33), University Libraries, Colorado State University, Fort Collins, Colorado 80523

Margo Sassé (149), University Libraries, Colorado State University, Fort Collins, Colorado 80523

Norman D. Stevens (79), University Libraries, University of Connecticut, Storrs, Connecticut 06268

B. Jean Winkler (149), University Libraries, Colorado State University, Fort Collins, Colorado 80523

Preface

New roles for librarians and other information professionals and new goals and new directions for libraries are the themes that tie together the topics covered in the 1993 volume of *Advances in Librarianship*, Vol. 17.

In his chapter, Huwe advocates a role shift for the profession, positing that collaborative reference services create information alliances by combining shared analytical skills and previously fragmented knowledge, thus creating added value. Huwe presents two models of effective collaboration between librarians and other professionals, one in law libraries and the other in academic libraries.

Major issues associated with the shift from library ownership of publications to libraries providing access to published information regardless of location or ownership are reviewed in the chapter by Rutstein, DeMiller, and Fuseler. Specifically, they address changing patterns in scholarly publishing, copyright issues, the impacts of a new electronic environment on users, staff, budgets, and long-range considerations.

Potter explores the many options facing libraries in planning to provide user-friendly as well as cost-effective access to electronic information. This chapter covers the technological developments that make the present plethora of options possible and lists the factors that need to be considered as part of any planning process.

Changes in direction for research libraries, both present and projected, are discussed in the chapter by Stevens from his vantage point as a longtime director of a Northern American research library. Evolutionary as well as revolutionary developments in such key components of library services as the catalog and access to published journal literature are addressed by Norgard and co-authors, who present a major review of the research and development concerning online catalogs. Sassé and Winkler analyze the challenges, especially in the areas of bibliographic control and user access, faced by libraries working to integrate electronic journal access into more conventional modes of information dissemination.

Developing methodology for outcome assessment has become mandatory for educational institutions, including libraries and learning centers, as governing bodies increasingly stress accountability. de Leon Clarke and Clawson present a case study, "Output Measures for Evaluating the Performance of Community College Learning Resources Programs," that provides valuable details on the practical and political processes involved in developing and gaining acceptance for a comprehensive set of measures. This chapter provides a valuable addition to the literature and will be especially useful for those beginning or refining the assessment process, be it in or beyond the community college audience.

"New Patterns for Scholarly and Business Communication in Denmark" are discussed by Clausen, who reports on a Danish delphi study, which was designed to predict future developments in the use of information technology in everyday life as well as in science and business. The implications of Clausen's findings go beyond Denmark, affecting the European Economic Community (EEC), where plans for a Pan-European integrated system of information provision are under way, and beyond the EEC for national and regional network designers in general.

More international connections are advocated by John, whose chapter covers the history of United States involvement in the International Federation of Library Associations, stressing an action plan for the future that would broaden the involvement of the United States library and information professional community.

When I became editor of *Advances in Librarianship*, one of my goals was to return the publication of this serial to an annual basis so that thoughtful analysis of current issues could be brought before the profession while they were of maximum use. I am pleased to present the current volume as a step toward meeting that goal.

Irene P. Godden

Information Specialists and the Cooperative Workplace: Challenges and Opportunities

Terence K. Huwe
Institute of Industrial Relations Library
University of California, Berkeley
Berkeley, California 94720

I. Introduction

Speculation about future trends in libraries is a risky endeavor. This is particularly true when change is driven by technological development. Yet speculation serves a purpose nonetheless, as librarians adjust to ongoing change, especially technological change. As the workplace evolves and work styles adjust to new technology, foresight can help us seize opportunities for innovation.

This chapter celebrates speculation and its hazards. It is an expansion of an essay that won the First Place prize in the 1991 Dow Jones/News Retrieval® Professional Researcher Essay Contest. This annual call is addressed to members of the Special Libraries Association, and its topics address issues of interest to corporate librarians whose organizations have expanded, restructured, "downsized," and "outsourced" over time. The 1991 topic was: *The need for information plays a vital role in keeping up with today's fast-paced business environment. What do you see as the role of the information professional over the next five years?*

The temptation to think ahead was particularly acute in 1991, since several new theories about the interplay of information technology and worker productivity were emerging at the time. It was interesting that some of the leading theorists were not examining libraries and library research, although enterprising special librarians were taking increasingly innovative steps to promote library skill. At the same time, academic librarians were beginning to take collaborative roles to administer expanded information services at research universities.

The 1991 paper called for collaborative alliances between librarians and knowledge workers outside of libraries, drawing on the theories of informa-

1

tion technologist Michael Schrage (1990a,b, 1992). Schrage's study of human interaction with high technology suggests that collaborative, interpersonal communication is a vital link for effective knowledge management. Schrage's analysis echoed remarkably the trend in libraries to merge technical skills using networked information with the reference skills traditionally performed at reference desks. The paper drew an analogy between Schrage's emphasis on interpersonal communication and technological innovation and reference interviewing using both traditional resources and new, networked information resources. In making this argument, the following ideas were advanced:

1. Knowledge—organized information, in every conceivable format—is stored in fragments. Reference connects the fragments, and the reference product has added value, because the librarian analyzes a multitude of sources while searching for the best answers.

2. Management researchers are exploring work styles that foster teamwork across departmental boundaries. However, when management researchers think about fragmented information and technological solutions to access, they overlook reference skill, because they are ignorant of the successful collaboration already occurring between librarians and specialists (Koenig, 1992).

3. Reference skill creates information alliances, pulling together shared analytical skills among diverse staff. When reference is effective, it improves productivity. As information technologies make retrieval increasingly complex or foreign to other specialists, effective reference becomes a collaborative, high-technology skill, because the librarian moves between various media to find answers.

4. Collaboration with influential staff outside the library sphere is necessary to bring library skill into the organizational mainstream.

This study expands upon the paper presented to Dow/Jones News Retrieval, using Schrage's ideas about "relationship management" and "new technologies of collaboration" as starting points to examine the ways that librarians can use reference skill in evolving organizational settings. Management research about organizations will be examined to show how alliances can shape the future role of the information specialist, drawing primarily on Schrage's theory of collaboration.

Two examples of effective collaboration already under way will be provided as a test of the theory. The first is the delivery of reference in private law firm libraries, and the second is possible, collaborative roles for reference in academic libraries. The examples will demonstrate that reference is an interpersonal skill that should be considered in management theory, and that librarians should collaborate in the development of information systems, particularly as networked information technologies become more accessible.

II. Reference as an Information Alliance

A. "What Were You Hoping to Find?"

Reference interviewing has always been an invitation to the researcher to turn a problem on its side and look at it with new eyes. When the librarian draws out the questioner by saying something like "What were you hoping to find?" shared space is created. This interviewing skill is the basis of public service in the profession. Effective reference librarians know they must help their patrons reframe their information needs to understand what is really needed.

The ability to help others define what they need to know is not taught widely. For example, a doctor might excel at diagnosis in clincial settings, but avoid the same intuitive and analytical approach when investigating investment opportunities or financial conditions. Reference librarians on the other hand enter new domains of knowledge as confident navigators. In both business and academic settings, this ability saves time for others, if they know to seek it out.

Information systems, including both online databases and in-house management information systems, tend to remove human interaction from search processes when the systems are extended to users who do not know their full capabilities (Schrage, 1990a,b). This eliminates an opportunity for shared understanding to be established, as it would be at a reference desk. Information technologists who do not consider the organic nature and two-way dialogue that characterizes information searches have not been designing systems that reflect users' search strategies; the reservoir of knowledge about search strategies lies in the library domain.

Since 1990, Schrage has been studying emerging technologies of collaboration. The goal he proposes is to make information technology mirror human interaction, rather than impose regimentation. Library thinking about reference interviewing is remarkably analogous to his conclusions. For example, human beings engaged in conversation can quickly establish agreed-upon strategies; this is the first step in an information search. Circulated reports that summarize unwanted data, or databases that do not allow users to search using their native intuitions, are electronic obstacles that block successful searches. Reference librarians who can build shared understandings are aware of this; they have already created cross-departmental strategies for filling information needs, and they can communicate this skill to the searcher. Librarians are also aware that internal information such as financial reports and client data is just as important as outside data. Special librarians in particular have been leading advocates in the overall integration of information systems.

Reference is a fundamentally collaborative activity that is not studied widely outside the library profession, but within the library domain, reference expertise guides systems development (Feng and Weise, 1988). Reference also clarifies communication, enabling specialists to share special knowledge. These qualities make reference expertise potentially valuable both in strategic planning and in the introduction of new information systems.

B. Management's Lost Skill Group

Management literature about information technology and information systems is directed at executives and nonlibrary information managers. These groups think about information as an internal resource (McKinnon and Bruns, 1992) or even a commodity (Roszak, 1986). At the same time, library literature offers compelling ideas about the uses of reference (and retrieval skills) as a strategic resource, but this literature is not mentioned or referred to by management. It is likely that managers miss it altogether.

Library and information science literature has examined the interplay between information services and productivity, and Koenig (1992) has carefully evaluated this literature and its message to managers. He finds that information services (particularly as provided by libraries) are "underrecognized" and "underinvested," and that in scattered research areas, the relationship between expert information services and productivity is slowly being discovered. Yet while management's theorizing flows into the library's conceptual world, a two-way interchange between library researchers and management researchers does not occur in a meaningful way. Koenig's recent research (1991, 1992) confirms the need for promotion of library skill. The means of successful promotion is the formulation or reformulation of alliances.

Librarians are trained to embark on information searches across conceptual boundaries and to assist people in identifying what answers they most need. Online reference techniques have brought speed and effectiveness to this work, but the interchange is still fundamentally interpersonal and intuitive. Heavy users of libraries are aware of this; they rely on reference librarians, even if only for brief consultations (Whitlach, 1990). Reference librarians analyze unclear communication for a living, as they locate knowledge and provide guidance to patrons. Data processors and information systems managers in business have not usually assumed this role, except by default. Bauwens (1993) argues that corporate libraries should be "client-centred" and "process oriented" to respond to the ongoing trivialization of expert information services by midlevel managers. He also advocates the dispersal of library staff into offices, and a new name that captures the potential of wide area networking, "cybrarians."

Bauwens's approach illustrates that it will be up to librarians to convince management that their skills in reference, retrieval, and management of knowledge resources have a role in the increasingly automated workplace. This is not a new idea, yet emerging theories about teamwork and technological change require a new emphasis on alliances with influential groups who map strategic planning and manage information technology. Teamwork may assist librarians, since teamwork reveals the skill of persons who improve productivity beyond their home departments.

III. Collaboration: Guidance for Alliance Building

Schrage's two theories (1990b) outline intriguing new ways for information technology to be used. They form the basis of the call for greater collaboration set forth in this article. These theories are important for librarians because they emphasize informal alliances between people, and the impact of these alliances on the quality and style of work.

A. "Relationship" Management, Not Information Management

Schrage (1990b) has been writing and speaking about a new approach to information technology, which he calls "relationship management." The basic premise of relationship management is that information technology should mimic informal human communication rather than demand conformity to set arrays of options. Schrage argues that information technology tends to hinder communication and the informal meeting of minds; he believes that informal communication, ranging from notes to conversations by water coolers, is the preferred means of building shared understandings. He is echoed by others in this criticism; McKinnon and Bruns (1992) have studied the ways that managers avoid management information systems altogether to do their work, despite substantial planning and investment in the new systems.

Existing systems for management information have not increased productivity as much as was hoped for, even though the electronic medium itself is highly flexible and could be configured differently to boost productivity (Schrage, 1990a). Schrage says that "systems that are designed to support relationships need to be different than systems that are designed to support information" (1992). Systems designers are not being flexible in their thinking about how people use information systems; they lack the flexibility that reference skill requires, and they lack information about what librarians have learned in using online systems.

B. New Technologies of Collaboration

In order to create a workplace where people use technology jointly, Schrage (1990b) believes that "new technologies of collaboration" are needed. These new technologies will unleash the linked potential of people who work in teams by matching systems design to human communication styles. Just as teamwork among individuals is leading to new organizational structures, "group work" utilizing information technology to speed communication and research among individuals is gaining the attention of information technologists (Schrage, 1990b). Rather than perpetuate cycles of working separately and then comparing progress, the new technologies would create an electronic commons where everyone can watch progress occur and have input all along.

Dialogues and conferences in electronic mail services approach this model, but the technology that supports seamless, simultaneous communication in a joint space is still being researched. The systems could range from shared electronic "chalkboards" to other, less familiar "colaboratories" (Schrage, 1990b). Xerox® Corporation released a report on its first commercial application of this technology in June 1992 (Clark, 1993; Elrod et al., 1992). The product is called LiveBoard, and it utilizes an oversize screen and stylus that enables group discussants to use a computer screen as they would use a chalkboard. It also enables remote groups to access the same screen. LiveBoard substantially improves upon teleconferencing techniques by eliminating the need for discussants to read telefacsimiles while maintaining eye–camera contact; both can be achieved simultaneously by writing with the stylus while viewing other discussants. Group participants are shielded from the difficulties of the Unix operating system platform by the stylus and the LiveBoard interface. LiveBoard's initial price is $49,500, making it an expensive innovation. Yet, it reveals a possible future in which collaborative technology can link staff in a new group relationship.

Reference relationships that use this technological approach to assess research needs interactively could greatly improve the effectiveness of work, by linking discussants with knowledge resources throughout their work process. An example may be seen in the explosive growth of the Internet, where prototypes for reference in networked communities are being tested. Bulletin boards and conferences are already bringing together librarians and specialists without regard for geographic or institutional boundaries, expanding possible alliances greatly. Indeed, information service vendors who have used LiveBoard indicate that the display of information searches on the large screen have a riveting effect on audiences of researchers, yielding many questions from the floor (C. Corcan Douglas, personal communication 1993).

Elrod et al. (1992) do not assess the potential of networked information or commercial online searching uses for LiveBoard. Schrage also does not address library roles in these colaboratories in his book *Shared Minds* (1990b). However, in his 1992 speech to the Library Information Technology Association (LITA), he emphasized the importance of "agents" in the electronic commons, and the value gained when the agent (a librarian) connects persons with information, or each other. He goes further, speculating that "in the future, libraries will be about the creation, care, and feeding of 'virtual' communities," and that librarians should plan a future role as "virtual agents" of information. Patrons would enter a virtual library and meet persons who would help them navigate to knowledge. This capability would recreate the consulting role librarians take when they leave reference and information desks, and rove through terminal banks to help patrons with their search strategies.

C. Remote Interactive Search Systems

The use of information technology to create collaboration between persons is an important objective for future information systems. In addition to the recent introduction of LiveBoard, other existing techniques explore interactive searching coupled with reference skill. The best example of an existing technology of collaboration used by librarians for reference service may be found in NASA's Far West Regional Technology Transfer Center at the University of Southern California, and Teltech, an information broker in Bloomington, Minnesota (Zimmermann and Erlandson, 1991). These firms use a real-time online research tool called a Remote Interactive Search system (RIS); others have called them simultaneous remote search systems (SRSs) (Anderson, 1984, 1985), or "conference call searching" (Trautman and King, 1983).

These RIS systems employ existing technology compositely, and are basic, as compared to Schrage's futuristic and highly complex systems. A librarian is connected to a database, and the search is relayed via a modem connection to clients who watch the information search scroll on their own monitor screens. Simultaneously, the clients are in telephone communication with the librarian, and are able to reframe the search as it proceeds, tailoring and changing the parameters as "pearls" are uncovered. This collaborative process often reveals the faulty reasoning of specialists unfamiliar with online search techniques. Simultaneously, it exposes poor-quality indexing within databases as the searcher "backtracks" to the salient information. As an online relationship, RIS merges the intuitive and systematic skill of the searcher with the cognitive biases that scientists find difficult to convey to lay people (Anderson, 1987; McCleary and Mayer, 1988).

At Teltech, searchers specialize in highly technical information areas and have midsize manufacturing firms as a key constituency. Lately, Teltech has been doing a landslide business (D. Cuming, personal communication, 1992). This demand occurs because the match between interpersonal communication and electronic communication speeds the power of scientists in thinking through what it is that they really want. The real-time availability of the information specialist linked by telephone and screen facilitates collaboration, exactly as Schrage claims. It also showcases the searcher, who takes a leadership role in shaping the conversation. This technology is a highly collaborative endeavor, and team members must view each other as respected equals for it to work.

Less exotic examples of intermediate technologies may be found within corporate firms where librarians use local area networks (LANs) for information dissemination. LANs are an accepted feature of highly automated offices, and they are conduits for research results and news as projects develop (Henderson, 1992). In addition, multiple CD–ROM disks may now be linked to LANs for expanded access; Bucknall and Mangrum (1992) studied user patterns in an academic library under this configuration. Real-time links between library reference providers and patrons using networked resources would add a new, organic feature to these systems.

Schrage suggests that the best use of technology hinges on interpersonal communication, a human characteristic. Effective special librarians spend a substantial amount of time reframing questions conceptually and then providing access and retrieval services. In this regard, we have learned a great deal about how to interpret patrons' expectations and analyze their information needs before going online. RIS technology and LANs are collaborative tools that are already having an impact. Participation in, and planning of, these and other emerging technologies will become a crucial aspect of the information alliance.

D. Impact on the Profession

1. Teamwork in Business Settings

In business, the electronic communities created by collaborative technology would allow multiple aspects of product development to occur simultaneously with input from every participant. The working group could be in electronic communication at all points of the process. Schrage envisions a technology that would allow multiple users to interact on the same computer screen, commenting freely on each other's output. The product could be virtually anything: a song, a report, an automobile. An online search played out on a corner of the community screen could have profound influence on the process.

Technology of this sort would offer a new means to circumvent departmental barriers to communication and information access. If this occurs, then the electronic commons itself could potentially become a constantly evolving organizational structure, linking together overlay groups of designers, accountants, librarians, lawyers, and anyone else whose input is needed (Savage, 1990).

2. Information Literacy

New technologies of collaboration such as LiveBoard offer a fresh venue for library skill. The new technology increases the potential of collaborative initiatives that have originated with librarians, such as the information literacy movement. Academic librarians envision information literacy training as part of every course (American Library Association, 1989; Breivik and Gee, 1989). To achieve this, they need allies among faculty and administrators, and a means of illustrating the benefits tangibly. Information literacy programs that do not forge links with allies beyond the library sphere remain out of the mainstream. Information literacy training in the corporate arena also requires alliances and a presence on teams.

Collaborative technologies are natural domains for savvy reference librarians searching for missing information, missing connections, and overlooked research. The effectiveness of LiveBoard as a display platform for online searching targeted at scientists and specialists confirms the power of this medium (C. Corcan Douglas, personal communication, 1993). Collaboration involving group work technology could lend new life to information literacy programs, both in academia and in business.

McCrank (1991) critiques information literacy unfavorably, precisely because many models for the training involve removing others from the mainstream and bringing them into library settings. Alliances and collaboration are the crux of his cure. McCrank says:

> If the aim is truly comprehensive information literacy, then libraries must cooperate with other information agencies more than ever. They will need alliances with nonlibrary administrators, civic and religious leaders, educators, and academicians.

Technologies of collaboration might bring information literacy training closer to the leaders and thinkers who need it most. Again, there is a market for reference expertise in the electronic workplace because reference skills are not taught to the technologists who plan systems. McCrank states that once people learn information literacy skills, the prototype (librarians) will not be needed any longer. In contrast, Schrage finds more value in the communities that technology creates than in the systems themselves (1992); and since communities are ongoing associations, the need for reference and training is likely to recur regularly. This theory about community comes from a technological thinker who was not considering library reference specifically, yet his emphasis on the importance of relationships is in harmony with reference librarians' emphasis on human interaction.

3. Librarians and Information Technologists

Beyond this variety of opinion within the library profession is a greater gulf between library thinkers and the technologists who create hardware and software. Koenig (1991) describes a bifurcation of information management theory in his study of library skills transfer, with much of the needed knowledge about users and their patterns for research locked away in the library's room, and excluded from systems development. Schrage's recipe for collaboration would start with informal alliances between skill groups (librarians and information technologists) that would create a "shared understanding" about what knowledge is needed, and by whom. This approach reiterates what special librarians already have been doing when they plan their service environments and do reference well (White, 1989).

Management has tended to view information from a data processing bias, which emphasizes numeric information and applications. This bias seems universal in business literature, and Koenig (1991) has provided a thorough analysis of the development of library information access priorities and business access priorities. At the same time, management researchers are taking a new look at how to connect people for more effective teamwork, and library managers who are aware of the trends in both information technology planning and human resources management may be able to enter the ongoing process as allies.

IV. Viewpoints on Information in Organizations

Intense competition in the international marketplace is driving American business researchers to formulate new organizational structures. Researchers interested in the interplay between high technology and worker productivity are examining the way people interrelate and work in teams. Certain theories that take a new look at information systems and teamwork support Schrage's theories about collaboration. A summary of some leading theories about how organizations should handle information follows below. First, an overview of research about information technology is provided. This is followed by four viewpoints on organizational change.

A. Information Islands

The development of computer systems that fostered repetitive, parallel, and multiple handling of internal information resulted in an "archipelago" of separate information islands, as documented by McFarlan, McKenney, and Pyburn (1983) and McKenney and McFarlan (1982). In these early years, high technology was used to pave the "cow paths" that were formerly employed by paper storage systems; in other words, financial records were not configured to interrelate with client records, or the content of client files, and so on (Hammer, 1990). This was later reaffirmed by Walton (1989) during the more mature technological era of the late 1980s, although new technologies, including LANs and databases, had already begun to bridge the islands by then. McKinnon and Bruns (1992), in researching how information is gathered in manufacturing and high-technology firms, declare that management information systems are likely to be avoided if they are hard to use. They also assert that most information is exchanged interpersonally whenever possible. This is echoed in the public sector. Survey research by Levin (1991) confirms that interpersonal communication is the preferred avenue of information gathering, taking up to 50% of public administrators' time. This lack of effectiveness in management information systems ultimately has led to Schrage's claim (1990a) that the price for information systems is too high.

As information technology becomes commonplace, the study of informal work styles has become a critical component of systems analysis. Work teams utilizing high technology in manufacturing and in services are increasingly considered in studies of organizational effectiveness (Brown and Reich, 1989; Lawler, 1992).

The information islands still exist in most large organizations. They exist in the research university, where information technology departments manage research programs, administrators manage records, and libraries manage "knowledge"; and they still exist in business settings, where external information resources (such as commercial databases) are handled by librarians and research specialists, and internal data such as client data and financial information are handled by data processing departments (Jester, 1992).

There is a similarity between this fragmented picture of information resources and emerging models for organizational change. Libraries and library skill at knowledge work are not mentioned by the authors below, as they describe ways to create "total qualilty management" (Lawler, Mohrman, and Ledford, 1992) "high involvement," new "architecture," "learning," and so on; yet collaborative approaches as defined by Schrage are echoed by these theorists. The absence of library collaborators in these theories supports the case for alliances with nonlibrary staff, since these researchers do not examine the ways in which corporate librarians provide research support (Linder, 1992).

B. Evolving Organizations

1. Reengineering

Hammer (1990) theorizes that a fundamental redesign of business organizations is necessary; rather than automate, obliterate and reconfigure. Davenport (1992) expands upon the reengineering theory and adds the appellation "process innovation"; he views information technology as the "enabler" of the structural changes that would reconfigure work roles more effectively. Penrod and Dolence (1992) and Heterick (1992) apply reengineering theory to higher education, with a particular focus on information technology units.

Hammer's obliteration is necessary because many organizational structures and information systems still in use were conceived when professionals were few, and both skilled and unskilled labor was plentiful. Furthermore, much of the organizational structure currently in place in offices and factories was established during the early post–World War II period; many production-oriented procedures (purchasing, accounting, manufacturing) evolved without conscious planning. Rather than perpetuate this ad hoc structure, Hammer believes that work should be organized around outcomes, with professionals fully subsumed into the work process. Parallel processing should be coordinated during the processes instead of when they are completed. Parallel processing of information evolved when organizations were "information poor"; now they are "information affluent," although information poverty is deeply embedded into systems, reducing overall productivity.

Parallel functions and multiple handling of data abound in most large organizations, and "turf" wars are regular features of working life. To solve the dilemma, reengineering emphasizes three broad management revisions, applied in concert: increased reliance on teamwork as defined by the total quality management movement; "empowerment" of individuals through more authority at lower levels; and reorganization of work to emphasize flexibility for ongoing change. Such approaches might make staff reductions a constant feature of corporate working life, as information technology and teamwork create new efficiency.

Hammer is interested in maximizing productivity while reducing staff who do not directly contribute to quality in the final product. Ehrbar (1993) outlines the growing popularity of reengineering seminars, which retrain managers to search out redundant work that is based on outmoded organizational structure. Presumably, new jobs will arise that replace old positions, although staff will be fewer in number. However, no one can forecast exactly what these jobs will be. Ehrbar reports that various executives forecast substantial shifts in employment patterns if reengineering gathers momentum; worker displacement could be great, even on a par with the changes brought about by the Industrial Revolution. But it is also presumed by reengineering trainers that new jobs will emerge, and that they will be more dependent on knowledge skills, falling in line with government and commercial advocacy for "high skill" employment (National Center on Education and the Economy, 1990).

Library skill in access to and delivery of knowledge would have a home in a reengineered organization that depends on prompt availability of information. Reference service already crosses conceptual boundaries, and it could go further still if it is understood by management as a transferrable skill with broad relevance.

2. The "Learning" Organization

Senge (1990) argues that organizations should plan for constant learning and avoidance of linear thinking in order to boost productivity. While the manipulation of information resources is not always the only concern, the benefits of ready access to online resources and internal information (such as library-administered records management) under this theory are obvious. Organizations that use reference skills are more likely to learn effectively. Further, information literacy training for the entire organization would be a powerful, collaborative role for the librarian under this model (American Library Association, 1989).

3. Organizational Architecture

Lawler (1992) favors a view of organizations that takes formal and informal communication into consideration, and matches persons to teams. These "autonomous work teams" work together, once again across corporate boundaries, to bring all the needed expertise together for product development or the rendering of high-quality services.

Manufacturing firms in particular see potential benefits in this arrangement; automobile manufacturing has witnessed the alliance of finance, engineering, sales, and production workers whose charge is to bring new models to market faster, and with fewer flaws.

The influence of an information specialist on a team with this kind of makeup could be great. Smaller manufacturing firms with fewer than twenty engineers, working in team structures, comprise a core constituency for the search staff at Teltech who perform RIS searches. The need of these smaller firms for highly skilled online help confirms that alliance-minded librarians can find a place in working teams.

4. Virtual Groups

Savage (1990) describes "virtual groups" of staff that overlay formal organizational structures via electronic links. Rheingold (1991) has investigated virtual technology thoroughly as a gateway to much greater social transformation, but business applications of this technology are concerned with ways to circumvent organizational obstacles via "overlay" groups. These overlay groups work together and share ideas on bulletin boards. Current electronic mail technology allows for interactive bulletin boards that attempt to achieve this effect. However, virtual groups for teamwork in corporate settings will become more effective if electronic mail evolves into a forum for simultaneous group discussion, and is accepted more widely.

Similarities exist between library theorists and generalists who study virtual reality and business. Kurzweil (1993) envisions a future in which editorial and library functions merge in virtual work groups. He sees a potential of virtual reference relationships and the possibility of paying for library skill by "person-minute." Yet the core potential he sees is in the librarian's role in making virtual information accessible through indexing, database structuring, and access planning. Atkinson (1993) echoes this idea, arguing that new virtual libraries must retain the information intermediary, given the existing access problems involving vast, unstructured information already found on the Internet. Atkinson argues that this role must be actively pursued so that access planning becomes a standard feature in electronically networked information resources.

V. Rethinking the Information Alliance

Among productivity and technological theorists such as Hammer, Savage, and Schrage there is a consensus that understanding informal group processes may improve overall productivity. Furthermore, a focus on group dynamics as a positive workplace asset, coupled with an open electronic plane of fully networked and interactive information systems, may finally lay to rest Frederick Taylor's theory of hierarchical, regimented management, even in manufacturing firms (Taylor, 1915). Reference skills have an increased value to firms in this changing environment, and in order to share them, participation in teamwork is increasingly important.

Several suggestions about how to view alliances follow. Some are not new, but I hope they will challenge enterprising librarians to think about ways they can collaborate to advance to promote library skill.

A. Shared Skills Build Alliances

Sharing of skills is being advocated throughout management literature as a way to improve products and services. In order for library skills to be shared, librarians need to ally themselves with the specialists that use library information strategically, and the technologists who configure information systems.

Alliances involve two-way exchange. For example, librarians are not "scientifically" trained in marketing techniques, but effective marketing is a principal survival technique for all types of staff (Prusak and Matarazzo, 1990; Borbley, 1988). An alliance with marketing or research department staff would start a two-way education about what each party does. Library talent would interest marketers and promote the librarian indirectly throughout the organization, while a marketer's viewpoint could upgrade the librarian's sense of how to advance the library. Likewise, alliances with technology managers can create productive, two-way exchanges, particularly since technology managers may be the first to know what new technologies are being released.

B. Shared Minds Build Alliances

Alliances multiply mind power. Koenig (1992) argues that managers are not aware of the contributions of libraries and information centers; alliances outside the library would help create awareness. Schrage roves far afield to substantiate the value of alliances, citing Rodgers and Hammerstein along with Watson and Crick, discoverers of the double helix structure of DNA (Schrage, 1990b). Both of these teams worked closely, bouncing ideas back and forth, and revising throughout. Reference as part of teamwork could mimic this give and take and could clear up misconceptions or gaps in knowledge as they appear. This type of alliance follows Lawler's (1992) high-involvement techniques and virtual communities online (Rheingold, 1991; Savage, 1990).

When combined, technology and teamwork create an ideal playing field for alliance-minded librarians. Team models also give librarians yet another opportunity to shift library skills directly into the organizational processes that managers are trying to alter. If they are considered irrelevant, corporate librarians may squander this conceptual window.

The most significant boundary to overcome is the unconscious belief that libraries are physical places rather than persons providing services (Schrage, 1992; White, 1989). White compares special libraries to other corporate departments; he takes a dismal view of their political prospects whenever they are evaluated as budgetary line items, since libraries are expensive. However, a valuable service becomes an income producer and an alliance-building device. Shared skills and mind power shift the focus from physical plants to processes, which is what White, Hammer, and Schrage all advocate.

Sharing skills in a virtual community is exactly what allied professionals should be planning to do. The RIS system outlined earlier is a working example of reference being performed with a transitional, composite technology. Virtual communities will discover the kind of interactive reference that Teltech is offering now, but the product will be much more effective if it becomes part of the work process, and is handled by librarians.

C. Manage Technology; Manage Research Support

Interactive technology that couples human beings for teamwork is a compelling new forum for good reference service. It is well documented that decision makers often lack critical knowledge, and they do not know what potential sources exist or how to find them. Truly interactive teams, utilizing shared electronic workspaces, would come to rely greatly on librarians' ability to do literature searches and other analytical work. For this process to advance, librarians must become more involved in technology planning. Examples of this involvement follow in Section VI,B,1.

When librarians are involved in technology planning, they become more

aware of the overall work and reference needs of their organizations. From this platform they can assume the allied role that is needed to keep management's attention long enough to help the firm "learn" better (Lawler, 1992; Jester, 1992). They can also manage the introduction of technology for the firm or substantially influence its introduction.

D. Work "Inside"; Work "Outside"

Special librarians may be better able to provide service as outside consultants, as Teltech and the NASA technology transfer center at the University of Southern California do when they perform conference searches using RIS systems. Moreover, they may be able to form larger scale firms similar to Teltech, or else band together as departments in full-service consulting firms. This would mirror the career development of managers or accountants, who may move "inside" or "outside" business during their careers. The influence of consultants can be seen in the regard information vendors extend to librarians when they market new electronic services to management. Sales representatives often invite librarians to collaborate in promoting new products. In this sense, both vendors and information brokers are pioneering new collaborative relationships at rates that are set by what the market will bear.

Special librarians already play a consulting role as information counselors. Bell (1990) discusses the difference between online searching in academic and corporate settings and its effect on collaborative relationships. In a virtual library where librarians can be agents of connectivity, reference could become a lucrative addition for large-scale consulting firms or enterprising individuals.

The pattern of "consulting" about research before going online is a fundamental collaborative technique of librarians. It is also an eminently movable skill.

E. Plan for Networked Systems

Networked access to diverse information systems emphasizes the workstation, where an end user will perform at least some of the searching. Interacting on a reference-providing level with end users on these networks will maintain expert human communication in the search process. New common graphical user interfaces, such the "Z39.50" project (Lynch, 1992b), will greatly increase end user interest in online search techniques as well. If searchers need to learn only one command set for multiple sources, their way will be made easier (University of California, 1992b).

The people who use these systems will need more help, not less, as Michael S. Hart points out in describing the role of librarians in electronic, full-text domains such as his "Gutenberg Project" (Wilson, 1992a). In commenting about the challenges of marketing new services to end users, K. Wayne Smith, president of the Online Computer Library Center® (OCLC), had the following to say:

> I'm not sanguine . . . . We know a lot about how librarians behave. We don't necessarily know a lot about how library patrons behave. (Wilson, 1991, p. A25)

A networked environment could be used to improve the librarian's training role, since large information vendors like OCLC, Dialog Information Services,® or Mead Data Central® are not going to be able to meet the challenge of training network users alone. Technologies of collaboration would augment end user searching positively; even with one common user interface effectively in place, not everyone will wish to take the time to search databases productively. They will turn to librarians that they already work with and trust. However, they will be doing this from remote locations. This user group will be a market for reference service, and technologies of collaboration may offer a new way to provide service to them.

F. Reengineering with Library Skill

All of these strategies are promoted in library literature. Moyer (1992) lists an overview of the strategies private law librarians should employ to inject library skill into the law firm, ranging from training to participation in every management decision-making group. Moyer's prescription is based on the success of the alliance between private law librarians and lawyers, which is evaluated below in Section VI,A. In Section VI,B, several initiatives at work in the academic environment are explored, including the Coalition for Networked Information (CNI), and the Higher Education Information Resources Alliance (HEIRA). These efforts indicate that forward-looking librarians are responding to the charge that management thinkers such as Senge, Hammer, and Savage give to executives: the entire organization should be reorganized to serve the outcome better, and new ways to manage technology and information resources are essential. Librarians can echo the call for reorganization.

The evolving role of the library at Apple Computer provides one well-publicized example of positive impact by librarians (Ertel, 1990). Experiments in electronically assisted collaboration, such as the RIS system described in Section III,C may also yield some answers. If organizations are reengineered without considering this kind of talent, a great value will be left out of the new structure. Librarians can use alliances with influential staff to participate in any reengineering that occurs (Prusak and Matarrazo, 1990; Linder, 1992).

Promotion of library skill is the best avenue available to librarians wishing to reengineer organizations. Indeed, the techniques that reference librarians employ are practiced by other professionals, and when they are reported on, they are often seen as innovative and new. For example, accountants are encouraged by Leinecke (1990) to perform "business advisory services": a rigorous level of attention to clients' hidden needs for new types of consulting services. This is reference interviewing applied to client contact by nonlibrary professionals.

VI. Information Alliances in Two Settings

Section III examined the importance of cooperative alliances with staff outside of the library, with an emphasis on managing relationships and new technologies. Can some of these ideas succeed in applied settings? To explore this question, two evaluations follow. The first examines alliances between private law librarians and lawyers. Research libraries will be used as a second example, although the scope of the analysis is intentionally limited, given their size and complexity.

A. Private Law Libraries

Private law librarians have been able to take advantage of several benefits that online media bring to the legal world. The role of the law library in the law firm, particularly firms involved in "defense" work, has changed dramatically, following the explosive growth of the legal profession and its current retrenchment. The teamwork that typifies day-to-day work in large-scale business law firms has been influenced by librarians, and the techniques that have worked for them should be of interest to librarians in other settings.

The principal advantages private law librarians have enjoyed flow from three areas. The first is that many lawyers understand the value of information, since legal practice requires a grasp of diverse kinds of knowledge (Rosen, 1990). Second, full-text online resources were pioneered with legal material, and most lawyers enter practice with at least some basic skill in online searching of the LEXIS and Westlaw® database families. This familiarity creates a foundation of shared understanding between librarians and lawyers about the importance of libraries, although librarians still have to justify the need for libraries in the firm. Last, the relative flexibility of the law firm is an advantage, as the organization tends to reward legal expertise on a higher plane than business expertise. The primacy of legal skills creates opportunities for private law librarians who can simultaneously understand and support legal practice while improving the business of the firm.

1. The Value of Information

Kregel and Howard (1987) provided an authoritative description of why and how private law librarians bill the cost of their research time to clients. This topic has been controversial, but the real value of the private law librarian's work is no longer disputed. Librarians who can provide the right information promptly tend to excel and enjoy support (Metaxas, 1986). In such cases, private law librarians may bill their time at a rate higher than legal assistants, perhaps even on a par with new associate lawyers. (Billing structures for leading law firms in 1992 can start at more than $100 per hour.) Librarian billing has improved library alliances with lawyers, because the recovery of costs and generation of income are entirely justified by the culture of the firm.

Another important role private law librarians play has to do with legal research training. Lawyers graduate from law school with a "foundation" in the law, but they lack practitioner skills. Legal research training is a key concern of private law librarians, and they continue the training that academic law librarians began. Indeed, a deficit in legal research skill has been identified in legal education, and law librarians have moved actively to fill this gap (Howland and Lewis, 1990; Myers, 1991). Therefore, possibilities for collaborative relationships involving legal research training constantly arise for private law librarians who are on the lookout for them (Cronin Fisk, 1991; Seer, 1991).

2. The Online Advantage: Use and Training

The rapid evolution of electronic information sources brings constant changes to legal practice and leaves many lawyers and administrators unprepared. These groups depend on the private law librarian to help them keep up. Three law firm groups are natural allies for private law librarians: the young lawyers who work under high pressure; the senior lawyers who avoid online databases and require mediated searching and other help; and administrative support staff in charge of information management systems.

The lawyer groups are aware of the vital importance of online and CD-ROM-stored information. The monthly tab for online research is a major expense for firms and daily use of databases such as LEXIS and Westlaw is essential for many lawyers. Private law librarians have two advantages that facilitate an allied role. The first is advanced skill in legal research, both manual and online (Scwharz, 1991a,b). The second is that libraries are the most logical sites for online systems administration. With this advantage, private law librarians can either help lawyers formulate their searches or do their research for them. Since large firms can require hundreds of passwords and several subspecialties in legal practice, alliances built on training and maintenance of online skill have been quite effective.

Law firm information administrators are typically less aware of the value of strategic information contained in databases and law library book collections. However, they manage vital data, including client files, billing records, and legal briefs or memoranda. Automation of these records can be relatively advanced if staff have been empowered by managing partners (Novachick, 1991a,b). In some cases briefs and memoranda (detailed summaries that record the analytical development of legal arguments) are transformed into full-text databases. Private law librarians are frequently tapped to participate in the creation of these databases because the information archived in them can save hours of research time (Schwarz, 1991b).

These databases can be absorbed into libraries, although this might be perceived as empire building and thus be detrimental to the collaborative model of teamwork. Alternatively, librarians might choose to join the committees that oversee the work and influence how the data are accessed and organized.

New technologies of collaboration, which would allow lawyers to search a "brief bank" of memoranda, update the case law with LEXIS or Westlaw, and "shepardize" the court cases (i.e., find out if the decisions have been affected by new legal developments), and then pose a research question to the librarian based on this work, would be attractive to lawyers interested in saving time and money. The injection of library skill into the process of legal research already boosts quality, and technologies of collaboration could improve upon this foundation.

3. Flexibility of the Organization

These kinds of activity and interaction are fundamentally collaborative. They fulfill Schrage's theory in an "applied" setting, since the relationships are the enabling factors. Informal collaboration between private law librarians and lawyers multiplies the existing talent, drawing together various skills for an improved product. The allied role of the librarian in providing reference throughout the process occurs when private law librarians can tailor their skills to have a maximum impact.

The overall organization of law firms presents a challenge to private law librarians intent on teamwork. Law firms are partnerships, and they have become more volatile as the legal profession has expanded. The actual nature of work within partnerships varies dramatically, ranging from bureaucratic, committee-driven models, to oligarchies of "star" lawyers, to autocracies. However, the skill of the librarian is transferrable to various kinds of office cultures. Moyer (1992) argues that involvement in firm planning groups is essential for librarians. When they are willing to be flexible, adjusting library goals to match the goals of the lawyers, they are more likely to enjoy support.

One example may be found in technical services planning, and the priority given to it in various settings. If resources in a particular firm are scarce, but the need for reference is keen, librarians could choose to keep all cataloging and classification at a bare minimum. Traditionalists might view this as unthinkable and miss the service opportunity, whereas librarians who emphasize reference could build support for future cataloging projects by providing good service (Huwe and Schut, 1991).

4. Chief Information Officer, or Chief "Collaborator"

Library thinking about "chief information officers" is split to a degree. Some, such as Mathaisel (1992) see the slot as transitional, while others (Sirkin, 1992) view it as the best course for survival past the millennium. The important question is, Does creating an integrated department truly improve legal practice? If structural reorganization changes reference librarians into office managers, this goal could backfire, because it is the reference alliance that has value. Schrage's collaborative model is based on product success, and for private law librarians, the product is legal reference.

"Chief collaborators" who can offer online assistance, clarify confusion, provide end user training, and play political hurly-burly to do so will remain in the line of production in law firms. Chief information officers might have to bring into line departments that do not emphasize reference service. The mission of law firms is to perform legal work for clients, and the heart of good legal practice is the analytical review of legal and nonlegal information. In this regard, online research in legal resources, coupled with complex business and social science research, involves a much higher level of collaboration than office information management. The allied professional will have to keep the product in mind, which is client success.

Alliances with this focus are likely to be cemented by participation in the "associate" lunches, briefings, and training sessions that act as pipelines for information sharing among lawyers. Team roles (both formal and informal) that are based on lawyers' goals would breed greater longevity in librarian–lawyer collaboration. Moyer (1992) emphasizes all of these forums and basically urges private law librarians to collaborate as closely as possible with lawyers. While it is difficult to forecast growth trends in the legal profession, it is likely that new technologies of collaboration will positively affect the allied role that law librarians play in the firm.

B. Academic Libraries

Academic libraries provide another setting that illustrates the effectiveness of alliances. They have a clear-cut mission to support teaching and research, primarily through collection development and reference service. These are competing goals that limited budgets often place at odds with one another, creating difficult choices about how much service is affordable. Furthermore, academic libraries operate as departments in large and typically bureaucratic organizations. A full review of how they evolve and change is not a goal of this study, which focuses more narrowly on collaborative roles across departmental barriers.

Technological change has had a significant impact on reference services at research universities. Three areas stand out in their potential for collaborative work: advances in networked information systems, end user instruction, and administrative integration of information-providing units. These are evaluated below.

1. The Networking Environment

a. Online Public Access Catalogs and Networks   Academic librarians have become active users of the Internet, a national system of networks connecting academic and research institutions. The Internet is heavily used for file transfer and electronic mail, but its uses are still evolving. Mainframe computers on large campuses link local networks into the Internet, providing a powerful new medium for electronic access. Online Public Access Catalogs (OPACs) of many universities may be searched on the Internet; in some cases these OPACs include indexing and abstracting databases and other useful subsets of information.

The vastness and diversity of networked information are creating a bewildering array of choices for scholars and other users of networks. This is a fertile environment for reference librarians whose skill in end user training is already proven (University of California, Berkeley, 1992a). The librarian's skill is especially important, since librarians tend to see information searches more as open-ended quests in which the searcher can rove about for answers "organically" (Battin, 1984). Librarians who oversee large OPACs, such as the University of California's MELVYL system, can launch initiatives to influence the networked information environment with the search patterns of the end user in mind. Recently, much attention has been given to the development of the Z39.50 protocol. Z39.50 would enable end users to search various databases with a single command language (Lynch, 1992b; University of California, 1992).

Librarians who ally with information systems designers to manage these networks are creating an important new role. The Internet is a major change agent in academic thinking, and new collaborative relationships using this high-speed communications network are currently being worked out. These range from professional networking and reference tips to speculation about electronic campuses as an alternative to building new physical campuses (DeLoughry, 1992; Watkins, 1992; Wilson, 1992b). Real-time reference, performed at academic workstations by collaborative teams, would influence the nature of research and study in sweeping ways, and would insert library skills into the research process.

Experiments in consulting alliances between librarians and faculty are also being studied in more traditional ways. One example of this may be seen in the Library Research Consultancy Project at Berkeley's Townsend Center for the Humanities, which was initially funded by the Council on Library Resources. The program was conceived to help humanities researchers navigate through both online and manual resources in their fields by establishing a personal, consulting relationship with librarians (University of California, Berkeley, 1992c). This is an example of collaborative thinking that expands the role of reference providers in the research process. "Meta"-reference relationships that are not based on physical presence at reference desks may follow the emergence of virtual communities at research universities.

b. Administering the Networked Environment   Librarians have had many opportunities to be active participants in the construction of the electronic information age; seizing these opportunities has been a principal challenge. The emergence of full-text databases requiring specialized and intuitive skills affected much of the profession's direction during the 1980s (Bell, 1990). The power of networked information, as witnessed in the Internet and the "wide area information server" (WAIS) model for retrieval (University of California, 1991), is beginning to define another level of information access, which Schrage addresses in detail in his 1992 speech at LITA. Academic librarians are likely to be leaders in understanding the full potential of the Internet and its role in emerging technologies of collaboration (Schrage, 1992).

Two large-scale initiatives provide excellent examples of the power of alliances beyond the library: The Coalition for Networked Information (CNI), and the Higher Education Information Resources Alliance (HEIRA).

The CNI is an example of collaborative planning between diverse professionals. The CNI was formed in 1990 by a diverse group of faculty, librarians, and publishers to brainstorm about the electronic environment and its impact on teaching, publishing, and organizations (Grycz, 1991; Lynch, 1992a). Continued involvement to top academic library administrators in the CNI is likely to achieve a much deeper integration of library skill into information networks. If so, such involvement may bring another chance for the profession to gain greater influence.

The Higher Education Information Resources Alliance (HEIRA) takes the CNI's goals further. The HEIRA is a vehicle for cooperative projects between the Association of Research Libraries (ARL), CAUSE, and EDUCOM. In October 1992, it sponsored a large-scale evaluation of the interplay of information resources in higher education, which led to the publication of a report addressed to college and university presidents. This document is titled "What Presidents Should Know . . . about the Integration of Information

Technologies on Campus" (HEIRA, 1992). The document is supported by five background papers written by coalitions of librarians, technologists, and chief campus executives from the five participating institutions. The report reflects a unanimity of opinion that collaborative uses of new technologies are now essential for productivity and justifiable as a capital expense. More important for librarians, the documents suggests that existence of a reservoir of skill in libraries and its importance to overall planning.

Networking technology is evolving so swiftly that Schrage's model for collaboration is essential in understanding what is happening. In the macro view, the kind of coalition that the CNI embodies will stimulate creative thinking, because publishers, professors, and librarians have different goals that overlap. On university campuses the critical alliances between the information systems and technology units, the library, and faculty should reflect this collaboration. In a sense, the pace of change has caused many information managers to see the value of broad collaboration, as Schrage advocates.

Collaboration between information technologists and librarians creates an important alliance that will help technologists understand how patrons use systems. According to Collins and Straub (1991), there are "information gaps" that need to be sown together; to respond, the OPAC could be extended to workstations via the network, joined with document delivery service (including book retrieval, full text of reserve reading), and "tailored" to individual needs. In a recent review of library automation at the University of California, Berkeley, the library's systems office defined this tailoring as a "toolkit" approach to building customized information access (University of California, Berkeley, 1992a). If access to finding aids and primary sources, matched with full-text databases and document delivery services, could be brought to a scholar's computer in an easily usable format, administrative support for this collaborative work could grow.

2. Bibliographic Instruction

Bibliographic Instruction (BI) as a mission of the academic library is constantly evaluated in terms of its cost, budgetary requirements, and effectiveness (Loomis and DeLoach, 1987). Online and CD–ROM resources, not to mention innovations in online catalogs, invite concerned librarians to invent new ways of reaching their users (Farah, 1989). However, Whitlach (1990) has shown persuasively that demand for reference and training always rises to meet supply in public institutions, and that reference librarians are "gatekeepers" as well as service providers. Therefore, many BI programs are geared toward introductory sessions and basic guidance as a survival mechanism. LaGuardia (1992) challenges the overall direction of BI, charging librarians to evaluate what students need to know about finding information, and whether subject-related discourses are really helpful. BI programs are controversial, prompting incisive and critical comments about their fundamental viability (Broidy, 1988; Eadie, 1990).

As networked access to the library catalog, abstracting and indexing databases, and full-text source databases become a reality, librarians may need to develop a new approach, networking BI programs and teaching research skills to the academic community in the virtual library. Innovations are certain to be ongoing, given the rapid pace of change in electronic reference availability and cost. Beth and Farber (1992) describe a program to introduce students to online searching using Dialog Information Services at Earlham College. This kind of collaborative program reflects heightened interest in the direct involvement of vendors, faculty, and students in library research skills development.

Loomis and DeLoach (1987) also support such programs, suggesting that BI should take place in the "larger academic community," by which they mean outside of the library. Taking training to the user, on users' turf, so to speak, is a common modus operandi for special librarians, many of whose firms are commercial and more flexible than universities. Given the pressure on library resources in academic institutions and the belief that demand for service will always exceed supply, alliances that stretch the training reach of librarians are increasingly important.

The scope of these collaborations for BI will be worked out over time, and may change shape as budgetary constraints pose new challenges. At a town meeting on reference service held at the University of California, Berkeley in March 1992, several speakers speculated about possible future allies outside the library, who might be enlisted to help in training. Graduate student instructors were considered as one possible secondary tier of trainers. This line of discussion had vociferous opponents, but it is evidence of collaborative thinking and alliance building in a dynamic process (University of California, Berkeley, 1992b).

3. The Integrated Academic Information Center

Matheson and Cooper (1982) formulated a thorough study of how information systems could be integrated in medical libraries. They called their model the integrated academic information management system (IAIMS). Much of what was planned in 1982 was pursued throughout the 1980s and has become accepted in information systems development and library roles (Broering, Feng, and Matheson, 1988; Lucier, Matheson, Butter, and Reynolds, 1988). The most recent evidence of advances is given by Lucier (1992), who describes the implementation of this model at the University of California, San Francisco's Library and Center for Knowledge Management.

Branin *et al.* (1991) (and many other researchers working with him) have also studied how information sources can be pooled in diverse academic and research settings. Branin's integrated information center (IIC) would link all information together via networks, and allow various staff to communicate electronically via workstations and LANs. The Council on Library Resources initially funded this research (University of Minnesota, 1991).

In both cases, the IIC model may be effective in blending together different concepts of information access. It may also showcase librarians' skills, particularly if a RIS system were added to the configuration. Branin in particular identifies a "group discussion support system" that follows Schrage's viewpoint on collaborative technology. The group decision support system is also addressed in Berkeley's "scholar's toolkit" scenario (University of California, Berkeley, 1992a).

Matheson and Cooper's model emphasizes the integration of systems, and Lucier (1992) rightly speculates that the Center for Knowledge Management he oversees will evolve as it is implemented. The careful planning that has gone into these integrated organizations will allow librarians to test new methods of collaboration outside of the library. Further, the future role of a scholar's workstation will also be clarified in these integrated settings, where document delivery, access to online databases, and print collections will be coordinated by librarians.

Integrated information centers provide an ideal test site for new technologies of collaboration, which would reintroduce a role for human agents in the workstation configuration. The IIC also extends current collection-sharing efforts by easing the technological interface between diverse organizations; this may also increase collaborative management of information resources. The promise of greater potential for collaboration is well articulated by Lynch (1992a) in his overview of the past achievements and future plans for the University of California's MELVYL. Lynch summarizes the importance of the Coalition for Networked Information and the mission of large-scale, networked OPACs as follows:

> No single institution will be able to house the entirety of the networked information resources that will appear in the 1990s; rather consortia, and collaborative efforts will be the order of the day as institutions work together to manage and provide access to all of this information on behalf of their user communities.

VII. Summary and Conclusions

Researchers in the public and private sector largely agree that organizational culture should encourage cooperation and collaboration and that skills should be shared through a variety of team models that accentuate informal communication. High technology challenges managers to consider collaborative work as it brings ongoing change to organizations. As collaborative work becomes more common, traditional library skills such as reference, end user training, and information management will have increased importance, particularly for systems development.

Alliances with nonlibrary planners should be cultivated both in the academic and in the corporate sector, for two reasons. First, the contemporary workplace requires more pooling of talent, and while library talent is vital, it has not hitherto been viewed as centrally important by nonlibrary information technologists. Second, emerging technologies of collaboration may greatly accelerate the deconstruction of organizational and technological boundaries, resulting in a much more cooperative workplace. This process will create overlay communities in which collaborative work will be promoted.

A highly integrated role for librarians within these overlay communities would improve organizational productivity and give analytical reference skills greater visibility. A focus on such alliances would support the many calls that are made to justify the value of information services to top managers, who are only now beginning to understand the interplay between productivity and information services (Koenig, 1992).

The actual design of the collaborative technology that will facilitate new styles of teamwork is still unsettled. This creates an early opportunity for librarians to influence design from the outset. Strong alliances between information technologists and librarians have already begun to take shape, particularly at research universities. These should be solidified.

The 1990s will be the decade of collaboration and networked information. The leaders in the cooperative workplaces of the 1990s will be allied professionals from many fields, working together to guarantee that future technologies will facilitate relationships and communities. These collaborative communities are the most promising new domains for librarians, as the public and the electronic commons become more closely aligned and linked.

Acknowledgments

The author wishes to thank the following people for their comments and assistance: Jennifer Collins, MLIS '92, for her library research; Denise Cuming of Teltech, for her comments on remote interactive search systems; Dow Jones/News Retrieval; Bernie Hurley, University of California, Berkeley Library Systems Office, for the use of LSO's "white paper 1.0" on library automation planning at Berkeley; Janice Kimball, for her library research; Michael Schrage, for his encouragement and interest in this line of research and the role of libraries; and Martin Zeller of the Far West Regional Technology Transfer Center at USC, for his comments on the development of remote interactive search systems.

References

American Library Association (ALA) (1989). Presidential Committee on Information Literacy. *Final Report*. ALA, Chicago.

Anderson, Verl A. (1984). Simultaneous remote searching: The system and the reality. *Library Hi Tech* **2**, 61–64.

Anderson, Verl A. (1985). Simultaneous remote searching. *Library Journal (Library Computing Supplement)* **110**, 167–169.

Anderson, Verl A. (1987). The Eastern Oregon Information Network. *Library Hi Tech* **5**, 66–70.

Atkinson, Ross (1993). Networks, hypertext, and academic information services: Some longer range implications. *College and Research Libraries* **54**, 199–215.

Battin, P. (1984). The electronic library—a vision for the future. *EDUCOM Bulletin* (Summer), 12–17.

Bauwens, Michel (1993). The emergence of the cybrarian: A new organisational model for corporate libraries. *Business Information Review* **9**, 65–67.

Bell, George (1990). Online searching in industry versus academia: A study in partnerships. *Online* **14**, 51–56.

Beth, Amy, and Farber, Evan I. (1992). Lessons from Dialog: Technology impacts teaching/learning. *Library Journal* **117**, 26–30.

Borbley, Jack (1988). The emerging role of the corporate library: Restructuring information service to fit the times. *Bookmark* **47**, 56–59.

Branin, Joseph, Finn, Charles, D'Elia, George, Rohde, Nancy Freeman, Cogswell, James, Gorman, Kathy, Adams, Carl, Beath, Cynthia Mathis, Bolan, Richard, and Straub, Detmar (1991). A model academic integrated information center. *Journal of the American Society for Information Science* **42**, 137–151.

Breivik, Patricia Senn, and Gee, E. Gordon (1989). *Information Literacy: Revolution in the Library*. MacMillan, New York.

Broering, Naomi C., Feng, Cyril, and Matheson, Nina W. (1988). Integration across institutions: IAIMS extended. *Journal of the American Society for Information Science* **39**, 131–134.

Broidy, Ellen (1988). Organizational structure: Politics, problems, and challenges. Essay presented at the California Clearinghouse on Library Instruction, Southern Section, spring meeting, April 4, 1987. *RQ* 28, 162–168.

Brown, Clair, and Reich, Michael (1989). When does union-management cooperation work? A look at NUMMI and GM-Van Nuys. *California Management Review* **31**, 26–44.

Bucknall, Tim, and Mangrum, Rikki (1992). U-Search: A User Study of the CD-ROM Service at the University of North Carolina at Chapel Hill. *RQ* 31, 542–553.

Clark, Don (1993). Xerox takes aim at boring meetings. *San Francisco Chronicle*, May 18, p. C3.

Collins, Rosann, and Straub, Detmar (1991). The delivery of information services within a changing information environment. *Journal of the American Society for Information Science* **42**, 120–123.

Cronin Fisk, Margaret (1991). Maintaining expertise. *National Law Journal* **13**, S1 (July 22).

Davenport, Thomas H. (1992). *Process Innovation: Reengineering Work Through Information Technology*. Harvard Business School Press, Cambridge, Massachusetts.

DeLoughry, Thomas J. (1992). Crucial role seen for technology in meeting higher education's challenges. *Chronicle of Higher Education* **39**, A21–A22 (September 23).

Eadie, Tom (1990). Immodest proposals: User instruction for students does not work. *Library Journal* **115**, 42–45.

Ehrbar, Al (1993). Re-engineering give firms new efficiency, workers the pink slip. *Wall Street Journal*, March 16, p. A1.

Elrod, S., Bruce, R., Gold, R., Goldberg, D., Halasz, F., Janssen, W., Lee, D., McCall, K., Pedersen, E., Pier, K., Tang, J., and Welch, B. (1992). LiveBoard: A Large Interactive Display Supporting Group Meetings, Presentations and Remote Collaborations Report Number CSL-92-6 [P92-00073], June, 1992. Xerox PARC, Palo Alto, California.

Ertel, Monica (1990). Getting a piece of the pie: R & D at the Apple Library. *Library Journal* **115**, 40–44.

Farah, Barbara D. (1989). Academic reference librarians: A case for self-evaluation. *Reference Librarian* **53**, 495–503.

Feng, Cyril, and Weise, Frieda O. (1988). Implementation of integrated information services: Library/computer center partnership. *Journal of the American Society for Information Science* **39**, 126–130.

Grycz, Czeslaw Jan (1991). Economic models for disseminating scholarly information. *DLA Bulletin* (University of California, Office of the President) **11**(25), 1–10.

Hammer, Michael (1990). Reengineering work: Don't automate, obliterate. *Harvard Business Review* **68**, 104–112.

Henderson, Tona (1992). LANs and information leverage in the special library. *b/ITE: Bulletin of the Information Technology Division of SLA* **9**(2), 1–8 (pullout pages).

Heterick, Robert C., Jr., ed. (1992). "Reengineering Teaching and Learning in Higher Education: Sheltered Groves, Camelot, Windmills, and Malls." CAUSE Professional Paper Series, no. 10. CAUSE, Boulder, Colorado.

Higher Education Information Resources Alliance (HEIRA) (1992). "What presidents should know . . . about the integration of information technologies on campus." HEIRAlliance Executive Strategies Report no. 1. (Note: Five separate background papers by each of the contributing institutions are also available.) HEIRA, Boulder, Colorado.

Howland, Joan S., and Lewis, Nancy J. (1990). The effectiveness of law school legal research training programs. *Journal of Legal Education* **40**, 381–391.

Huwe, Terence K., and Schut, Alan (1991). Classification, cataloging, and private law libraries: A survey. *Legal Information Alert* **10**, 1–6, (July/August).

Jester, Roger E. (1992). To the ends of the earth: Librarians and management information needs. *Special Libraries* **83**, 139–141.

Koenig, Michael E. D. (1991). The transfer of library skills to nonlibrary contexts. In *Advances in Librarianship*, **15**, (I. Godden, ed.), pp. 1–27. Academic Press, San Diego.

Koenig, Michael (1992). The importance of information services for productivity "under-recognized" and under-invested. *Speical Libraries* **83**, 199–210.

Kregel, Charles E., and Howard, Sally J. (1987). Charging clients for information specialist time: Toward improved library service, overhead reduction, and fairness in billing. *Law Office Economics and Management* **27**, 460–469.

Kurzweil, Raymond (1993). The virtual library. *Library Journal* **118**, 54–55.

LaGuardia, Cheryl (1992). Renegade library instruction: Teaching students what they really need to know. *Library Journal* **117**, 51–53.

Lawler, Edward E., III (1992). *The Ultimate Advantage: Creating the High Involvement Organization.* Jossey Bass, San Francisco.

Lawler, Edward E., III, Mohrman, Susan Albers, and Ledford, Gerald E., Jr. (1992). *Employee Involvement and Total Quality Management.* Jossey Bass, San Francisco.

Leinecke, Linda M. (1990). A different approach to serving clients. *Journal of Accountancy* **169**, 53–60.

Levin, Marc A. (1991). The information-seeking behavior of local government officials. *American Review of Public Administration* **21**, 271–286.

Linder, Jane C. (1992). Today a librarian, tomorrow a corporate intelligence professional. *Special Libraries* **83**, 142–144.

Loomis, Abigail A., and DeLoach, Marva L. (1987). Library instruction trends and resources: A delicate balance in academic libraries. *Bookmark* **46**, 14–19.

Lucier, Richard E. (1992). Towards a knowledge management environment: A strategic framework. *EDUCOM Review* **27**, 24–31.

Lucier, Richard E., Matheson, Nina W., Butter, Karen A., and Reynolds, Robert E. (1988). The knowledge workstation: An electronic environment for knowledge management. *Bulletin of the Medical Library Association* **76**, 248–255.

Lynch, Clifford (1992a). The MELVYL System: Looking back, looking forward. *DLA Bulletin* (University of California, Office of the President) **12**, 1–32.

Lynch, Clifford (1992b). *Z39.50 in Plain English: A Non-Technical Guide to the New NISO Standard for Library Automation Networking.* Digital Equipment Corporation, Marlboro, Massachusetts.

McCleary, Hunter, and Mayer, William (1988). Expert systems the old fashioned way: Person to person. *Online* **11**, 15–24.

McCrank, Lawrence J. (1991). Information literacy: A bogus bandwagon? *Library Journal* **116**, 38–42.

McFarlan, F. W., and McKenney, J. L. (1983). The information archipelago—governing the new world. *Harvard Business Review* **61**, 91–99.

McFarlan, F. W., McKenney, J. L., and Pyburn, P. (1983). The information archipelago—plotting a course. *Harvard Business Review* **61**, 145–156.

McKenney, J. L., and McFarlan, F. W. (1982). The information archipelago—maps and bridges. *Harvard Business Review* **60**, 109–119.

McKinnon, Sharon M., and Bruns, William J., Jr. (1992). *The Information Mosaic: How Managers Get the Information They Really Need.* Harvard Business School Press, Boston.

Mathaisel, Bud (1992). Putting the I back in IT. *Special Libraries* **83**, 145–146.

Matheson, Nina W., and Cooper, John A. D. (1982). Academic information in the academic health sciences center: Roles for the library in information management. *Journal of Medical Education* **57**, 1–93 (Part 2).

Metaxas, John C. (1986). Firm librarians no longer mere keepers of the books. *National Law Journal* **8**, p. 1 (July 14).

Moyer, Holley M. (1992). Law librarians positioning for tomorrow. *PLL Perspectives* (Newsletter of the Private Law Librarians/SIS of the American Association of Law Libraries) **4**, 1–6.

Myers, Ken (1991). Research literacy a topic at law librarians' convention. *National Law Journal* **13**, p.4 (July 15).

National Center on Education and the Economy (1990). *America's Choice: High Skills or Low Wages!* National Center on Education and the Economy, Rochester, New York.

Novachick, Deborah (1991a). No longer a back-office function; sophisticated computers need sophisticated management. *Legal Times* **14**, p. 20 (October 28).

Novachick, Deborah (1991b). Strategies for automation and staffing. *National Law Journal* **13**, p. 9 (August 12).

Penrod, James I., and Dolence, Michael G. (1992). "Reengineering: A Process or Transforming Higher Education." CAUSE Professional Paper Series, no. 9. CAUSE, Boulder, Colorado.

Prusak, Laurence, and Matarazzo, James M. (1990). Tactics for corporate library success. *Library Journal* **115**, 45–46.

Rheingold, Howard (1991). *Virtual Reality.* Simon & Schuster, New York.

Rosen, Peter K. (1990). Let your fingers do the searching: Computer-assisted legal research can make short work of a tough job—but you have to know where to look. *California Lawyer* **10**, 47–54.

Roszak, Theodore (1986). *The Cult of Information: The Folklore of Computers and the True Art of Thinking.* Pantheon, New York.

Savage, C. M. (1990). *Fifth Generation Management.* Digital Press, Bedford, Massachusetts.

Schrage, Michael (1990a). The healing power of high tech. *Los Angeles Times*, November, 18, p. 9.

Schrage, Michael (1990b). *Shared Minds: The New Technologies of Collaboration.* Random House, New York.

Schrage, Michael (1992). "The Myth of the Information Age, or Why Information Technology Isn't." Keynote speech, Library and Information Technology Association (ALA) (audio tape), Denver, Colorado.

Schwarz, Deborah (1991a). Firms' librarians seek broader role; leaving the card catalog behind. *National Law Journal* **13**, p. 26 (April 22).

Schwarz, Deborah (1991b). Law librarians look past the stacks to explore new roles within firms. *New York Law Journal* **205**, p. 46 (April 15).

Seer, Gitelle (1991). Research training benefits firms, summmer clerks. *National Law Journal* **13**, p. S22 (July 22).

Senge, Peter (1990). *The Fifth Discipline: The Art and Practice of the Learning Organization.* Doubleday, New York.

Sirkin, Arlene Farber (1992). Librarians in the twenty-first century—endangered species or future chief information officer? *SpeciaList* **15**, 1–3.

Taylor, Frederick W. (1915). *The Principles of Scientific Management.* Harper & Row, New York.

Trautman, Rodes, and King, Christee (1983). Interactive simultaneous remote searching: Evolution of conference call searching to a reliable procedure. *Online* **7**, 90–97.

University of California (1991). *The Role of the MELVYL System in University of California Library Automation: the Next Five Years.* Technical Report no. 5. Office of the President. Division of Library Automation. October.

University of California (1992). *Development of a Prototype Graphical User Interface for the MELVYL System.* Office of the President. Division of Library Automation. January.

University of California, Berkeley (1992a). *Berkeley Library Automation Review Focus Paper.* Draft 1.0. The Library. June 5.

University of California, Berkeley (1992b). *Report to Library Administration on the Reference Services Committee Town Meeting on Reference Service.* The Library. Reference Services Committee. March 25.

University of California, Berkeley (1992c). *Townsend Center Newsletter.* Townsend Center for the Humanities. The Library Research Consultancy Program. March.

University of Minnesota (1989). *Academic Integrated Information Center Project.* Final Report Summary. (Council on Library Resources Grant no. 8004). July.

University of Minnesota (1989). Academic integrated information center project: Final report summary. Council on Library Resources Grant 8004.

Walton, Richard E. (1989). *Up and Running: Integrating Information Technology and the Organization.* Harvard Business School Press, Boston.

Watkins, Beverly T. (1992). Computer link for each professor and administrator is the goal of 2 year college system in Florida. *Chronicle of Higher Education* **39**, A18–A19 (March 11).

White, Herbert S. (1989). The quiet revolution: A profession at the crossroads. *Special Libraries* **80**, 24–30.

Whitlach, Jo Bell (1990). *The Role of the Academic Reference Librarian.* Greenwood Press, New York.

Wilson, David L. (1991). Researchers get direct access to huge data base. *Chronicle of Higher Education* **38**, A24–A28 (October 9).

Wilson, David L. (1992a). Electronic versions of public-domain texts draw fire and praise. *Chronicle of Higher Education* **38**, A15–A16 (October 12).

Wilson, David L. (1992b). Huge computer network quickens pace of academic exchange and collaboration. *Chronicle of Higher Education* **39**, A17–A18 (September 30).

Zimmermann, Roy, and Erlandson, David (1991). Power searching at Teltech: Gaining power through customer focus. *Database Searcher* **7**, 32–37.

Ownership versus Access: Shifting Perspectives for Libraries

Joel S. Rutstein, Anna. L. DeMiller,
and Elizabeth A. Fuseler
University Libraries
Colorado State University
Fort Collins, Colorado 80523

I. Introduction: The "New Paradigm"

In a recent interview published in the *Christian Science Monitor*, Richard De Gennaro summarized in a succinct manner the issues confronting librarianship as the twenty-first century approaches. "Research libraries in the next decade or two are going to be evolving very rapidly toward this new paradigm where it's not just what you own in any particular library, but it's what your library is able to provide access to," he stated. "This evolution toward making access rather than ownership the priority calls for increased cooperation between libraries" (Walters 1992, pp. 12–13).

The purpose of this article is to develop the issues relating to debate over how librarians will respond to this perceived shift from the traditonal ownership of resources toward an uncertain future relying more on electronic information technologies. Debate in the literature from the past few years may be sorted out under various categories, and this article is formatted to reflect the major concepts. The first part deals with collection development because this "paradigm shift" directly impacts the way we build and manage collections. Further, in the realm of collection development, traditional collecting methods meet head-on with the electronic information environment. The second part examines the creation of information itself, its packaging and distribution, and how automation is altering traditional bonds between librarians, scholars, and publishers. In the following section, the overriding issue of information ownership is discussed. Copyright is the legal means for controlling the incentive to freely develop ideas while protecting the rights of the creators and disseminators of these ideas. In a world of digitized information, copyright plays a crucial, yet uneasy and ill-defined, role. In the section after copyright, the theme centers on how the library confronts these changes. The potential future shape of this brave new world will be deliberated in the conclusion, and what librarianship might expect from the vantage point of the 1990s.

II. The Changing Pattern of Collection Development

A. What Collection Development Is Supposed to Do

It all begins with collections. Collections define the essence of a library. Library buildings are constructed primarily to house and maintain on-site materials. Two-thirds of the operating budget is directed toward the acquisition, processing, and preservation of these resources. Collections are also a status symbol for a library. The size of the collections, their scope and depth, their unique specialties, and the appropriate staff to service these collections indicate to the scholarly world and the reading public the meaning and place of a particular library.

Collection development is an active expression to denote the systematic growth of collections. The term is fairly recent, because until the post-World-War-II period, collections grew in a less than systematic fashion. Often, libraries were founded and later prospered because of generous donor bequests, faculty bibliophiles, and active community support groups. Collection development was the library control response to a new age of affluence characterized by an exponential growth in the production of knowledge, the great infusion of public funds to acquire this knowledge, and the low costs of processing incoming resources.

Collection development (often used interchangeably with "collection management"—denoting a more encompassing role) became responsible for not only selecting resources and managing materials budgets, but also ensuring that resources added met institutional objectives, and provided a degree of accountability for administrators.

Although a recent managerial function in libraries, activities carried on by collection development librarians have followed practices not markedly different from their counterparts over the years. As long as the written word could be expressed in a fixed medium, be it tablets of stone, wax, parchment, or paper, the need to collect and house information in repositories remains unchanged.

This process continues into the 1990s. However, fundamental changes are occurring that challenge the traditional acquisition and maintenance roles that are hallmarks of collection management. As Clifford Lynch notes, "the historical philosophy of collection management is changing radically. It is partly affected by the current breakdown of the existing system of scholarly publishing" (Lynch, 1991, p. 8).

B. The Serials Crisis

Although libraries as repositories have not changed drastically since the beginnings of recorded time, the scholarly journal is a relatively recent historical adaptation to the way information is formatted. This medium can be traced back to the seventeenth century, when one of the earliest learned associations, London's Royal Society, first began publishing its journal. Since that time, the substance of the scholarly and scientific journal has remained the same: to publish at regular intervals the most recent communication, notes, queries, and essays in order to enhance and expand the interchange and sharing of knowledge. In time, the trappings of bibliography were added: running headings, abstracts, footnotes, indexes, and cumulative bibliographies.

The groundwork for the serials crisis was laid after World War II, as America witnessed a surge in population accompanied by a robust economy, easier access to higher education, as well as the rise of an enlarged reading public. The "information explosion" was the result, accelerated in the "Sputnik era," when the federal government actively intervened to promote the advancement of scientific research. By the 1960s, the journal was undergoing a quiet revolution of its own.

A large portion of the research journal market was a product of the many scholarly associations developed within the university environment. The intellectual connection fostered initially with the Royal Society continues unabated at the end of the twentieth century. Inundated by the influx of public funds to university researchers, scholarly societies found it increasingly difficult to maintain their publishing equilibrium. Univeristy presses were unprepared to initiate many new journals, since their emphasis has traditionally been the monograph, and continues so today. When an academic department or scholarly society concludes that journal editing and production are no longer feasible as "pro bono" work, it has commenced the process of being transformed into "a creature of a commercial publishing house" (Metz and Gherman, 1991, p. 320).

As the costs of organizing and running ever larger conferences and symposia increase, scholarly societies themselves often struggle to remain financially solvent. These societies are faced with either raising membership dues, increasing the price of their journal to individuals and libraries (frequently at differential rates), or allowing the journal to be subsumed by a for-profit publisher.

In a fast-paced entrepreneurial world where marketing and sales are the driving force of competition, commercial publishing houses seized an opportunity from the more sheltered precincts of dispassionate scholarship. Most research is produced in the university, while faculty and their research associates are literally paid (via grants) by federal, state, and some private agencies to disseminate their findings through the print medium. Further, the "sacred engine" of tenure and promotion requires such production on a practically limitless scale. The marketplace of ideas, as readily seen by the private sector, became a genuine market. Information equals money.

Commercial publishers also discovered that the pricing of research, primarily scientific journals, carried no "elasticity of demand." This means the consumer reaction to any price increase is, for all intents and purposes, nonexistent. Also, "it is clear that many scientific and scholarly journals are exempt or nearly exempt from the pressures a perfect world would exert to limit their prices. Each journal . . . is a monopoly by its nature. No other can substitute for it" (Metz and Gherman, 1991, p. 317). The mechanics of collection development exclude competition as a method for building collections. Collections are supposed to be comprehensive, in-depth reflections of the production of knowledge. As long as a title carries new information, new ideas, or new arguments about existing information, it is worthwhile to acquire. Herbert White (1992, p. 11) remarks that the real cause of journal price increases can be attributed to the lack of balance between supply and demand. "Publishers see us as purchasing agents rather than customers." The "real" customer—the library patron, so to speak—has no financial obligation.

Although this will be addressed in more detail later, the very nature of copyright law, its main premise being protection of the author, generally favors the publisher, since in order to fix the author's ideas in a medium of expression, that author usually releases copyright to the publisher. Thus, the publisher creates a monopoly that "prohibits the redistribution of property that has been ceded to them by its creators" (Metz and Gherman, 1991, p. 317).

> We are drifting from an era in which information was perceived as a public good toward one in which information is marketed as a commodity. Our financial predicament and collections crisis are inevitable consequences. (Hazen, 1992, p. 14)

For librarians, these circumstances are exacerbated because the larger scientific journal publishers like Elsevier, Pergamon (now part of Elsevier), Springer-Verlag, Gordon and Breach, and Taylor-Francis are based in Europe. As Europe moves closer toward a genuine barrier-free economic community, the U.S. dollar has fared poorly against their currencies. Irony abounds as librarians witness information created by American researchers packaged by European publishers and then sold back at high cost to the very institutions that nurture this environment. Charles Hamaker (personal communication) uses the phrase "information colonialism" to describe this process.

Not all blame, if this term is appropriate, should be attributed to European houses. The world's largest publisher, the United States government, has been divesting some of its crucial data gathering functions. Once part of the public domain, the private sector is now able to sell information that was once received on free deposit to libraries. This action stems from recent presidential administrations that have emphasized a more entrepreneurial approach to government, encouraged by a perceived public demand to trim the costs of a colossal bureaucracy.

A congeries of statistical data, much of it gathered by the Association of Research Libraries (ARL), bears out the consequences of the concomitant rise of serial prices and information expansion. Here are some samples:

> Journals from the major sci-tech publishers appear to double in size in about 11–12 years and double in price in about half that time. (Okerson, 1992, p. 8)

> Ulrich's database describes close to 120,000 serials of all kinds produced worldwide, and reports that in the decade between 1978–1987 over 29,000 science titles were started. (Okerson, 1992, p. 4)

> With increase in titles, plus costs, the ARL serials universe has declined from 33% of total in 1973–74 to 26% in 1986–87. (Metz and Gherman, 1991, p. 316).

Materials budgets since 1981 have grown by 244% in ARL libraries, but collection size has grown by only 12%. During the same time period, average cost of a book is up 49%; journals, 105%. Up to 80% of acquisition budgets for institutions that are heavily science oriented go to journals (Baker and Jackson, 1992, p. 4).

In the period 1986–1991, users in ARL libraries have grown by 10–16%; new information resources in the same period declined by 15% for books and 2% for journals. In 1990, the average ARL library cancelled $120,000 of subscriptions, and the figure is higher for 1991 (Thatcher, 1992, p. 4).

With this sobering data, a parallel rise in interlibrary loan traffic is predictable: since 1981, resource sharing in ARL is up 155% for lending and 206% for borrowing. Forty to sixty percent of interlibrary loan traffic by ARL libraries is with other ARL libraries. Since 1971, borrowing has risen 7.61% to $18.00 an item, and the cost of lending up 5.82% to $11.00 an item. Interlibrary loan has become less a courtesy and more an essential service (Baker and Jackson, 1992, p. 4).

In both words and deeds, reaction by librarians has been vociferous, though often ineffectual. Traditional countermeasures include efforts to control and stabilize costs, largely through cancellation of "offending" journals. Others include boycotting particular publishers, lobbying for more funds from parent institutions and funding agencies, seeking out cooperative resource sharing agreements, and persuading universities and scholarly societies to retain physical and copyright control of their publications (Smith, 1991,

p. 233). Richard Dougherty has argued that academic libraries should be a major player in these surroundings, even to the point of promoting the university as the primary publisher with libraries "as retail distributors of resource sharing networks" (Alexander, 1990, p. 189).

But this is an uneasy role for librarians unaccustomed to confronting those purveyors of print who once were an integral component of the librarian–scholar–publisher triad. This is exemplified by the failure to establish a concerted boycott of commercial publishers, fearing both a legal tangle on the restraint of trade issue, as well as a potential dampening of the free flow of information—a hallmark of the profession (Smith, 1991, p. 234). Murray Martin (1992, p. 11) suggests the situation may be "incurable," and cites the high costs of core journals that serve as the bulwark of any self-respecting collection and which would be politically dangerous to cancel. Also, monographic purchases, still the trademark of library collections, are not prone to significant reductions, since so many disciplines are still book oriented. Perhaps, says Herbert White (1992, p. 12), we need to rethink how we acquire information. "We have rapid bibliographic access, but not rapid document delivery. This suggests that a reversal of our present tactic of diverting funds from other activities to acquisitions might be in order."

C. The Advent of Automation

While collection development librarians were observing the rise in serial prices in the 1970s and 1980s, the long-awaited age of automation implanted itself on the library infrastructure. Once the MARC format became a practical entity, large bibliographic utilities supplanted the NUC and enabled simultaneous online cataloging and processing transactions. At first, the utilities generated catalog cards, since local online catalogs were rare. This activity is similar to the record of other technological innovations, which at first mimic the superseded technology, much as the first printed books copied exactly the written codex format.

For a long time, collection development was among the last segments of the profession to embrace automation. Librarians in general are circumspect about new incentives that alter centuries of tradition. For example, the problems in implementing AACR 2 left many leery about potential upheavals in the workplace (Molholt, 1989, p. 132). Unlike cataloging, and to some degree circulation, collection developers could keep their distance, at least for a while.

By the late 1980s, the "paradigm shift" began to affect collection management. Online public access catalogs became prevalent, including the capacity to mount abstracting and indexing services as well as local catalogs. At the same time, CD–ROM technology became a common feature, vying with standard print indexes in use and importance. Collection development librarians had no choice but to be involved in technological decision making, much like their cataloging and circulation colleagues a decade ago.

The online catalogs themselves could be devoted only to monographic collections, leading to efforts at retroconversion programs in order to capture older materials not available on MARC tapes. This is an interesting paradox. Library automation dollars pursued more traditional information resources, while acquisition budgets became increasingly dominated by serials. Of course, there is logic to this dichotomy, since economic factors made online public access catalogs possible, originally based on the development of bibliographic utilities. Concerning serials, "access to journal literature . . . from private database producers, required piecemeal licensing, plus huge files, and few libraries could afford the disk space to mount them" (Lynch, 1991, p. 9).

Today, collection development librarians view the onset of electronic information technology as inevitable, but with some trepidation. Whether computers will impact collection management is no longer an issue; most discussion centers on the degree of technology's influence and how best to incorporate it into the workflow. Many librarians perceive automation as a panacea resolving the serials crisis. They fully expect access to myriads of databases, whether through abstracting and indexing products as menu items on OPACs, mediated online searches with vendors like DIALOG, and/or CD–ROMS. Eldred Smith (1991) envisions a great leap forward to a centralized electronic resource database, without the messy implications of copyright.

Most opinions are conservative. Large portions of the debate develop around the basic issue of differences between access and ownership. Vicki Anders (Anders, Cook and Pitts, 1992, p. 37), for example, itemizes circumstances when ownership takes precedence. She mentions archiving priorities, distinct popular formats like newspapers, and when access is simply inconvenient. Access will prevail over issues like cost effectiveness, timeliness, or enhancing information. Sheila Intner (1989, p. 5) takes an even broader position, defining "accessed" resources, which are either interlibrary loan material, databases housed at remote locations, or a "shared ownership" status, referring to material like films, which could be jointly held or purchased on a collective basis for school districts or consortia. She claims some librarians see accessed information treated more like a "service," and printed information treated as "materials."

> Collection developers should expand access to wanted materials by increasing the number of database services, especially full text services, interlibrary loans, and shared collecting agreements, and reserve their purchasing decisions for items that cannot be obtained except by owning them (Intner, 1989, p. 8).

Peggy Johnson (1992, p. 4) suggests collection development goals be tightened as access technology becomes more pervasive. Instead of building comprehensively, collection policies should focus on primary clientele, core material requirements, and developing consortial protocols. The latter is essential because "the consequences of reducing purchasing power are homogenous collections across the country and a loss of richness and depth in the national collection."

For collection developers, Sassé and Smith (1992, p. 138) ask the unthinkable. Will automation be the demise of the selector? If approval plans already allow a degree of mechanical selection, why not utilize an enlarged databank derived from local systems to enhance the ability to automatically acquire even more material, leaving selectors "free to concentrate on fringe material." Abandoning the concept of the selector as a primary agent is a premise also proposed by Jasper Schad (1992, p. 5). No longer, he avers, can selection be the activity it once was in the 1960s and 1970s. Today, the planning function looms in importance as librarians cope with rising costs, dwindling collections, and electronic information access.

Michael Keller (1992, p. 7) asks that cooler heads should prevail. "Let's not get carried away with access and deny all the good we've done in the past." Even in an age of access, collection development librarians need to reaffirm their basic tenets: continue to support instructional programs, continue to support current research, build for the future, and proceed with "collection-based" acquisition programs. Like other collection development librarians, Keller (1992, p. 7) places some faith in cooperative collection development, if libraries can move beyond local prerogative. Even that old standby, the Center for Research Libraries, should be exploited.

Donna Goehner (1992) calls this "a revolution, but with constraints" and asks that most troubling of questions: "do we allocate more funds from our materials budget or do we pass a portion of this to our users via fees? How much do we reallocate? Can we gauge such activity through interlibrary loan and online database demand?"

In the final analysis, there probably will be a balance between onsite holdings and accessed information. Core collections that are high demand will always be required. As the "new paradigm" slowly transpires into whatever shape the future holds, nationally networked collections will play a larger intermediate role once the political and economic conflicts are resolved.

III. Scholarship, Information Dissemination, and Publishing

A. Communication among Scholars

If the "new paradigm" confronting libraries and librarianship confined itself only to the way information is packaged, then its significance would be little more than ornamentation. In a deeper sense, advent of electronic information technologies is having a widespread impact on the very soul of scholarly communication. Serious consideration is given to the notion that a revolution is occurring, rivaling the invention of movable type in the fifteenth century.

Librarians should be cognizant of three discrete components of communication affecting the potential of electronic information: (1) the ability to match speed of thought with simultaneous speed of communication; (2) the varying and complex development of access points to information; and (3) the capacity for interaction and collaboration.

The first relates to the idea that written dialogue can never maintain pace with the act of thinking, and that oral speech more closely resembles the natural speed of thought. Steven Harnad (1991, p. vii) places this in the context of four progressive, chronological revolutions since the dawn of civilization: first speech, then writing, then the advent of print, and finally, "electronic skywriting," which restores scholarly communication "to a tempo much closer to the brain's natural potential." Ann Okerson (1992, p. 7) aludes to this when she declares that even with our most advanced print format, the journal, delays in publication can take months or even years. Often, scholars need to share information long before publication. The ability to communicate electronically will greatly facilitate this process.

Accessing information is another area that will change radically in this "fourth revolution." Although the codex page format is a linear process, its access has always been nonlinear; yet, this capability has evolved slowly over the centuries. The invention of movable type provided the means to record and accumulate knowledge quickly, thanks to its portability and mass production. But as books proliferate, finding information becomes more elusive. Page numbers were introduced after 1500. Today, knowledge is more interdisciplinary, leaving the standard bibliography less effectual (Summit, 1992). The journal is more amenable to different access points, since indexing is more sophisticated. James O'Donnell (1992, p. 11) thinks the monograph may be in jeopardy because it is too linear, it is access inefficient, and "looks more like a dinosaur."

The third upheaval in communication relates to scholarly interchange. The highest form of intellectual potency in a university is the concept of a scholarly community, and the hallmarks of such a community are collaboration, instruction, and publication. The electronic medium will enable collaboration to increase to the point where "invisible colleges" will develop, transcending physical proximity (McCarty, 1992, p. 6). Michael Schrage, in his book *Shared Minds: The New Technologies of Collaboration* (1990), argues that environments must be designed that support collaborative interaction, and a primary tool for accomplishing this is the computer. Society may value the solitary work, but in many instances, scholarship and creativity require collaboration.

B. Publishing in the Electronic Age

The shape of access technology can be defined by the growth and characteristics of the database industry. Today, there are 7000 database producers compared to 300 thirteen years ago, translating to four billion records compared to 52 million. Seventy-two percent of databases are of "word type" variety, while 22% are numeric. Full-text databases have mushroomed 300% since 1985. Orientation by subject shows 33% of databases related to business, 23% for science and technology, and 11% for health and life sciences. Online databases comprise 51% of the industry, batch-mode 16%, and CD-ROMs 13%. Seventy percent of the market is commercially derived, the United States government produces 16%, and other nonprofit sources comprise 12% (Williams, 1992).

The pervasiveness of this industry has provided researchers and others in the business of information to develop or extend new mediums of expression for formal communication. For example, the journal will "behave" differently in the electronic world in ways not previously possible. The quality of nonlinear access to information will grow and improve. Keyword searching will virtually eliminate the use of LC subject headings. The source of information will become less important to the user as boundaries separating one information source from another will lose distinctness (O'Donnell, 1992, p. 13). This mutability of electronic information has the potential to create confusion and disorder for archiving, integrity, and security of data. The medium itself becomes a change agent, echoing the earlier themes of Marshall McLuhan.

The electronic journal has received much attention, less for what has actually occurred, than for possessing the potential to redefine the scope of formal communication and publishing. The print industry has long been criticized for delays and constraints in publishing ideas and new data in a timely manner. Peer review, refereeing, editing and revising, and final manifestation consume months and years, often resulting in materials considered obsolete. Many authors look to electronic journals, bulletin boards, and discussion groups on the Net to resolve the print world's inability to stay abreast of the information explosion.

Some authors have adopted the view that print journals and monographs are merely methods to validate research, rather than spreading new ideas. One math professor reported that sharing and collaboration in his discipline is primarily through electronic networking (Thatcher, 1992, p. 7). Even with ASCII text, the network medium is attractive because of connectivity, interactiveness, and speed. Okerson (1992, p. 13) sees the journal transformation to electronics determined by three factors: (1) technological advances; (2) economic priority of research and education; and (3) social and academic conventions. In an electronic environment, articles may be deposited in select databases, and will assume an official gloss when they are eventually refereed. In the meantime, as long as researchers are cognizant of the situation, these articles will be available for access.

The migration to electronic media from print will be a long and slow process. "Publishers, especially commercial publishers, have no incentive to give away what they can sell; they'll regard electronic journals with the same suspicion as the entertainment industry has had for dual VCRs, or digital audio tape—both of which have faced legal and economic roadblocks despite their technological feasibility" (Metz and Gherman, 1991, p. 321). In an electronic medium, the journal itself may be broken up as publishers discover the advantages of selling single articles on demand, not just full subscriptions (Lynch, 1991, p. 12).

There has been speculation that electronic journals will be a cost saver since it is expected to be less labor intensive than print journals. Metz argues to the contrary. Conventional production costs like typesetting, paper, and postage will be discarded, but "it is likely that as editing, management, and capital costs have soared, traditional costs of printing have become less significant" (Metz and Gherman, 1991, p. 322). We might be better off, he states, if the electronic journal is considered not as "a replacement of the paper journal, but a new means of communication" (1991, p. 323).

One of the largest scholarly scientific publishers, Elsevier, is making available 42 of its materials science journals over the Internet. This is an experiment (called TULIP, The University Licensing Program) to examine economic, legal, and technical issues in electronic journal transmission, including a look at user attitudes (Wilson, 1992, p. A17). According to Elsevier spokesperson Karen Hunter, the company is aware of the high cost of journals, and is hopeful that this project will be successful. Outside of the usual equipment and software expenses, there is no direct charge for the service, although participating libraries must carry the equivalent paper subscriptions. Exemplifying the industry's circumspect approach, Hunter cautions, "we don't want to create the expectation that somehow electronic information is going to be a lot cheaper than information on paper" (Wilson, 1992, p. A17).

The Association of Research Libraries is making efforts to support noncommercial scholarly publishers in the transformation to electronic media. As a joint program with the American Mathematical Society, ARL has created a Consortium For Electronic Publishing (CEP), "positioned with resources to assist other organizations with planning and implementing innovative electronic and publishing initiatives" (Okerson and Rodgers, 1992). The Consortium's premise is based on the difficulties confronted by not-for-profit printing houses with electronic publishing. CEP seeks to develop a set of uniform working relationships suitable for electronic networks, and be able to successfully compete with the commercial sector.

The "fourth revolution" alluded to above has yet to occur. Barriers include the chaotic nature of the Net, the conservative approaches of a university community, the inertia of the publishing industry, and concern about a stable atmosphere allowing quality information exchange and security of data files. Harnad speculates that the library community will accelerate this transformation, since it is in their best interests to see that information is transmitted to the scholarly world as soon as possible (Harnad, 1991, p. x).

IV. Impact of Copyright Law on the Electronic Environment

A. Copyright Law

Copyright was envisioned by Congress to make sure creators were compensated for their works and had control over how they were used. This basic economic system would thereby ensure the continued creation of new knowledge (Garrett, 1991). In 1974, Congress established CONTU, the National Commission on New Technological Uses of Copyrighted Works. Its charge was to look at the issues raised by photocopier and computer technology. While CONTUs' report was not adopted by Congress, it is used as guidance by the courts in computer-related cases.

The 1976 Copyright Act gives the copyright holder five rights: (1) to make copies; (2) to prepare derivative works; (3) to distribute copies; (4) to perform the work publicly; and (5) to display the work publicly. The new act (17 U.S.C. §102, 1988) was written to be technologically neutral. It talks about "original works of authorship fixed in any tangible medium of expression, now known or later developed, from which they can be perceived, reproduced or otherwise communicated, either directly or with the aid of a machine or a device." This act provides protection for the author from the moment of creation (17 U.S.C. §302, 1988).

B. The Debate in the Courts

The courts continue to define and evolve electronic copyright law on a case-by-case basis (Samuelson, 1992). In *Feist Publications vs. Rural Telephone Service Co.* it was found that the telephone directory white pages were a compilation of facts lacking sufficient originality to be copyrighted (Samuelson, 1992). Originality of the work was determined to be the basic principle on which copyright is grounded. Up until this time, the labor dedicated to the compilation could be used to justify copyright. Now, originality in the arrangement or selection of data is also required (Lewis, 1992).

The CONTU report offers little guidance regarding the protection of compilations. In *Fiest*, the Supreme Court stated a low threshold of originality is required in order to obtain copyright protection. Since most electronic databases depend on the selection of materials from a larger set, it is likely they would be protected under copyright (Lewis, 1992, p. 7).

C. Issues Surrounding Access

The copyright issues surrounding access in the electronic environment are complex. Many of the arguments are developed from the basic nature of electronic media. Information is easily downloaded and manipulated so that the original ownership is no longer traceable. At issue is the rights of the creators of the information as well as the users. There are arguments on different aspects of the applicability of copyright to electronic formats.

According to the Office of Technology Assessment, for copyright to work there must be a physical representation of a document, which can be archived and not changed (Oakley, 1991). There also is debate as to whether electronic bytes can be "fixed," since they constantly change. Authors rarely keep earlier drafts of their works. On the other hand, the Library of Congress Networking Advisory Committee believes in the soundness of copyright and its suitability in meeting the demands of the new technology (Avram, 1989). They cite the adaptability of copyright to motion pictures and music as examples.

The 1988 copyright amendments provide that a copy of software can be produced as an "essential step in the utilization of the computer program in conjunction with a machine and that it is used in no other manner" (17 U.S.C. §117, 1988). This allows users of software the right to make copies and assumes it would not be unlawful for the user to utilize copies converted into RAM or on a screen (Oakley, 1991). The principle is similar for printed works. Under fair use, the user can make a copy to read, but not produce multiple copies or create derivative works.

Issues involved in the sharing of information through electronic bulletin boards have yet to be tested in courts. However, writers making use of bulletin boards regularly apply notice of copyright to protect their interests, even though such notice is not required.

D. Possible Solutions

Several ideas have been proposed to protect authors in the electronic environment. Most are based on the ability of the computer to record use. Whatever the solution, it must be easy for the user to understand and easy for the library to administer. For example, using the model of the online database, the user could be charged for connect time, per search, or per hit (Lesk, 1992). However, this would not meet the criteria for ease of understanding by the user and administrative simplicity for the library.

The Coalition for Networked Information proposes a national site license model (Grycz, 1992). Under this system a license would be granted to an appropriate large site area. The price would cover, for example, "first copy" acquisition and data preparation costs, and would allow the licensee to redistribute the material using any medium deemed appropriate. Site licenses are currently being used for most CD–ROM and tape databases. They meet the criteria by being invisible to the user and easy to administer for the library. However, site license fees have been rising in a manner similar to journal prices. This is a handicap for libraries that are unable to afford the additional fees that allow access from more than one site.

The areas covered most frequently by licenses include printing, downloading, networking, and transmission. Since licensing agreements can be quite complex, before they are signed it would be appropriate for the interested library to seek purchasing or legal advice. Site licensing for libraries grants use, but not ownership. If the formatted information must be returned when the license is no longer paid, then the library loses that information from its collection.

Patents protect the "look and feel" of software (Ogburn, 1990) and offer protection to the patent holder for 17 years. But in the electronic environment, 17 years may be well past the time for a new version to be offered. Also, patents are more difficult and costly to obtain than copyright, and the work may be superseded by the time a patent is granted.

The arrangement between users and creators in the music industry may hold some answers for the electronic information tangle. Under Section 116 of the Copyright Act, jukebox owners pay a set fee per year, which is distributed to music copyright holders based on whatever share they are entitled to (Jensen, 1992). Users and owners may negotiate other arrangements that supersede the copyright law agreement. Cable television has compulsory licensing on a sliding rate scale. Smaller agencies have reduced fees. This is similar to agreements in libraries for some print indexes, like *Reader's Guide*.

Noncommercial broadcasters are granted a compulsory license for transmission of performances and artistic works (Jensen, 1992). The rates are set by the Copyright Royalty Tribunal and vary as to the kind of use. The rates are less for those stations affiliated with educational institutions. Most composers have transferred their copyright rights to a central group, ASCAP or BMI, which then licenses the works for public performances (Jensen, 1992). Licenses may be granted on a flat-fee basis, or a percentage of gross receipts for the performance on a song-by-song basis, or a flat fee for all songs in a performance. This kind of licensing arrangement could be handled by a central information agency like the Copyright Clearance Center to pay for downloaded information. This can be easily monitored and paid for by libraries as one fee for a specific amount of time. The need to negotiate a license with every publisher would be eliminated and provide some uniformity on how information is purchased.

In the future, a variety of arrangements can be expected between authors and users designed to meet their diverse needs. Libraries need to lead in determining what these methods will be if they are to ensure the continued access to information by all patrons.

V. Impact of the Electronic Environment on Libraries

A. The Influence of the User

1. The User-Centered Perspective

If the trend in ARL libraries is indicative of a more widespread phenomenon, then libraries are indeed making the shift from an ownership institution to an access service. According to a January 1992 survey of ARL libraries in which 74 out of 109 participated, 59 (80%) of the libraries indicated that "they were developing or implementing policies, services, or reallocations that emphasize access over ownership" (Schiller, 1992c, pp. 4–5). Francis Miksa (1989, pp. 781–785) predicts a fundamental shift in the operational paradigm of libraries, particularly the basic assumptions that librarians bring to their work and which shape their activities. The reasons he and others cite for this usually are connected to the advent of the information age (Sections II and III above). While useful in providing insights into the context and environment found in the academic research library, he contends that focusing on these aspects individually obscures the essential core of the change. He argues that the information revolution pivots on tailoring information retrieval to the specific information transfer requirements of users, that is, a user-centered perspective.

Whether or not one embraces this perspective totally, the fact remains that the concept of the library as a warehouse of information is losing its validity (Shaughnessy, 1991, p. 1). The supply-oriented library, no longer able to afford collecting for potential use, a "just-in-case" approach, is adopting a "just-in-time" philosophy. In this scenario, a library acquires only materials that its users need right away, freeing up funds to purchase access. In such an environment it is thus esential that a library know its users intimately: who they are, what their information needs are, how their needs are changing, and how they use information. In turn, the library needs to ask itself how best to meet those needs and uses, and particularly, what role collection building should serve in meeting those needs (Miksa, 1989, pp. 787–788).

2. Rising User Expectations

Without a doubt, user expectations have risen in concert with the rapid increase in computer literacy. This is especially true for the user group that has grown up with computers. These users are comfortable with using terminals and have little difficulty mastering basic protocols for computer use. Such knowledge increases their awareness of possibilities and heightens their expectations (Brown, 1991, p. 17). Rosenthal (1992, pp. 10–11) details some of these expectations:

1. Users expect that the online public catalog represents everything in a given library's collections—whether this is true or not, and regardless of signs to the contrary and the existence of card catalogs or other manual files.

2. Users want to be able to use just one computer terminal for traditional card catalog information, journal articles, and technical reports. Increasingly they also expect to obtain abstracts and, ideally, the full text of articles and reports.

3. Users expect to find bibliographic information for all forms and formats of material in the OPAC (i.e., books, serials, maps, manuscripts, sound recordings, machine-readable data files, films, and other audiovisual items).

4. Users want to determine if information relevant to their needs exists, regardless of where it is physically located or who has it.

5. Users want to be able to select data from files, combine and organize data from multiple sources, download or print the results, and transmit such information to others.

6. Users want to do all these things and gain access to all this information in locations and at times convenient to them; they want such capabilities on a reliable basis with a user-friendly interface. Furthermore, all this should be at little or no additional out-of-pocket cost to them.

3. Bibliographic Access Increases Pressure for Physical Access

Access can be defined in a number of ways. Often a distinction is made between bibliographic access and physical access (whether in paper, microform, or electronic format). With the proliferation of CD–ROM databases, online databases, and library catalogs through national, regional, and local networks, users have dramatically increased their bibliographic access. At the same time, libraries have been cutting back on collection development budgets, limiting on-site physical access to materials. Libraries frequently experience the phenomenon of acquiring new CD–ROM or online databases and having their interlibrary loan office swamped with requests for material not held on site (Moody, 1990, p. 157). To meet these increased user demands, libraries are expanding their traditional interlibrary loan services as well as turning to alternative access sources.

Document delivery services and full text databases are two alternatives being closely reviewed by libraries. Khalil (1993) and Wessling (1992) describe many of these services. Document delivery services concentrate on journal articles and deliver via mail, fax, or the Internet. One advantage appreciated by users is the ability to access systems at home and office without coming into the library. However, there is a hefty per-item fee, which includes copyright charges. Among the first of these services was UnCover2, offered by CARL, the Colorado Alliance of Research Libraries. Document delivery is provided from its UnCover database, containing well over three million articles. CitaDel, offered by the Research Libraries Group, offers document delivery of articles from four of its ten databases. OCLC developed ArticleFirst to deliver the contents of over 7000 journals from its Contents First database. Faxon Research Services offers documents from the 11,000 journals in its Faxon Finder database via Faxon Xpress.

Full-text projects do not require delivery: the text is available and can be searched, read, and in some cases manipulated, then printed or downloaded immediately. Libraries vary in whether they opt to charge users an extra fee for using these databases. The method of access ranges from full-text files on separate commercial systems, such as LEXIS/NEXIS, to such materials as encyclopedias and reference works mounted on a local library's online system. Some libraries offer access to texts via a campus network and the Internet. One example is the University of Michigan's UMLibText system, which provides scholars in the humanities access to software and texts for textual analysis. Other full-text projects are available on CD–ROM workstations. One of the most extensive of these is ADONIS, an international effort sponsored by various agencies both public and private. It provides the full text of more than 360 of the most heavily used biomedical journals and is stored on CD–ROM. Other examples include UMI's Business Periodicals Ondisc system, the Human Relations Area Files Cross-Cultural CDs developed by SilverPlatter, and the projects by IEEE and IEE to provide full text of their journals, magazines, conference proceedings, and standards. These products are not without cost, and as more of them become available, libraries will need to deal with complicated access issues. Just as some major microform sets can be purchased only selectively, these products may be limited to just a few libraries (Moody, 1990, p. 159).

Much has been written about the electronic journal. A few pioneering libraries interested in providing access to e-journals are currently trying to come to grips with the challenges of storage, cataloging, and user access. In the 1992 ARL survey noted above, less than half of the responding libraries (36, or 49%) indicated they now subscribe or intend to subscribe to electronic journals. Of these, four are in the early planning stages. Concerning electronic monographs, an even smaller number (31, or 42%) of the responding libraries are involved in digitizing text for electronic storage, retrieval, or dissemination. Of these, eight are exploring or proposing such projects (Schiller, 1992b, p. 4). *Superbook*, which was developed at Bellcore, the Bell Communications Research Laboratory, is a precedent-setting example of just such an electronic monograph. As the technology for digitizing improves and as the costs come down, this activity will increase not just for document delivery purposes, but for preservation of extant texts as well.

B. Problems of Budgeting

1. Redefining the Materials/Collection Budget

It is no longer sufficient to think solely in terms of a library materials budget for buying books, periodicals, and/or media. Librarians must be concerned with the process of information transfer rather than just with the process of acquisition (Martin, 1992, p. 7). If libraries are to take on the role of information brokers or gateways to information, they must look beyond their own catalogs and collections. User expectations have risen and librarians will need to become experts in exploiting library collections and electronic information resources wherever they are located.

It is ironic that as libraries are having to cut collection budgets, implying the purchase of fewer materials, user expectations are expanding, not only for even more materials, but for increased access. At the same time, the tools for access, that is, the various technologies, are competing for these same scarce resources (Anders, Cook, and Pitts, 1992, p. 38). Equipment purchase or leasing costs, maintenance, replacement of outmoded equipment, servicing, networking charges, computer storage, and staff training quickly devour large portions of a library budget.

2. Determining the Balance

The challenge for collection development librarians will be to achieve a balance between access and purchase, while serving the needs of their primary users. In doing so, it is helpful to think of access and ownership not as opposites, but as places on a continuum of information provision (Martin, 1992, p. 10). It is clear that there may be overlap as well. Libraries often choose to own a particular printed index as well as provide electronic access to the leased database either on site or through dial-up. Because of differences associated with one or both, each serves a potentially separate group of users. Examples include ease of searching for the novice or sophiesticated strategies for the expert, availability of enhancements, such as a thesaurus or abstracts, location of user, availability/location of terminals, and downloading and printing capabilities.

It will become increasingly important for libraries to determine whether acquisition or access, particularly for expensive items, is the most cost-effective measure. It is not a given that ownership is less costly. Of course, timeliness of access is still a factor in the whole equation, since access delayed can be access denied. Some libraries are already cancelling such costly titles as *Beilstein* and turning to on-demand database searches. The annual cost of a subscription far exceeds the cost of these searches. The quest for an answer to this equation is particularly important in the case of expensive periodicals (Johnson, 1992, p. 6).

A controlled test was conducted in 1990–1991 by Colorado State University Libraries with SABR (Selected Articles By Request), a document delivery service. The library subscribed to the table of contents from 48 journal titles in the Institute for Scientific Information's Research Alert. Requests were then faxed to ISI through their delivery service, the Genuine Article. Costs, usage, and turnaround time were monitored for 20 months. After assessing the results, the library decided that use warranted subscribing to five of the titles. At the same time, because of a serials cancellation project, 22 titles already owned by the library were targeted for cancellation, but were then added to the SABR list. In an effort to further control costs, the library is currently investigating document delivery through an alternative source (Fuseler, 1993).

Eldred Smith (1991, pp. 234–235) raises the question of whether such strategies as this will eventually work at lowering library expenditures. He suggests that publishers, both scholarly and commercial, are prepared to increase their prices in order to compensate for reductions in research library sales volume. Fewer copies may be purchased by libraries, but the total expenditure's rate of increase is expected to remain nearly the same. Certainly, differential serial subscription prices for libraries and individuals have been around for a long time. Monographs have been exempt from this differential pricing, though it is suspected that the high prices of some reference books usually bought only by libraries, not individuals, is higher than the end product warrants. With the issue of their "Nutritional Anthropology" catalog, the publisher Gordon and Breach has broken ranks. Monograph prices are listed separately for libraries and individuals, with the library price being, in one case, $68 more. This may be the harbinger of things to come.

3. New Measures of Quality

Libraries have always provided access to materials needed and wanted by their users. Historically, this has been made possible by providing access to materials in the local library's collection, with traditional interlibrary loan taking up the slack. This view is broadening dramatically to mean access to all library collections and electronic information resources worldwide. In the future, it is likely that "users will no longer evaluate a library by what it has, but rather, by what it can provide access to" (Bierman, 1992, p. 71). Some libraries have even reorganized themselves around this concept, with the library materials/collection budget being replaced by one access budget (information resources budget, collections access budget), which encompasses buying, borrowing, and leasing resources and information.

Both the Association of Research Libraries and the Association for College and Research Libraries (ACRL) are looking at ways to get away from the concept of quantity as a measure of quality. At ARL's 117th annual meeting in 1990, it was suggested that membership and ranking should now be determined by quality of access to online and computer network resources, not quantity of resources. Its Committee on Statistics is working to develop indicators of quality based on this premise (Bierman, 1992, p. 71). ACRL has made a start in this area as well by developing some tools for measuring library performance. Providing some assistance is the new publication *Measuring Academic Library Performance* by Nancy A. Van House and others (Chicago: ALA, 1990; Martin, 1992, p. 9). Although it is doubtful that traditional ownership-based measures will be dropped in the near future, it is probable that measures of access (both qualitative and quantitative) will be constructed and used with increasing frequency (Shaughnessy, 1991, p. 5).

4. Who Will Pay for Access?

Many librarians are not comfortable with the idea of user fees. For most it is a moral dilemma. Free access to information is essential in an enfranchised society, whereas fees erect barriers to the pursuit of knowledge. Although it can be said that information was never literally free, it is also true that the costs were controllable, predictable, and largely independent of the amount of use. Kenneth Bierman (1992, pp. 75–79) argues that in the future, less information will be available within the collections of a particular library, and there will be greater dependence on user fees. Because these costs, based directly on the amount of use, are neither predictable nor controllable by the library, the historical premise that information should be free to all users will become increasingly difficult to administer and support. Moreover, because there are more and more sources of information, libraries that do not charge fees may be forced to deny access or limit access to a significant portion of the information base. Viewed positively, fees can be a management tool to limit waste and overconsumption as well as provide an incentive for borrowing libraries to more clearly meet their primary clientele requirements.

Recently, there have been significant changes in the practices of libraries regarding charges for interlibrary loan service. An analysis of this service, conducted by Kendon Stubbs of the University of Virginia, shows that between 1985–86 and 1990–91 interlibrary lending increased by 45% and interlibrary borrowing increased by 47%. In the past year a survey of ARL member libraries on trends in interlibrary loan was conducted. Of the 82 responding libraries, 31% have changed their fee policies: 13% introduced fees, 26% increased fees, 11% established reciprocal agreements, and only 3% eliminated fees. The trend is clear. Furthermore, another 31% of respondents indicated they expect to make changes in their ILL fee structure in the coming year (Dearie and Steel, 1992).

In a program sponsored by the LAMA/LOMS Financial Management Committee at the 1990 ALA summer conference ("Alternatives", 1992), three libraries shared their strategies for dealing with costs and budgeting issues in providing alternatives to collection ownership. These were Arizona State University, California State University at Chico, and George Washington University. Each has chosen a number of ways to control costs, including limiting amounts of information, subsidizing only certain user groups, and establishing parameters for what is supplied and who supplies it. For the most part their materials budgets will support this access with help in individual cases from "new " monies and start-up grants.

C. Resource Sharing

Resource sharing holds promise as a means for libraries to deal with some of the troubling questions posed by the access versus ownership dilemma and the rising costs associated with both. Once resource sharing is developed, libraries will be more readily able to develop their core collections (the 20% that satisfies 80% of need), provide timely access to that information not owned (the other 80%), and work out cooperative collection development agreements to collect peripheral materials. Whereas developments in computing and telecommunications have given libraries the means to implement resource sharing, historic traditions of library cooperation and interdependence have also served an important function (Cohen, 1989, p. 84).

An important element in resource sharing is interlibrary loan, and any cooperative collection development effort must be closely linked to an efficient delivery system. Interlibrary loan can take many forms, from the traditional borrowing and lending practiced by virtually all libraries, to more formal reciprocal arrangements. One example of the latter is an arrangement initiated in the early 1970s between the libraries of Stanford University and the University of California at Berkeley. Not only are the delivery of materials facilitated, but faculty members and graduate students are transported between these two institutions in a van that runs several times daily (known as "The Gutenberg Express"). In this way scholars at both institutions have been assured of quick and direct access to these two research collections, with full reciprocal borrowing privileges. A more recent example of an innovative interlibrary loan arrangement is the service agreement initiated in 1989 between the libraries of the University of Texas at Austin and at Permian Basin. Patrons at the Permian Basin campus can receive copies of articles via fax from the library at Austin on the same day (Perryman, 1991, p. 78).

Although there were a number of early efforts to promote cooperative collection development, exemplified by the Farmington Plan of 1947 and the Midwest Inter-Library Center (which later developed into the Center for Research Libraries), these efforts did not meet expectations. The Research Libraries Group in the late 1970s also made an attempt at practical resource sharing. Its cornerstone was the creation of a conspectus of each library's holdings. The conspectus mapped each library's strengths and weaknesses and could be viewed by all members of the group. Primary collecting responsibilities for various subjects was divided among member libraries. Some success at a practical level was achieved in cooperative acquisitions for South Asian materials and for the areas of German literature and geology as described in the RLG Conoco study. In reporting on the aftermath of this study, Hacken commented that "although small efforts have been made in light of the Conoco study findings, acquisitions in the vast majority of institutions, both inside and outside of RLG, proceed in the traditional manner (Hacken, 1992, p. 22).

If only these disappointing efforts at the national level are considered, it would seem that the virtues of cooperative collection development in the academic library world have been more often extolled than implemented. Perhaps Michael Keller (1992, p. 8) is correct when he stated that regional efforts may prove less costly and more immediately beneficial than the national schemes. Many such initiatives are now taking place on a regional or state level. This is often occurring in conjunction with individual library involvement in consortia or networks (Schiller, 1992b, p. 4).

D. Rethinking the Organization and Staff

A whole host of changes in information technology, institutional and societal imperatives, and user expectations are forcing libraries to reexamine not only their basic services, but also the organizational structures that have been created over time to support those services (Larsen, 1991, p. 79). The shift is away from a collection-centered organization concerned with handling of materials and toward a focus on users, which emphasizes human needs assessment and personal interaction with users (Miksa, 1989, pp. 789–790). The old adage that form follows function is an applicable expression. Even if a library does not make radical changes in its basic structure, shifts and changes can still be expected at varying organizational levels in order to accomodate new functions.

Patricia Larsen's (1991) survey of library organizational structures between 1985–1990 bolsters this view. The survey focused on public and technical service divisions and whether those divisions had undergone changes within this time period. She found the division between public and technical services basically unchanged. Of the 118 responses mailed to 216 libraries, 79% continued to have public services divisions and 81% to have technical services divisions or equivalent nomenclatures. Functions included in these divisions are by and large the traditional ones, although there is considerable variation in the location of preservation, systems management, and collection management. Whereas collection development and selection activities most often reside in public services rather than technical services, these activities often overlap. In 27 libraries, collection development is a separate division. New functions most often reported include systems management, database management, and preservation, while a number and variety of functions in public and technical services are shared. Larsen (1991, p. 92) found a direct correlation between the extent to which restructuring has taken place and where libraries are located along the continuum of technological change. The report by Kathleen Carney (1991) on the experience at O'Neill Library, Boston College, lends credence to this theory. The migration from one automated system to another and the described "virtual explosion" of technology-based services at O'Neill Library were the impetus for efforts to integrate services provided by reference, cataloging, and circulation.

There are only a few examples of major organizational changes reported in the literature. Often cited are the University of Illinois at Urbana-Champaign and Penn State. In both these institutions, cataloging functions and reference functions were combined. Less widely reported is a similar combination of functions gradually taking hold at the State University of New York College at Oswego. Automation is a prime factor for this blurring of divisional lines, and although it provides advantages, there are implications for management (Davenport, 1991).

The situation in Oswego exemplifies what experts are predicting in response to advances in technological innovations and user orientation (Anders, Cook, and Pitts, 1992; Creth, 1991; Larsen, 1991). The result is a flatter organization requiring a great amount of cooperation and communication among staff members. They must be creative and flexible individuals, with success achieved by those who are self-motivated and self-directed. Cross-training for everyone has become de rigeur and reference and collection development librarians have acquired many technical skills. There is an emphasis on staff development and pursuit of other work-related projects.

Although the role of support staff at SUNY Oswego was not specifically addressed, this is another area frequently mentioned in the literature as an area for change. The ratio of support staff to professional librarians is expected to increase with the demand for programmers, system analysts, telecommunication specialists, media technicians, and conservators (Anders, Cook, and Pitts, 1992, p. 39). Paraprofessionals will assume a larger proportion of reference service, paralleling a similar growth in responsibilities in cataloging work and other technical service operations. Reference librarians can then be freed to function more as consultants to their clienteles (Rosenthal, 1991). Soon, librarians may even function as a gateway to the gateways, interpreting the means of access for their patrons (Anders, Cook, and Pitts, 1992, p. 40).

VI. Conclusion

The movement from ownership to access is no longer within the realm of debate for libraries. Whether the change is tantamount to a "fourth revolution" in the history of communications, as prophesied by some pundits, is an issue to be resolved in the twenty-first century. What matters is that librarians and information specialists are fully aware that a metamorphosis is occurring in the way we produce, store, and disseminate information, due largely to the impact of computerized technologies. This chapter has examined the primary issues in the forefront of this change, which is summarized as follows: (1) Access to electronic information databases proliferate, and libraries have commenced incorporating them as an integral part of their collection development program. (2) Choices are now being considered between ownership of material and external availability through an electronic medium. (3) With the existence of electronic networks, especially the Internet, scholars are bypassing the traditional publishing infrastructure and are exchanging, modifying, and creating ideas and information among themselves. Publishers in turn are responding to these challenges through new methods of charging, licensing, distribution, and database control. The entire issue of copyright is being reexamined in order to determine its role in this fast paced environment. That most conservative of institutions, the library, that is the library as a repository of the written and printed word, is reevaluating its place in the knowledge industry chain.

Like the term "paradigm shift," another expression has entered the vocabulary of transition, namely, the "virtual library." This term has become pervasive as a defining force for change. In 1992, ARL conducted a survey that resulted in a Systems and Procedures Exchange Center (SPEC) Kit on the "emerging virtual research library." In the introductory flyer, the virtual library is described as follows:

> In describing the research library of the future, the phrase 'the virtual research library' has been used to describe a vision of the library of the 21st century in which computer and telecommunications technologies make access to a wide range of information resources possible. . . . Like a 'virtual machine,' the virtual library gives its users the 'illusion' of access to resources far greater than those actually present (Schiller, 1992a).

The survey revealed that 85% of the libraries in ARL answering the survey are employing or considering electronic document delivery services, electronic journals, and text digitization. The SPEC Kit goes on to examine the meaning and implications of such activity in areas of service, staff training, and organization (Schiller, 1992a).

The evolving strategies in libraries for the rest of 1990s will be to integrate and account for the virtual library concept. Each library will concentrate on its own idiosyncracies, but in the overall picture, certain factors will transcend local prerogative. Among these will be:

1. Ways to cooperate with publishers
2. Concerns about copyright
3. Shifting budgets more toward access, and less reliance on onsite resources
4. Closer interaction among collection development and interlibrary loan units
5. More regional and common network collaboration as libraries are designated as last copy holders of journal titles
6. More distribution of resources among consortial libraries
7. More common use of text digitization and ownership of full-text databases
8. Reconfiguration of OPACs as database menus continue to expand
9. Libraries acting more as gateways to information networks and librarians becoming gateway navigators and monitors
10. The breakdown of present organizational hierarchies in libraries, paralleling the growing need for staff retraining.

Libraries are in the middle of a transition phase in which they are leaving the comfort of the print medium and moving toward an uncertain, relatively immature technology. The social and economic pressures during this conversion will be high. How the shape of the library will be determined in the twenty-first century largely depends on decisions made now, in the 1990s. Libraries have survived previous revolutions in communications, and they will no doubt survive this one, as long as the primary mission is preserved: to provide free access to knowledge in order to improve and enlighten an enfranchised society.

References

Alexander, A. W. (1990). Intellectual property rights and the 'sacred engine': Scholarly publishing in the electronic age. *Advances in Library Resource Sharing* 1, 176–192.

Alternatives to Collection Ownership: Costs and Budgeting Issues. (1992). Program sponsored by the LAMA/LOMS Financial Management Committee ALA Annual Conference, San Francisco, June 30.

Anders, V., Cook, C., and Pitts, R. (1992). A glimpse into a crystal ball: Academic libraries in the year 2000. *Wilson Library Bulletin* 67, 36–40.

Avram, H. D. (1989). Copyright in the electronic environment. *Educom Review* 24, 31–33.

Baker, S. K., and Jackson, M. E. (1992). Maximizing Access, Minimizing Cost; A First Step toward the Information Access Future. Prepared for the ARL Committee on Access to Information Resources, September.

Bierman, K. J. (1992). How will libraries pay for electronic information? In *Library Management in the Information Technology Environment: Issues, Policies, and Practice for Administrators* (B. G. Hobrock, ed.), pp. 67–83. Haworth Press, New York.

Brown, R. C. W. (1991). Issues in networking. In *The Future of the Academic Library: Proceedings of the Conference Held at the University of Wisconsin in September 1989* (E. P. Trani, ed.), pp. 7–23. University of Illinois at Urbana-Champaign, Champaign, Illinois.

Carney, K. M. (1991). On becoming team players. *The Reference Librarian* 15, 55–60.

Cohen, D. (1989). Are we ready for access? *Serials Review* 15, 83–85.

Copyright Act of 1988, 17 U.S.C. §102, §302, 1988.

Creth, S. D. (1991). Personnel realities in the university library of the future. In *The Future of the Academic Library: Proceedings of the Conference Held at the University of Wisconsin in September 1989* (E. P. Trani, ed.), pp. 45–62. University of Illinois at Urbana-Champaign, Champaign, Illinois.

Davenport, S. E. (1991). The blurring of divisional lines between technical and public services: An emphasis on access. *The Reference Librarian* 15, 47–53.

Dearie, T. N., and Steel, V. (1992). *Interlibrary Loan Trends: Making Access a Reality* (SPEC flyer no. 184). ARL Office of Management Studies, Washington, D.C.

Fuseler, E. (1993). Providing access to journals: just in time or just in case. In *Aquatic Information Resources: Tools of Our Trade. Proceedings of the 18th Annual IAMSLIC Conference.* (E. Fuseler and S. Wiist, eds.), pp. 127–132. IAMSLIC, Bremerhaven, Germany.

Garrett, J. R. (1991). Text to screen revisited: Copyright in the electronic age. *Online* 15, 22–25.

Goehner, D. M. (1992). Steady as she goes: Moving from print to electronic forms of information with budget reductions. *The Journal of Academic Librarianship* 18, 9–10.

Grycz, C. J. (1992). Economic models for networked information. *Serials Review* 18, 11–18.

Hacken, R. (1992). The RLG Conoco Study and its aftermath: Is resource sharing in limbo? *The Journal of Academic Librarianship* 18, 17–23.

Harnad, S. (1991). Post-Gutenberg Galaxy: The fourth revolution in the means of production of knowledge. Originally published in the *Public Access Computer Systems Review* 2, no. 1, 39–53.

Hazen, D. C. (1992). Is money the issue? Research resources and our collections crisis. *The Journal of Academic Librarianship* 18, 13–15.

Intner, S. S. (1989). Differences between access vs. ownership. *Technicalities* 9, 5–8.

Jensen, M. B. (1992). Making copyright work in electronic publishing models. *Serials Review* 18, 62.

Johnson, P. (1992). When pigs fly, or when access equals ownership. *Technicalities* 12, 4–7.

Keller, M. A. (1992). Moving toward concrete solutions based in fundamental values. *The Journal of Academic Librarianship* 18, 7–9.

Khalil, M. (1993). Document delivery: A better option? *Library Journal* **118**, 43–47.

Larsen, P. M. (1991). The climate of change: Library organizational structures, 1985–1990. *The Reference Librarian* **15**, 79–93.

Lesk, M. (1992). Pricing electronic information. *Serials Review* **18**, 38–40.

Lewis, G. J., Jr. (1992). Copyright protection for purely factual compilations under Feist Publications, Inc. v. Rural Telephone Service Co.: How does Feist protect electronic data bases of facts? *Santa Clara Computer and High-Technology Law Journal* **8**, 196.

Lynch, C. A. (1991). Serials management in the age of electronic access. *Serials Review* **17**, 7–12.

Martin, M. S. (1992). The invasion of the library materials budget by technology serials and databases. *Serials Review* **18**, 7–17.

McCarty, W. (1992). "A potency of life: Scholarship in an electronic age." Plenary address at the North American Serials Interest Group Conference, University of Illinois at Chicago, June 18–21.

Metz, P., and Gherman, P. M. (1991). Serials pricing and the role of the electronic journal. *College and Research Libraries* **52**, 315–327.

Miksa, F. (1989). The future of reference II: A paradigm of academic library organization. *C&RL News* **50**, 780–790.

Molholt, P. (1989). Research issues in information access. *School Library Media Quarterly* **17**, 131–135.

Moody, M. K. (1990). The impact of CD-ROM on resource sharing. *Advances in Library Resource Sharing* **1**, 154–165.

Oakley, R. (1991). Copyright issues for the creators and users of information in the electronic environment. *Electronic Networking* **1**, 23–30.

O'Donnell, J. J. (1992). "St. Augustine to NREN: The tree of knowledge and how it grows." Paper presented at the North American Serials Interest Group Conference, University of Illinois at Chicago, June 18–21.

Ogburn, J. L. (1990). Electronic resources and copyright issue: Consequences for libraries. *Library Acquisitions: Practice and Theory* **14**, 257–264.

Okerson, A. (1992). "The role of journals in scholarly communication." Paper presented at the North American Serials Interest Group Conference, University of Illinois at Chicago, June 18–21.

Okerson, A., and Rodgers, D. (1992). "Consortium for Electronic Publishing (CEP)." ARL draft concept document 3.1, August 7.

Perryman, W. R. (1991). The changing landscape of information access: The impact of technological advances upon the acquisition, ownership, and dissemination of informational resources within the research library community. *The Journal of Library Administration* **15**, 73–93.

Rosenthal, J. A. (1991). Crumbling walls: The impact of the electronic age on libraries and their clienteles. *The Journal of Library Administration* **14**, 9–17.

Samuelson, P. (1992). Legally speaking: Copyright law and electronic compilations of data. *Communications of the ACM* **35**, 27–33.

Sassé, M., and Smith, P. A. (1992). Automated acquisitions: The future of collection development. *Library Acquisitions: Practice and Theory* **16**, 135–143.

Schad, J. G. (1992). The future of collection development in an era of fiscal stringency: A symposium. *The Journal of Academic Librarianship* **18**, 4–7.

Schiller, N., comp. (1992a). The Emerging Virtual Research Library (SPEC Kit Number 186). ARL/OMS, Washington, D.C.

Schiller, N. (1992b). Toward a realization of the virtual library: First in a two-part series. *ARL Newsletter* **163**, 3–4.

Schiller, N. (1992c). Toward a realization of the virtual library: Second in a two-part series. *ARL Newsletter* **164**, 4–6.

Schrage, M. (1990). *Shared minds: The new technologies of collaboration*. Random House, New York.

Shaughnessy, T. W. (1991). From ownership to access: A dilemma for library managers. *The Journal of Library Administration* **14**, 1–7.

Smith, E. (1991). Resolving the acquisitions dilemma: Into the electronic information environment. *College & Research Libraries* **52**, 231–240.

Summit, R. (1992). "Reflections and projections beyond the year 2000." Paper presented at the 13th National Online Meeting, New York, New York, May 5–7.

Thatcher, S. G. (1992). "Document delivery and copyright in a university environment." Paper presented at workshop on document delivery, sponsored by the AAP, September 18.

Walters, L. S. (1992). Costs pinch university libraries: Rising expenses, tight budgets force them to redefine their mission. *The Christian Science Monitor*, May 4, 12–13.

Wessling, J. (1992). Document delivery: A primary service for the nineties. *Advances in Librarianship* **16**, 1–31.

White, H. (1992). Collection development is just one of the service options. *The Journal of Academic Librarianship* **18**, 11–12.

Williams, M. (1992). "Highlights of the online database industry." Paper presented at the 13th National Online Meeting, New York, New York, May 5–7.

Wilson, D. L. (1992). Major scholarly publisher to test electronic submission of journals. *The Chronicle of Higher Education* **38**, A17–A20.

Access to Electronic Information: Exploring the Options

William Gray Potter
University Libraries
University of Georgia
Athens, Georgia 30602

I. Introduction

There are many ways for libraries to provide access to electronic databases. Using commercial time-sharing vendors, purchasing the database on CD–ROM, and mounting the database on a local mainframe computer are just three of the possibilities. Each approach has advantages and disadvantages. This article will explore the technological developments that have given libraries this variety of options. It will then discuss the options currently available to libraries and outline the factors that any library should consider when deciding which method to use for a particular database. These factors will be illustrated with examples from the University of Georgia. While improved access to an increasing variety of databases is welcomed by librarians and users alike, there is a basic problem in using different methods to access these databases. Confronting many databases on several diverse platforms can be confusing to the user. The prospects for integrating these platforms will also be considered.

II. Background

Over the past twenty-five years, access to electronic databases has become increasingly widespread in libraries. Commercial services like DIALOG and BRS were , until recently, the primary sources for online searching of electronic databases. Libraries usually paid a fee based on elapsed time of a search and the number of records captured from a search. In many cases, all or part of this fee was passed on to the library patron, a practice many librarians found abhorrent but which they were compelled to follow because online searching

ADVANCES IN LIBRARIANSHIP, VOL. 17

was costly and there was no way to set a fixed budget for this service. Online searching was perceived to be a sophisticated and arcane practice, one better left to those who were thoroughly trained in its mysteries. Therefore, the search was conducted by a professional searcher, usually a librarian, who acted as an intermediary between the database and the user.

This situation prevailed because online searching through a commercial service was expensive. The cost of storing and maintaining the database on a mainframe computer was high, as was the care and feeding of the computer. Given the cost of the hardware and of the personnel to support the system, the only way to make electronic databases widely available was through a time-sharing system where everyone who used the system paid for their use. This spread the cost and made electronic databases somewhat affordable to most libraries.

III. Developments in Computer Systems

Over the past five years, many of these same electronic databases have moved from the commercial time-sharing systems to local computers, allowing libraries to provide unlimited searching by owning the computer on which the database resides and thus fixing costs. This has become possible because computers have become cheaper and faster in three areas: storage, power, and connectivity.

The disk storage needed to house a database has become less expensive over the past few years. The most dramatic example of this is CD–ROM, which can store up to 600 megabytes of data. It became possible to store a database on a CD–ROM that could be attached to a microcomputer. Thus, a large database that would cost a certain amount per minute to search on a commercial time-sharing system could now be purchased on a CD–ROM and made available for unlimited searching for a reasonable fixed cost. At the same time, the cost of conventional magnetic disk storage has been dropping for both mainframe computers and microcomputers. This is making it possible for libraries to consider mounting databases on the local computers they use for their online catalogs.

At the same time, the processing power of computers is improving and becoming less expensive, especially with microcomputers. Prices for the central processing unit (CPU) that drives most microcomputers has plummeted, allowing many libraries to purchase more powerful machines that can support more users and larger databases. The cost/performance ratio for larger or mainframe computers has improved dramatically over the past few years, allowing many libraries to expand their systems to support databases locally.

The ability to connect computers into networks at the local, regional, and national levels has also improved dramatically over the past few years. Local Area Networks (LANs) are widely used in libraries to allow users to access a cluster of CD–ROM databases. Universities are becoming increasingly wired with campuswide networks that allow ready access between LANs and with the central, mainframe computer. State and regional telecommunications networks are providing the basis for increasing library cooperation by giving libraries a means for linking their computer systems and providing access to shared resources. Foremost among developments in connectivity, however, is the emerging national telecommunications network that provides an electronic highway that gives libraries a ready-made way to share information. The current incarnation of the national network is the Internet and over the next few years it should evolve into the much more capacious National Research and Education Network.

As computer storage becomes cheaper, as computer processing becomes both cheaper and more powerful, and as the means to connect computers becomes more prevalent, libraries are finding alternatives to commercial time-sharing systems to provide access to electronic databases. Moreover, these trends affect all sizes of computer systems, from microcomputer to mainframe. Indeed, the distinctions that existed only a few years ago are beginning to blur. At one time, there were three distinct sizes of computers— mainframe, minicomputers, and microcomputers. Today, the line between minicomputers and microcomputers is becoming increasingly difficult to draw. This is especially true because LAN technology has allowed the use of interconnected microcomputers to do jobs once performed by smaller minicomputers.

IV. Types of Databases

Advances in technology, then, are permitting libraries to mount some databases on local computers. This is being done through CD–ROM technology in some cases or mounting databases alongside an online catalog in others. Before describing how this has been done, however, it is important to define what databases are involved.

For the most part, the electronic databases that libraries are working with are standard abstracting and indexing services: ERIC, *Psychological Abstracts*, *Engineering Index*, *Modern Language Association Bibliography*, *Readers' Guide*, *Bio-*

logical Abstracts, and MEDLINE. These are essentially databases that provide access to the literature of a particular discipline, especially to the journal literature.

Looking beyond the abstracting and indexing services, libraries are increasingly concerned with full-text databases. These can be divided into three categories: reference works, core journals, and high-end journals.

The full text of several reference works are available in electronic form. Grolier's *Academic American Encyclopedia* is perhaps the most widely available. Others include *The Oxford English Dictionary*, *Peterson's Gradline* (a guide to graduate schools), *Statistical Masterfile*, and many federal documents that are now published on CD–ROM.

Libraries are interested in making the full text of core journals available to their users. These 1500–2000 journals are those that are most commonly held by academic libraries and that are indexed in Information Access Corporation's *Expanded Academic Index*, University Microfilm's *Periodical Abstracts*, and the central H. W. Wilson indexes. The problem facing libraries is that they have provided improved bibliographic access to these journals by making electronic databases that index them widely and freely available to their users. As a result, it is increasingly difficult to keep the journals shelved and available because of the increased demand. Access to the full text of these journals would greatly improve a central service of all academic libraries. Information Access Corporation and University Microfilm are both working on ways to provide access to the full text of these core journals.

At the other end of the spectrum are the high-end, expensive journals whose prices are escalating beyond the means of many libraries to acquire them. These are often high-cost journals but, unlike the core journals, are not heavily used. It is possible that it might be less expensive to acquire the articles from some of these journals as they are needed rather than subscribing to the whole journal. This is often referred to as "just-in-time" acquisition rather than the "just-in-case" method used now. The problem is securing an article for a patron with the same turnaround time that would be realized if the journal were owned and shelved in the library. Several efforts, notably the ADONIS project, are attempting to provide the full text of these high-end journals in electronic form (Stern and Campbell, 1989).

Currently, libraries are most concerned with abstracting and indexing databases, but there is increasing interest in full-text files. It is expected that reference works will become increasingly common, followed by the core journals, and then the high-end journals. The focus in this article, however, will be on the abstracting and indexing databases because that is where most activity is taking place.

V. Alternatives for Access to Electronic Databases

There are many methods available today to provide access to electronic databases. A library might choose to focus on one over the others, but will likely use a combination of several approaches. Eight different approaches are outlined below.

A. Commercial Online Vendors: Pay Per Use

DIALOG and BRS are the two chief examples. A library establishes an account with the vendor and then pays for every use of a database.

B. Commercial Online Vendors: Subscription Based

Several vendors permit a library to pay a set annual fee that permits a certain level of use. Mead Data offers academic libraries a flat-fee pricing structure for LEXIS/NEXIS that allows a fixed number of users to access the system at any one time. CARL Systems, Inc. also will permit a set number of simultaneous users to access its UnCover database.

C. Bibliographic Utilities

The Online Computer Library Center (OCLC) and the Research Libraries Group (RLG) offer access to electronic databases that they have mounted. OCLC's First Search offers a wide range of databases in addition to World-Cat, a version of OCLC's Online Union Catalog. OCLC charges by the search, but has recently announced subscription-based pricing. RLG's CitaDel system also offers a variety of databases and pricing is subscription based (Chen, 1992).

D. Library Consortia

Several library consortia have mounted databases as part of a shared online system. The Florida Center for Library Automation, for example, provides an online integrated library system to the nine publicly supported universities in Florida. They have loaded *ERIC*, Information Access Corporation's *Expanded Academic Index*, and several other files that are available to these nine libraries. Several other consortia have undertaken similar projects, including the Division of Library Automation of the University of California, the Illinois Library Computer System, and OhioLink, all groups of academic libraries.

E. Local Mounting on Mainframe Computer

Several libraries acquire electronic databases from the publisher. The databases are received on magnetic tape and loaded onto their mainframe computer system, usually the same system that supports their online catalog. Libraries that do this include Georgia Tech, the University of Virginia, the University of Michigan, Dartmouth, Clemson, Arizona State, and the University of Georgia (Potter, 1989). One chief advantage of this approach is that people use the same commands that they use in the online catalog to search these other databases.

F. Local Mounting on a Local Area Network

The most common way to mount databases on a Local Area Network is to connect a cluster of CD–ROM drives to the microcomputer that functions as the network's server (Bailey, 1992). This approach allows several workstations to use the same set of CD–ROMs. Also, large-capacity magnetic disks can be attached to the server to store these databases. Magnetic storage can support more simultaneous users with faster access times than CD–ROM.

G. Stand-Alone CD–ROM

This arrangement involves one CD–ROM drive attached to one microcomputer workstation so that the database is accessed one user at a time. A slight variation is to have five or more CD–ROMs stored on a mini-jukebox and the user selects which CD to search. This is especially useful if a given database, for example, *Dissertation Abstracts*, spans several disks. The essential characteristic here, however, is that only one user can access a given disk at any one time.

H. Print

With all the attention paid to electronic databases, it is easy to forget sometimes that most indexes still appear in print. In many cases, print may be the most appropriate medium and should be considered. Print might also be considered in conjunction with an electronic database. For example, it is possible to purchase the indexes to *Chemical Abstracts* on CD–ROM and rely on the print volumes for the actual abstract.

VI. Selecting the Best Method of Access

Libraries are using technology to provide improved access to information by taking advantage of what is available and affordable today. There are many ways to provide access to electronic databases, many more than there were a few years ago and more are coming. Each library needs to consider which method best meets its own circumstances and it must consider this for each database.

There are many factors to consider when deciding which method to use for which database. The financial cost of hardware and software certainly must be considered, but cost is not always the overriding factor. Other conditions might make the cheapest method less attractive.

There are seven factors that a library should consider when deciding how to offer a database. These are anticipated use, cost of hardware, cost of subscription or license, functionality, need to support remote users, possibilities for cooperation, and political considerations. Each of these factors is discussed below.

A. Anticipated Use

The use a database will receive should be analyzed. If a database will be heavily used, then mounting it locally alongside an online catalog or on a Local Area Network might make economic sense, rather than relying on an outside vendor and paying by the search or by connect hour or by simultaneous user. On the other hand, if little use is anticipated, then relying on a vendor, a stand-alone CD–ROM product, or even print might be preferable.

It should be kept in mind that when dealing with electronic databases, the means of access can be readily changed. For example, a library might assume that a database will be heavily used and mount it on its mainframe computer. Actual experience might show that the database is not used, in which case the library can cancel the subscription and use another means of access. The disk space that was allocated to the database can be used for another database that will be more heavily used.

B. Cost of Hardware

The costs of acquiring and maintaining hardware for a database should be considered. The larger the database, the more expensive it will be to store locally. Of the local options, mainframe disk storage is the most expensive, followed by magnetic disk on a Local Area Network server. CD–ROM is likely to be the cheapest method of storage next to paper, and may in some instances be less expensive to house and maintain than paper. Therefore, the larger the file, the more expensive it will be to mount on a mainframe system. Even for a heavily used database, the cost of disk storage on the mainframe may be prohibitive.

Beyond disk storage, other hardware costs include the charges a computer center might make for searching. Some libraries are billed by how much the computer is used. Other costs might include the start-up costs of setting up a

Local Area Network if one does not exist, including wiring and the costs of a server.

C. Cost of Subscription or License

Unlike books and journals, electronic databases are leased to the library under the terms of a license agreement. This agreement usually lasts a year and it spells out who may use the database, how much the library will pay, and other obligations of the library. It also might limit use of the database to a set number of simultaneous users. The license for a stand-alone CD–ROM will cost less than a license to network a CD–ROM, which will be less than a license to load a database on a mainframe computer.

These first three factors—use, hardware cost, and license cost—are fairly straightforward and can be quantified and even made part of a formula for determining the best method of access. Richard Meyer has developed a model to quantify and weigh these factors (Meyer, 1993). Meyer's model is valuable in evaluating the cost factors which, in many cases, will be overriding. However, as Meyer also points out, if cost were the only factor, libraries would not even use electronic databases and instead would force patrons to use the print versions. There is a basic acceptance that online searching is easier and more responsive to the needs of the user. That is why libraries work to provide it. The remaining factors have less to do with cost and more to do with providing the best possible service.

D. Functionality

Online searching is fundamentally superior to searching a printed index. It is faster, more comprehensive, and provides more points of access. Search results can be captured and stored. Further, online systems give us the opportunity to develop systems that instruct and inform the user. It is this improved functionality that makes online searching attractive to librarians and to users.

There are also significant differences among the various methods of online searching and these differences in functionality should be considered when deciding how best to offer a particular database. For example, a stand-alone CD–ROM search product may be considerably less expensive than using DIALOG or BRS, but the search engine may not be as powerful. If a user requires keyword searching of words in the abstract, then a CD–ROM product that does not provide this will not be of much use. As mentioned earlier, using the same search engine as that of the online catalog allows the user to transfer skills learned from searching the online catalog to searching another database. Also, loading an index to periodicals on the same system as the online catalog can provide the ability to link holdings information to article citations, as NOTIS does. These and other differences in functionality might be important enough to justify the additional cost of one approach over another.

E. Need to Support Remote Users

One of the chief advantages of online searching is that a user does not have to be in the library to conduct a search. Even with commercial vendors, accounts can be set up for users to access databases, with the library picking up the tab. Of the various alternatives for access listed above, all except print and stand-alone CD–ROMs permit remote access. However, some do a better job than others. Local Area Networks can be used remotely, but this can be tricky, depending on the network software used. Loading databases on the main-frame makes remote access relatively simple. The exact circumstances will vary from one library to another, but remote access will be possible for some alternatives and not for others.

A library needs to consider the importance of remote access. A large research university will have many faculty and researchers working in offices and laboratories throughout the campus and possibly at remote research stations. Providing them with 24-hour-a-day access to the files they need for their research could be important. A multicampus institution might also find remote access important as would an institution with many commuter students who would welcome the opportunity to search these databases from home. Efforts at distance learning could also be supported by remote access. On the other hand, some libraries with a heavy population of users who live on campus may find that this is not as important or that for some databases remote access is not critical. Again, this is a factor that needs to be considered.

F. Possibilities for Cooperation

The ability to share a database with other libraries may be an important factor in controlling costs. Most vendors will offer a sliding price scale, making it cheaper for the second and subsequent libraries to license a database. Also, more potential users drives up the use of a database and thus brings down the cost per search. There are also economies of scale in sharing hardware re-sources.

There are several models for cooperation. A consortium of libraries might share a platform, or several libraries with locally mounted files might elect to share the databases each has loaded. There are probably as many different models for cooperation as there are library consortia. The important point is that the economics of acquiring a database may change if that database is acquired as part of a group effort.

G. Political Considerations

This last factor is the most subjective, but political considerations cannot be overlooked. For example, when considering sharing a database with a consortium of libraries, the importance a parent institution places on cooperation may have an overriding effect. Also, if a library has loaded a set of scientific databases on its online catalog, it might be politic to consider one or more databases in the social sciences and humanities as a way to strike a balance. The campus environment should be considered carefully. If the president has said that a given discipline is going to grow over the coming years, it might be wise to support a database in that discipline.

These seven factors discussed above provide a framework that can be useful in deciding how best to provide access to a particular database. Other authors have developed other models (Pagell, 1991; Meyer, 1993) that are also valuable. These seven factors are illustrated below using specific examples.

VII. The University of Georgia

Examples of how specific databases have been loaded at the University of Georgia will be used to illustrate the points made in the preceding section. First, some background on the situation at Georgia is in order.

Two systems are used to provide direct user access to databases at Georgia. The first is the library's online catalog, called GALIN, an acronym for the Georgia Academic Library and Information Network. GALIN is a locally developed system operating on an IBM ES/9000 mainframe computer with over 250 dedicated terminals, of which 110 are public access. In addition, any terminal on campus connected to the mainframe or to the campus broadband can access GALIN. Dial access is readily supported for a wide variety of terminals.

In addition to the online catalog, the following databases have been loaded on GALIN:

Academic American Encyclopedia
Art Index
Biological Abstracts
Books in Print
Business Index
Current Contents (Sciences and Social Sciences)
ERIC
Expanded Academic Index
Newspaper Abstracts
Psychological Abstracts

Also, *Public Affairs Information Service* is being readied for loading. GALIN uses twenty-seven gigabytes of storage for these databases, which grows by about five gigabytes per year. Several other academic libraries in Georgia also use these databases. They pay the incremental license fee for the databases they wish to use and they pay a fixed annual fee for the computer overhead incurred by their searching. The library has also been exploring the possibility of sharing databases with Clemson University, which has loaded several files on their system.

The other system used at Georgia is a Local Area Network called LIBRA. Based on an IBM PC compatible database server, LIBRA uses Novell Netware 3.1. It supports twenty-eight CD–ROM drives using SCSI Express from Micro Design International, a Novell network loadable module that uses the standard Small Computer Systems Interface (SCSI) to control the CD–ROM and hard disk drives. LIBRA currently has twenty-five dedicated workstations split between the Main and the Science libraries. It is connected to the University's campus broadband and can be accessed by any Novell compatible network on campus. LIBRA currently supports the following databases:

Agricola	*MathSci*
America: History & Life	MEDLINE
Analytical Abstracts	*MLA Bibliography*
CAB Abstracts	*Peterson's Gradline*
Compact Disclosure SEC	*Social Work Abstracts*
GPO Monthly Catalog	*SocioFile*
Historical Abstracts	*Statistical Masterfile*

Development continues on LIBRA, with plans for dial access and improved network support. A second server is envisioned that would support large magnetic disks, thus allowing large files such as MEDLINE to be mounted as one file rather than spread across several CD–ROMs. LIBRA will also become the platform for offering access to other systems across the Internet. For example, a menu system has been set up on LIBRA that provides access to twenty-three online catalogs of other libraries around the country. Also, up to three simultaneous users can access Mead Data's LEXIS/NEXIS system through LIBRA.

Several stand-alone CD–ROMs are also housed in the libraries for products that, for various reasons, could not be placed on the Local Area Network. These include *Dissertation Abstracts, Social Science Citation Index, ABI Inform*, and *Science Citation Index*. The reasons for maintaining some of these databases on stand-alone CD–ROMs will be explained below.

Given this background on the situation at the University of Georgia, the decision process that went into deciding how to make some of these databases available can be examined, using the seven factors outlined above.

A. Expanded Academic Index

Produced by the Information Access Corporation, *Expanded Academic Index* covers about 1500 core journals. It is similar to University Microfilm's *Periodical Abstracts* and to a combination of several of H. W. Wilson's core journal indexes. Others have compared these files and decided to load one over the other (Beaubien, 1992). Georgia decided to load this index because it matched *Infotrac*, a CD–ROM product that was in use and familiar to students. In deciding to load *Expanded Academic Index* into GALIN rather than leaving it as a CD–ROM product, the seven factors mentioned above were considered:

1. Anticipated use. Use was expected to be high, given the fact that this database covers core academic journals used by a wide variety of undergraduates. GALIN supports far more simultaneous users than LIBRA or a stand-alone CD–ROM, so it can better handle heavy use.

2. Cost of hardware. The records are relatively small and the database grows by about 350,000 records per year. Disk storage costs were minimal.

3. Cost of subscription or license. This was a wash, with the cost of a subscription to the tapes running at about the same cost as the CD–ROM-based *Infotrac*.

4. Functionality. At the time the decision was made (Fall 1991), GALIN provided much better searching capabilities than the CD–ROM version. Improvements have been made since then in the CD–ROM version, but GALIN still offers superior features, such as sorting by author, title, or date.

5. Need for remote access. This was not an overriding concern, but it was deemed important. GALIN supports remote access better than any other method.

6. Possibilities for cooperation. At the time, it was thought that other libraries in Georgia would be interested in using our implementation of this file.

7. Political considerations. This is a safe database politically because it covers many subject areas.

Based on this analysis, it was decided to put this database on GALIN.

B. Current Contents

From the time loading databases on GALIN was first contemplated, *Current Contents* was a top contender. Only the Science and Social Science sections were considered because they included abstracts, which the Arts and Humanities section did not. The database covers 5000 journals in the sciences and 1500 in the social sciences and adds about 850,000 records per year. It is current and has considerable name recognition among faculty. It is a research-oriented file and, because it has abstracts, the library intends to keep it up indefinitely rather than roll off the older years.

Applying the seven factors led to the following analysis:

1. Anticipated use. Heavy use was expected, especially in the sciences, given the volume of funded research on campus.

2. Cost of hardware. Disk space requirements are high, over three giga-bytes per year.

3. Cost of subscription or license. The database license is expensive, but works out to less than $6 per journal covered. Given the high subscription price of these research journals, providing this level of access is worth the cost.

4. Functionality. The subject headings used by this file are broad and not useful. GALIN permits keyword and phrase searching in all fields, including the abstract, which is essential for searching this database. GALIN can also be programmed to search by journal title and then display the issues of a journal in reverse chronological order. Given the nature of the database, this was also deemed essential.

5. Need to support remote access. As stated, there is a large volume of funded research on campus, primarily in the sciences. Thus, there are many researchers working in laboratories and offices who need access to their literature from their workplace. They also need round-the-clock access.

6. Possibilities for cooperation. This database offers great potential for cooperation. Other libraries in the state have expressed more interest in this file than in any other.

7. Political considerations. From a political standpoint, this is an excellent database. It provides in-depth access to research journals in a variety of fields, it is timely, and it provides access to tables of contents on a timely and regular basis. This is important for journals we own and also for those we do not subscribe to or have cancelled.

Based on this analysis, it was decided to load *Current Contents* on GALIN.

C. MEDLINE

While the University does not have a medical school, there is considerable research in allied fields across campus. The central index to medical litera-ture, MEDLINE is an important database and the library wants to provide access as widely as possible. The options considered for making this file available included loading it on GALIN or loading CD–ROM version on LIBRA. Applying the seven factors led to the following analysis:

1. Anticipated use. Use was expected to be heavy, given the amount of work in the biosciences across campus. This would favor GALIN.

2. Cost of hardware. This file requires tremendous resources for disk space on GALIN and five or six CD–ROM drives on LIBRA.

3. Cost of subscription or license. Because MEDLINE is produced with federal funds by the National Library of Medicine, the subscription cost for either GALIN or LIBRA is minimal.

4. Functionality. Loading MEDLINE on GALIN would require extensive programming to take full advantage of the features of the database. However, the GALIN search engine would probably be adequate for most users and more sophisticated users could be referred to the BRS or DIALOG version. The CD–ROM version from SilverPlatter is tailored to the database. However, the CD–ROM version is also spread across five or six disks, requiring the user to carry a search from one disk to the next.

5. Need for remote access. Remote access is important for this file.

6. Possibilities for cooperation. If MEDLINE were loaded on GALIN, there would be considerable opportunities for cooperation with medical and research libraries in Georgia. On the other hand, LIBRA is limited in its ability to support other libraries.

7. Political considerations. While there was considerable interest from users in having this file available, there was no preference for one method over another.

Based on this analysis, it was decided to place MEDLINE on CD–ROM on LIBRA primarily because of the cost of acquiring disk space to load it on GALIN. This might be reconsidered in the future. Alternatively, it may soon be possible to load MEDLINE as a single file on LIBRA using magnetic disk instead of CD–ROM.

D. Science and Social Science Citation Index

The citation indexes from the Institute for Scientific Information are extremely valuable research tools. Analysis was conducted to consider whether to load them on GALIN or LIBRA or as stand-alone CD–ROMs.

1. Anticipated use. While these are valuable databases, it was not expected that these files would be used heavily. Thus, there was no need to load them on GALIN and attention focused instead on LIBRA or a stand-alone station.

2. Cost of hardware. The cost of hardware was considered a wash whether the files went on LIBRA or a stand-alone station.

3. Cost of subscription or license. The cost difference between a license for a stand-alone station and a library or campus network is significant.

4. Functionality. There was no real difference between LIBRA and a stand-alone workstation.

5. Need for remote access. While this would be an attractive feature, it was not considered to be critical.

6. Possibilities for cooperation. The two methods under consideration, LIBRA or a stand-alone workstation, do not readily support interinstitutional cooperation, so this was not a factor.

7. Political considerations. Political considerations did not enter into this decision.

Based upon the above analysis, it was decided to place these two citation indexes on stand-alone CD–ROM workstations. The critical factor was the steep price of a network license.

These four examples illustrate how these seven factors can be applied. The University of Georgia Library has found that they work well, but other libraries might apply the same criteria to the same databases and come to different conclusions. Every library is different and must make its own decisions. The analysis of the databases listed above was carried out by the library administration. Recently, a Database Access Committee has been established to make recommendations on databases.

VIII. Conclusion

Recent advances in technology have given libraries new ways to provide access to a variety of electronic databases. While this discussion has focused on abstracting and indexing databases, the availability of full-text files is fast approaching and the alternatives for access and the factors to consider are much the same. No matter what alternative we use to provide access to these files, the users are empowered in ways few thought possible even a few years ago.

There is a downside to the current situation, however. While access to these databases has given library users unprecedented power and an increasing diversity of information resources, they are also confronted by a confusing hodgepodge of interfaces, search engines, and displays. The online catalog, the local area network, databases shared by consortia, commercial services, and other online catalogs available on the Internet almost all use different commands and protocols. We can create a pleasing menu to help users select a database, but once they get into it, they are on their own. At Georgia, users confront GALIN terminals, LIBRA workstations, several stand-alone CD–ROMs, and OCLC terminals all in the same area. It is difficult for them to tell which terminal does what, let alone know how to maneuver within a system.

Librarians need to work to unify these different interfaces and displays. There are several positive developments in this direction. There is a standard that would allow one system to talk to another and interpret the searches and the search results to the user in a manner the user understands. This is the Open Systems Interconnection standard Z39.50. As more vendors and systems adopt it, much of the problem of diverse systems might be resolved (Lynch, 1990). However, this is some years off. An intermediate step is to adopt the Common Command Language, a proposed National Information Standards Organization standard that sets forth a set of commands for searching (Crawford, 1992). Other possible solutions include Wide Area Information Servers (WAIS) that can gather and interpret information from a variety of information sources and not require that the user know a specific set of commands (Nickerson, 1992).

The best interface will be the one that is most transparent to the user. Regrettably, such an interface may be many years away. In the meantime, it is some consolation that despite the hodgepodge, users are enthusiastic about the array of information resources libraries are able to deliver today. It is also something of a comfort that they do tend to use a few databases in their particular fields and learn these well. Also, at Georgia, having the heavily used databases on GALIN does present a common search language and a common display to patrons, while on LIBRA most of the CD–ROMs are from SilverPlatter and use the same interface. So, the problem of diverse interfaces has been minimized, but remains a concern.

New technology, then, is permitting libraries to provide increased access to an increasing variety of databases at no direct cost to the user, despite the poor economic conditions of recent years. This technology is also allowing libraries to reach out to people in their homes and offices with services they can use every day. It has long been known that libraries are not the first place researchers turn for information. Instead, they rely on personal collections and on colleagues. As more and more people have computers on their desks that they use routinely, and as computers become increasingly networked, libraries are well positioned to offer services that people can access at the touch of a keyboard, services that they will turn to first when they need information. That is the real value of offering electronic databases, providing services that are efficient and powerful and that people can use in their daily lives.

References

Bailey, C. W. (1992). The intelligent reference information system project. A merger of CD–ROM LAN and expert system technologies. *Information Technology and Libraries* **11**, 237–244.

Beaubien, D. M. (1992). Wilson vs. IAC on tape: A comparison. *Database* **15**, 52–56.

Chen, C. C. (1992). Redefining information access to serials information. *Microcomputers for Information Management* **9**, 61–66.

Crawford, W. (1992) Starting over: Current issues in online catalog user interface design. *Information Technology and Libraries* **11**, 62–76.

Lynch, C. A. (1990). Information retrieval as a network application. *Library Hi-Tech* **8**, 57–72.

Meyer, R. W. (1993). A matrix framework for selecting electronic alternatives. *Information Technology and Libraries* **12**, 173–180.

Nickerson, G. (1992). Getting to know Wide Area Information Servers. *Computers in Libraries* **12**, 53–55.

Pagell, R. (1991). Planning your technology mix: Decision factors that meet user needs. *The Electronic Library* **9**, 319–324.

Potter, W. G. (1989). Expanding the Online Catalog. *Information Technology and Libraries* **8**, 99–104.

Stern, B., and Campbell, R. (1989). International document delivery: The ADONIS project. *Wilson Library Bulletin* **63**, 36–41.

Research Libraries: Past, Present, and Future

Norman D. Stevens
University Libraries
University of Connecticut
Storrs, Connecticut 06268

> Damn'd neuters, in their middle way of steering,
> Are neither fish, nor flesh, nor *good red herring*.
> —John Dryden, *The Duke of Guise*, 1682

I. Introduction

A. Content

What does Dryden's quotation have to do with the past, present, and future of research libraries? Apart from perhaps piquing the reader's interest, it aptly describes the dilemma that research libraries face in an extended period of transition that began at least thirty years ago and promises to continue well into the twenty-first century. Almost all libraries, of course, are now dealing with the innumerable changes brought about by new technologies that have altered the way in which information is disseminated. Research libraries, which have a unique role as a bridge between the past and the future, are now faced with particularly critical choices as they seek to identify and establish an appropriate role for themselves in a new environment that will enable them to continue to serve not only current users but future users for many generations to come. The date of that quotation (1682) also suggests quite vividly the complex problems that research libraries face as they seek to deal with materials dating back hundreds of years, as well as more recent and contemporary materials, and as they also contemplate the kind of materials they will have to deal with in the future.

This article will examine in broad outline the history of research libraries and their current state as a prelude to a more detailed consideration of the likely future of such libraries. In the context of this article, research libraries

ADVANCES IN LIBRARIANSHIP, VOL. 17
Copyright © 1993 by Academic Press, Inc.
All rights of reproduction in any form reserved.

are defined, as is discussed in more detail in Section II below, as those large libraries with extensive collections of printed books and other materials, that serve to support a broad range of current and future users conducting research in a variety of disciplines in the humanities, sciences, and social sciences. It will review, in passing, some of the most significant of the substantial quantity of articles, books, papers, and reports that, over the years, have offered the comments of others on the future of the libraries. All of those comments, as must always be kept in mind with any predictions of the future, are speculative and subjective even though they may be based on specific experiments or projects. Many of those comments deal with libraries in general and those that do specifically deal with research libraries tend to treat them as a broad and ill-defined class of libraries. The quantity of such previous speculative works is considerable (Roberts, 1987) and has undergone dramatic growth in recent years. With respect to research libraries, there are a few classic works (Bush, 1945; Clapp, 1964; Hirsch, 1951; Licklider, 1965; Rider, 1944; Shera, 1967; Wasserman, 1965) that are still essential to any consideration of the current situation. There is also a body of interesting, if generally less useful, works (Fussler and Bryan, 1978; *Future of Libraries*, 1982; Holley, 1975; Hubbard, 1986; Hyatt and Santiago, 1987; Lathem, 1978; Poole, 1977) that provide some additional ideas and considerable background information. There is another larger body of works (Anders, Cook, and Pitts, 1992; Billings, 1991; Billington, 1989; Cline, 1983; Crooks, 1982; Dowlin, 1984; Edelman, 1986; Hayes, 1981; Lancaster, 1982; Licklider, 1965; Ostrow and Zich, 1990; Overhage and Joyce, 1965; Seiler and Surprenant, 1991; Shera, 1967; Shuman, 1989; Smith, 1990; Taylor, Mann, and Munro, 1988) that deal specifically with the impact of technology on the future of research libraries, generally in an optimistic and positive tone. Finally, there are a few works (Birkerts, 1991; Smith, 1982; Stevens, 1984) that offer a more balanced and cautious view of the future.

This article will, in its conclusions, also offer some new, and perhaps innovative, personal comments on the future of research libraries including, especially, some on different ways of contemplating the future of individual American research libraries as those responsible for them seek to make intelligent choices that, hopefully, will not turn out to be red herrings.

B. Background

Almost all of the material, past and present, that deals with the future of libraries typically provides insufficient background information to enable the reader to grasp why the author holds a particular set of views. I feel it is important to provide some brief information about myself, without dwelling on the details of my professional history, that may place my thoughts into a more comprehensible perspective. The phrase "Damn'd neuters" in Dryden's quotation serves to describe my role as an observer of, and commentator on, Our Profession as well as my view of the likely state of research libraries in the twenty-first century.

I received an MLS in 1957 and a Ph.D. in 1961 from the Graduate School of Library Service at Rutgers University, where I was influenced by, among others, Ralph Shaw. Shaw was noted, on one hand, for his innovative uses of technology but also, on the other hand, for his cautious approach to the appropriate applications of the then emerging computer technology in libraries (Shaw, 1965). His old-fashioned approach was perhaps most notoriously highlighted in the controversy generated by an article by Jesse Shera (1967) that offered an expansive and optimistic view of the future of computers in libraries but, in passing, took Shaw to task for having said, "Let us think kindly of those who would frighten us by slogans and catchwords about the great and growing mass of the world's literature, and of those who would take pity upon our benighted state to solve all of our problems with machines they have not yet thought about" (Shaw, 1953, p. 10). To a far greater degree than in 1953, or even in 1967, the recent literature describing current applications of technology in research libraries is more reliable in that it does describe realistically, and sometimes even honestly, a true situation, rather than depending on machines we have not yet thought about. Shaw's statement remains, however, a valid way of characterizing much of what many writers now say about the future of libraries that is, often, based on machines that the authors may have perhaps thought about, yet do not exist. Now that we have seen the dramatic improvements in library service that have been accomplished through technology, our imagination is unchecked.

Since entering the profession in 1957, most of my career has involved the administration of academic research libraries. In that capacity, I have been involved only indirectly, and not always successfully, with the introduction and application of new technologies. I have participated actively in the development, governance, and planning of library networks at the multistate and state level. Although not trained as a library historian, I have a strong interest in library history, including the history of library technology, the broader aspects and implications of technology for libraries, and especially the history of information (Stevens, 1986).

I hold a conservative, and cautious, view of the likely future of the research library, and indeed of most libraries, in the twenty-first century that does not envisage a major transformation in the fundamental nature of those libraries. The changes in information technology that are now taking place are only part of a long continuum of changes in the diffusion of knowledge that have occurred over many centuries. They may seem more dramatic and rapid to us than the changes of the past but that depends on your point of view.

"The invention of printing," Victor Hugo (1958, p. 171) wrote, was "the greatest event in history. It was the supreme revolution. It meant the complete renovation of humanity's mode of expression, the discarding by human thought of one form to reclothe itself in another, the complete and final casting of the skin of that symbolic serpent, which, since Adam, had served as the representation of intellect. In the form of print, thought becomes more imperishable than ever; it is winged, intangible, indestructible. It mingles with the air. . . . It is turned into a flock of birds, winging its way in all directions, and occupying at the same time every corner of air and space."

II. A Definition

Many commentators on the future of libraries treat all libraries the same and fail to recognize or distinguish the unique nature of true research libraries. Other commentators who do deal specifically with the future of research libraries never define the distinguishing features of such libraries, but somehow assume that we all recognize and understand those features. Research libraries can most easily be defined simply as those 108 university libraries, and 12 independent libraries, in the United States and Canada that belong to the Association of Research Libraries (ARL). That simple definition is, in many ways, as unsatisfactory as no definition at all. The statistical measures that ARL uses as its membership criteria fail to speak, in a meaningful way, to the underlying purpose of research libraries that gives them their unique character. In considering how their role and responsibilities have developed over time, have already changed substantially in the past two decades, and might change further in the years ahead, a more specific definition is essential. Research libraries cannot be defined in terms of the size or stature of their collections. They must, rather, be defined in terms of their long-term commitment to the acquisition, preservation, and transmission of information not just to meet the immediate needs of current users but also to meet the largely unknown, and unknowable, needs of future generations of users. It is, in particular, their commitment, and their obligation, to serve scholars who are using their information resources to build and extend society's knowledge that sets research libraries apart. Research libraries do not exist primarily for casual, temporary, short-term purposes, although they may appear to, and often do, serve such purposes. They are primarily a vital link between the past, the present, and the future of society. Given that fundamental purpose, research libraries cannot undergo the kind of revolutionary transformation of their collections, services, and even purpose that a special library, for example, might attempt and even achieve. Many other libraries, including in particular special libraries, support research in scientific and technical disciplines, but their collections and services, unlike those of broad-based research libraries, focus on recent and current information. Those libraries have less commitment to the past, and less obligation to the future, and can, therefore, adapt more readily to changes in information technology. Research libraries—grounded in the past, serving the present, and building for the future—can only undergo a more gradual, evolutionary transformation of collections, functions, and services. In this regard, Swanson's (1980) views on the importance of evolutionary growth warrant special attention. Research libraries cannot, and should not, radically change their basic purpose in a short span of time.

III. The Past

A. The Role of Research Libraries

The traditional role of research libraries, as that role has developed in a little more than a hundred years, is, for better or for worse, likely to continue for some time. That is a role that emerged primarily out of a well-defined function involving primarily the acquisition and preservation of the printed word. It has been, therefore, size that has long been regarded as the primary attribute of research libraries. In the current environment size is no longer necessarily regarded as a virtue and may sometimes be a disadvantage when it comes to managing the kinds of changes that research libraries must deal with.

The primary role of research libraries to date has been, and largely continues to be, the collecting of materials. The antecedents of that idea of the importance of acquiring as much material as possible may be found in the great library at Alexandria that flourished in the third century B.C. That library, which represented an attempt to build a comprehensive collection of the world's knowledge as it was then defined, may have contained between 400,000 and 700,000 volumes (Smith, 1980, pp. 4–5) representing, in size and probably in content, a collection that was unmatched in most later research libraries until well into the twentieth century. In 1849, as the largest library in the United States, the Harvard College Library contained only 68,000 volumes; by 1876 its collections, then surpassed by the Boston Public Library and the Library of Congress, both of which contained about 300,000 volumes, had grown to 160,000 volumes, while the Yale University Library, as its nearest rival, contained 100,000 volumes; it was only over the next half century that those collections, along with those of other research libraries, grew to the point where they were larger than the library at Alexandria (Hamlin, 1981, pp. 230–237). While there were undoubtedly sound intellectual reasons for developing that collection at Alexandria, it is also more than likely that much of the motivation lay in the desire to acquire a vast array of unique material.

Other antecedents of contemporary American research libraries can be found in the various national, royal, and private libraries that developed largely after the Renaissance, and the invention of printing, again sometimes for intellectual reasons but just as often as the result of greed and pride of possession. It was the tradition of those libraries, which often were not connected with another institution, that eventually led to the development, in particular, of independent research libraries such as the New York Public Library.

It was also at Alexandria that the issues of bibliographic organization created by the size of collections first appear to have arisen and where the simple solution of using the alphabet as a means of organizing material was discovered (Daly, 1967). Just as the Alexandrian library spurred the discovery that the alphabet could be used to arrange materials, so later large accumulations of materials by libraries spurred similar discoveries and tools. The amassing of private libraries into a national collection during the French Revolution, for example, led to the use of the backs of playing cards for the recording of bibliographic information (Riberette, 1970). Those were, of course, issues that were to resurface over the intervening centuries, but that were to come to true fruition only as the growth of research libraries in the United States in the last quarter of the nineteenth century again created collections that demanded attention to bibliographic organization.

B. The Origins of Research Libraries

The true origins of contemporary research libraries lie in the changes in the pattern of information flow that took place, in what was simply another step in an information revolution that dates back at least to the invention of printing, in the first half of the nineteenth century. A multitude of changes occurred that increased dramatically the availability of information, the speed with which it was spread, and the quantity of information that was produced, and that brought about the final shift from the previous reliance on oral transmission to the printed word. As Brown (1989, pp. 288–289) points out, "The production and distribution of newspapers, periodicals, and books—a small-scale enterprise in the colonial era which relied chiefly on imports and never involved the full-time labors of more than one hundred people at any time—became a big business, so that by 1850, 22,000 men (and a lesser number of women and children) were not only printing and binding billions of items annually but producing the river of ink, the mountain of paper, and the type required for all this printing. Sales and distribution of printed goods, while not usually a full-time, specialized occupation, and the production of printing machinery and the textiles and leathers used for bindings, involved thousands more people who were scattered through virtually every county in the United States. . . . Diffusing information was a great national enterprise." It was, in large measure, this new availability of printed information, and, more importantly, the reliance on printed information as a significant intellectual resource, that led to the development of American research libraries.

The last half of the nineteenth century brought about a dramatic transformation in American scholarship. According to Rothstein (1955, p. 7), in 1850 "research activity—the extension of knowledge by scholarly inquiry—was insignificant in quantity and character, and the ideal of research all but unknown." The development of graduate and research programs in American universities, which is symbolized by the founding of The Johns Hopkins University in that year of all years 1876, based on the German model, led most directly to the large university libraries that now constitute the major exemplar of the research library. In 1850 research libraries could hardly have been said to exist; by 1900 there were collections of considerable size with well-established catalogs in libraries that were a key component of research and scholarship (Hamlin, 1981; Rothstein, 1955). As Rothstein (1955, p. 11) comments, "by the end of the [nineteenth] century . . . the statements 'the library is the heart of the university' and 'the library is the center of the university' [were] only commonplaces."

The dramatic development of both independent and university-based research libraries in the twentieth century—and that development is a twentieth century phenomenon—is due more to a sense of the need to acquire information for intellectual purposes than for purposes of pride or show, although the latter element has not altogether disappeared. Research libraries are testimony to a strong belief that the acquisition and retention of information, in printed and other forms, from all times and from all places is important to the growth and development of society. We learn from both the positive and negative experiences of the past as recorded in the information, which endures over a long period of time, that forms the core of research libraries.

C. Comprehensiveness and Access

It is commonly thought that from its origins research libraries have held an unwavering commitment to comprehensiveness and universality. As those libraries now strive to cope with another massive increase in the availability of information and another major shift in information technology, along with greater financial limitations than they may have ever known, critics suggest that an unbridled desire to continue to adhere to that commitment by collecting as much as possible lies at the heart of the problems of research libraries. The simple solution, they argue, is a shift in emphasis from acquisition to access. In fact, by the start of the twentieth century, President Eliot of Harvard, which then as now had the premier American academic research library, recognized the impossibility of even that institution's library acquiring everything as he proposed, at an American Library Association conference (1902), the development of cooperative storage libraries. The research library landscape is strewn with cooperative proposals and efforts, which have had varying degrees of success, to acquire, catalog, preserve, and/or share access to resources. The goal of building a comprehensive collection of the world's information resources has always been a shared goal of American research libraries. That goal often has been vague in terms of its failure to adequately and fully define and agree upon its scope, and at times limited in terms of its failure to recognize the value of information from some other parts of the world, or of nontraditional, or popular, information from this country.

There is one other important, and more recent, historical transformation in the role of research libraries that is critical to an understanding of their future. In the initial stages of the development of the research library, the acquisition, and to a lesser degree the cataloging and housing, of collections was viewed as their primary functions. Rothstein (1955, p. 13) points out that "for most scholars, the overwhelming preoccupation with the accumulation of materials cast a shadow of indifference over all library matters other than the acquisition function. Certainly this was true for problems of library staffing and service." Even as the concept of reference work emerged in the period from 1896 to 1916, the typical policy in research libraries was a cautious one that provided, at best, limited assistance to users. Even as the service concept was broadened in the period from 1917 to 1940, a conservative approach continued to be strongly favored by most university librarians (Rothstein, 1955). It was not until after 1945 that serious attention was given to the concept of service through the organized provision of assistance to users in finding their way through the mass and wealth of information contained in research libraries. The very idea of service, which includes the idea of access to information not locally held, is not only a recent one, but is, indeed, one that is not necessarily firmly implanted in the professional credo of research libraries.

The original concept of research libraries as places that largely accumulate materials continues to dominate in many respects. That is demonstrated by the widely varying commitment to service found among contemporary research libraries, including the common emphasis on protecting, at all costs, the acquisitions budget in times of severe financial constraint such as now exist. It is also demonstrated by the continued hesitance to pursue vigorously cooperative ventures and the current debate over acquisition versus access.

In any examination of the future of research libraries, it is important to know and understand some of these, and other, historical considerations that led to their creation, have molded their present form, and will, for some time to come, continue to have a considerable influence on their future shape. The sheer size and the well-established functions of research libraries make it difficult for rapid changes to occur. It must also be kept in mind that the basic concept of research libraries, in what might be regarded as their traditional form of a massive collection of partially and/or inadequately cataloged printed materials housed in a monumental building, is one that developed and reached its peak only in the last hundred years.

IV. The Present

A. The Introduction of Technology

The present state of research libraries, that has emerged primarily in the last thirty years, is obviously one of transition brought about by a variety of factors that are dominated largely by rapid, and as yet not entirely clear, changes in information technology. Society is at a point similar to those described so eloquently by Hugo (1958) and Brown (1989) but one that cannot yet be put into historical perspective.

While the substantial impact of technology on research libraries has been a recent development, it has historical antecedents that are important especially for what they reveal about the attitudes of librarians toward the proper role of technology in the research library. Despite the occasional warning from critics, such as Shaw (1953, 1955, 1965), about the necessity of dealing with technology in an appropriate manner, librarians have long had a fascination with equipment and technology that dates back at least to Ramelli's sixteenth-century scholar's bookwheel that was an ingenious device designed to help deal with the masses of new printed information that were becoming available. That fascination truly began, however, with the inception of modern librarianship in the late 1800s. As early as 1879, Melvil Dewey, for example, established an independent business firm, which was to become the Library Bureau, as a means of providing equipment to libraries to help them manage rapidly growing collections (Flanzraich, 1990). Dewey played a vital role in such seemingly simple matters as the development of vertical filing systems that allowed not just libraries but business and industrial firms to cope with the growing mass of paper information sources that were essential to their growth and development (Yates, 1989). Despite limited budgets, and generally a lack of appropriate expertise, individual librarians, especially those in research libraries, often undertook to incorporate new technologies such as the typewriter and the telephone into their work. Critics spoke of the mechanical appliance craze as one of the chief hindrances to progress in library work. "There is a subtle and fell fascination," Jast (1900, pp. 83–84) wrote, "about these things, which if allowed full play becomes a positive disease. It may begin innocently in the purchase of some book-supports [and then proceeds to the acquisition of automatic steps and other equipment but] the fascination grows with what it feeds on, until the funds of the library, and the time and thought of the librarian are frittered away in the pursuit of these mechanical accessories."

From the standpoint of research libraries, one of the most significant early successful adoptions of technology was that of photographic copying systems including, in particular, microfilm. While the origins of this technology date back only to the second half of the nineteenth century, by 1906 Otlet and Goldschmidt (Veaner, 1976, pp. 100–108) had set forth a proposal for a microphotographic book. As research libraries developed, these techniques were quickly seen to have special significance in their work. By 1912 several independent research libraries, including the Library of Congress, were using photostat cameras. Research libraries saw the potential of photostat and microfilm systems as a substitute for the inadequate means of transcribing by hand information for, and from, its collections. As that technology was perfected over the next several decades, it became a substantial means by which research libraries augmented their collections, and increased access to information for scholars, by copying in a permanent format a wide range of materials owned by individuals and/or other libraries, institutions, and organizations. Subsequently, of course, massive commercial programs for the microfilming of both manuscript and printed materials have enabled American research libraries to vastly broaden the scope of materials they can make available locally (Meckler, 1982).

In the 1930s and 1940s some libraries, including especially a few research libraries, began to experiment with the use of computers largely, initially, to handle internal routines such as circulation. Those experiments met with varying degrees of success. They were severely hampered, on one hand, by the inadequacies of the technology and, on the other hand, by the fact that libraries did not represent, or were not seen to represent, a viable commercial market by the emerging computer companies.

In the 1950s and the early 1960s the potential of computers for library routines was more fully recognized. Libraries, especially research and special libraries, struggled to adapt equipment and systems designed for other purposes to meet their needs. That was often under strong pressure from outsiders, including faculty members, who did not fully understand the nature and complexity of bibliographic records, especially for serials, and library routines, but who were certain that it would be simple to develop computer programs to manage those records and routines. Some limited-scale programs were successful, many larger scale efforts were not, and above all in too many cases, proposed solutions, as Shaw (1965) was fond of pointing out, were described in the literature as real accomplishments. Wasserman (1965) found the attitude of academic library directors and their assistant or associate directors to be either concern and inaction (50%), wait-and-see (~15%), concern and action (less than 20%), and dismissal (15%). It should be noted, incidentally, that one machine that was quickly adopted at that time, and has become a basic component of library service, was the photocopy machine. While this may seem, like the telephone, a commonplace tool, many scholars, as Case (1991, pp. 75–76) found, regard the availability of photocopy machines in research libraries as one of the most significant technological advances of recent years.

In the late 1960s and the 1970s the development of the MARC formats, the emergence of OCLC and of successful commercial circulation services, improved computer technology, and, above all, a better understanding of the issues involved in applying that technology to library needs enabled American research libraries, in particular, to adopt computer services and systems as the primary means for manipulating the basic internal routines of acquisitions, cataloging, circulation, and serials control. Along the way, as outsiders lost interest in the operation of research libraries as a problem that they could solve with computers, librarians recaptured the initiative and took control of planning for computer applications largely on their own. How research and other libraries will deal with their internal technical routines in a new environment has long been a matter of concern (Gellatly, 1983) for librarians. In a little more than twenty years, with some notable failures along the way, a standard, if somewhat too uniform, pattern has been firmly established. For most research libraries that pattern has consisted of reliance on a national online bibliographic database to provide records for a substantial percentage of its cataloging records, and a local integrated library system, which is often developed and managed in cooperation with an academic computer center, to provide for the management of basic internal routines and to offer an online public access catalog to its users. Changes in the availability of technological resources some studies suggest (*Technical Processing in Large Research Libraries*, 1992), may subject even that relatively recent pattern to substantial change.

In the 1990s the emergence of a vast array of CD–ROM products has led to the widespread use of those technologically based services and systems for the manipulation of indexing and abstracting services as a primary information resource in research libraries. Their adoption, as a tool that can be managed almost entirely within the library, has taken place far more rapidly, and far more easily, than the earlier adoption of bibliographic utilities, automated circulation systems, integrated library systems, and online public access catalogs. Initially, online services, such as those offered through

DIALOG and BRS, although heavily used in special libraries and by individual scientists, presented special challenges to many research libraries because of their pricing structure, their seeming complexity, and the felt need to provide them as mediated services. The experience gained with CD–ROM products, which can be offered in what appears to be a more normal operating situation, is resulting in a movement to integrate a proliferation of online information services, as well as other full-text and numeric databases, into the reference services of many research libraries.

Research libraries, with few exceptions, have tended to ignore, over this same period of time, developments in other information formats, such as audio and video, perferring to leave responsibility of those information sources to others. That is a decision that may come back to haunt those libraries as a greater integration of information technology continues to occur in the coming decade.

B. The Application of Technology

Above all it must be noted that the primary application of technology in research libraries, as in other libraries, has been to date as a substitute for, or alternative to, traditional manual routines, services, and systems, whether those applications have been developed locally and/or cooperatively or purchased commercially. Nevertheless, most librarians now regard the application of technology to the management and operation of research libraries as a primary responsibility and have a clear understanding of how best to do so.

More ambitious attempts to use technology to transform the basic nature of research libraries have been proposed and attempted in the past and lie ahead. Project Intrex (Overhage and Joyce, 1965), for example was undertaken at the Massachusetts Institute of Technology in the mid-1960s. It was, in most respects, a failure; it had virtually no impact on the operation of the MIT Library, or of any other library, and it has largely been forgotten. Still, there are important lessons, which have been forgotten or overlooked, to be learned from that experiment. Directed by Carl Overhage of the MIT faculty, that experiment took place largely outside the control of the MIT library at a time when machine-based information applications were still in their infancy. The failure of Project Intrex lay not so much in its vision of how libraries and information transfer at MIT might change by 1975 but more in the lack of a technology adequate to meet that vision and financial considerations. The planners of Project Intrex saw it as a way of providing more comprehensive access to the body of scientific literature needed by research faculty at MIT through enhanced techniques such as the entry of the table of contents and indexes of monographic material into a bibliographic database. The successful completion of that project would, they concluded, greatly increase the magnitude of the information available in 1975 but could also require as much as a 15-fold increase in the budget of the library. Although that change would have resulted in an annual expenditure of only approximately $1000 per user for library purposes, it would have required MIT to devote at least 10–12% of the institutional budget to library and information services compared to the 3–4% it was then devoting to those purposes. That would have required, of course, a major reallocation of institutional resources that, at that time, no major academic institution was prepared to make on what was largely speculation.

Since that time there has been no other major effort to experiment with the redesign of the fundamental way in which access to scholarly information is provided in research libraries. There have been numerous theoretical discussions of how that might be accomplished, often in much the same context as the vision of Overhage and his colleagues, and, more recently, in the context of the potential of electronic journals and other kinds of full-text access. Another bold Intrex-type experiment is needed to test the potential of contemporary information technology, which is certainly far more adequate to the task than that of the 1960s, as well as to identify the relative costs of such applications. Only through such an experiment might it be determined if research institutions are now prepared, in what is now a far more difficult finacial situation than existed in the mid-1960s, to make the kind of substantial reallocation of institutional resources that may still be required to accomplish the transformation that some futurists foresee. Such a positive reallocation of institutional resources seems increasingly unlikely to occur. In reality, research libraries are more likely to be faced with a substantial reduction, or at least a stabilization, of total resources and, perhaps, a decrease in their percentage of institutional resources. Such a bold experiment is unlikely even to be conducted if it depends on greatly increased institutional support for its initiation. If it is conducted, it is certainly unlikely to succeed if it depends on greatly increased institutional support for its continuing operation.

C. The Transformation of Collections

One popular current notion is that the vast existing resources of research libraries, either individually or collectively, will somehow magically be converted into one or more new electronic formats. Another is that somehow those resources can, or will, be simply ignored or discarded. It seems most unlikely that either of those scenarios will come to pass in the foreseeable future.

The reality of the economics of institutional support for research libraries, in a context in which support of higher education and research appears to be declining rather than expanding, makes the conversion in the near future of the vast wealth of information now contained in those libraries into electronic form extremely unlikely. That popular notion has considerable historical antecedents, as librarians and scholars have always been fond of proposing ways in which the latest technology might be harnessed to capture and store the world's information.

Often cited as a source of inspiration for future theorists, Bush's landmark article (1945) was among the first to suggest the potential applications of computer technology for scholarly access to information. Like the later Project Intrex, it had no practical impact on the development of information technology. Bush's article and related writings clearly have had substantial impact on the thinking of others who continue to offer, largely in theoretical ways, their ideas about the application of technology to the storage of vast amounts of information. The notion that somehow the contents of the Library of Congress, or its equivalent, can be stored in a device no larger than a shoebox, or now perhaps a matchbox, remains with us.

In considering technological solutions, however, it is essential to look at the entire process and not just one part of it. Even with current and likely technology, the conversion of even a reasonable fraction of the world's information into digital and/or other forms would be a massive and costly task. Even though devices to store the entire contents of the Library of Congress in a shoebox, or even a matchbox, may be available, the massive funds needed to accomplish the conversion of that material may not be. To do so, as Project Intrex demonstrated, would require a major shift in societal and institutional priorities leading directly to a major increase in the level of funds provided for libraries and information. That seems most unlikely to occur.

While the Librarian of Congress complains of the enormous backlog of unprocessed materials contained in LC's collections, and struggles to secure the funding to bring that material under simple bibliographic control (Weeks, 1991), funds to convert collections of that size into some new format are not likely to be forthcoming. While the Commission on Preservation and Access and the National Endowment of the Humanities struggle to adequately maintain a cooperative program to convert into microfilm the most essential parts of the enormous volume of materials in research libraries that is now disintegrating, funds to subsequently convert it and a vast array of other material into digital form are not expected to be procured. The 120 research libraries that are members of ARL now report holdings approaching 400,000,000 volumes and over 300,000,000 microform units. They are still adding roughly 7,000,000 volumes annually plus an almost equal number of microform units. There is little real likelihood that all of the material—even taking into account duplication between collections—will ever be converted into some electronically accessible form. Nor should such ideas and efforts be encouraged considering the nature, value, and use of that material. That material, and the information it contains, needs to be maintained and preserved for the future. Some portion of it needs to be maintained in its current physical format for artifactual and intellectual reasons. The bulk of it is not material that is now, or is ever likely to be, in high demand. It does not need to be instantaneously available to scholars everywhere. The nature of the collections of research libraries is that they contain enormous quantities of material and information that is ultimately needed, even over an extended period of time, by a relatively small body of serious users. The notion being advanced by the Library of Congress in its American Memory Project, and by others through similar multimedia projects, that greatly expanded public access to much of the information contained in research libraries is an important concept is due more to efforts to secure added funding than a realistic assessment of the true value and intended use of those collections. For better or for worse, given the range of problems that now face American society, the allocation of funds for the magical transformation of the collections of its research libraries into a matchbox available on everyone's desk is neither a likely nor a desirable goal.

Far more dangerous are the emerging notions that much of the material can be discarded altogether, or that a winnowing process will occur that will provide for the conversion of a limited amount of the most valuable information into digital form, or, as T. Mann (1991; personal communication, December 19, 1991) points out, that, at the very least, the kind of structured cataloging of information that research libraries have traditionally provided can be abandoned in favor of minimal records or free-form full-text searching. The winnowing notion, as expressed by Seiler and Surprenant (1991), for example, may recognize the fact that the resources to support the massive conversion of material of limited social utility will not be available. It fails to recognize the long-term permanent value of that material. The collections of American research libraries, as diverse and idiosyncratic as they are, do serve a social purpose of considerable value. They are, and are likely to remain, the fundamental basis for scholarly research in a variety of disciplines. They are important to the growth and development of knowledge. They are, and are likely to remain, permanent repositories of the results of scholarly research so that those results subsequently may be recovered and used by others.

The nature of those collections, both in content and format, may indeed continue to change as the forms in which new information is accumulated change. The old forms we will have with us for the foreseeable future if not, indeed, indefinitely. It is critical, therefore, to continue to discard the notion that the basic nature of research libraries will be transformed radically in the foreseeable future.

V. The Future

A. Biblical Adages

"Consider the lilies of the field, how they grow; they toil not, neither do they spin." That biblical adage might be said to characterize, in some respects, the past of research libraries. In that golden age, growth was viewed as good, inevitable, and something that simply happened as the sun and rain of an institution came down upon its library.

"Take therefore no thought for the morrow: for the morrow shall take thought for the things of itself. Sufficient unto the day is the evil thereof." This may characterize the past attitude of many regarding the future of research libraries.

Those responsible for the planned and intelligent growth of research libraries, as the twenty-first century approaches, cannot continue to live, if they indeed ever had, by either of those adages. They can no longer consider research libraries as the lilies of the institutional field nor can they take no thought for the morrow that those libraries face. If they do so, the evil of that day may well be more than sufficient to destroy the basic concept of research libraries.

Like all good preachers, I will now attempt to specify what thought those responsible for research libraries should take for their morrow. I will, first, address some general themes; then, outline some of the likely changes that may take place in the organization and management of those libraries; and, finally, offer what I hope are practical suggestions for a course of action that are not simply red herrings.

B. General Themes

First and foremost, research libraries must continue to give special heed to the collection and preservation of unique resources in any format, from all times, and from all parts of the world. They must do so, as they always have, in the context of not necessarily knowing what materials may be of interest and value to future generations of scholars and, therefore, of not being absolutely certain what materials it is important to collect. While there may be a shrinking base of commonly held material that individual research libraries can afford to acquire, a failure to emphasize the uniqueness of each research library, and the necessity for it to acquire materials not acquired by other research libraries, would be a major national disaster.

In continuing to build those unique collections, research libraries must give thought to their responsibility for seeing that the information created in the past fifty years, and that which will be created in the next fifty years, that is technology dependent remains as accessible as that contained in the manuscripts and books dating back hundreds and thousands of years now contained in their collections. There is already, unfortunately, ample evidence that some technology-based information is no longer accessible. One classic example is a quantity of World War II American military records that now exist only in a microfilm version of IBM punched cards. As we have experimented with and discarded information-based technologies we, as a society, have been too quick to discard the information contained in those technologies. Despite our best efforts, intentions, and plans (Lesk, 1992), we must recognize that we will inevitably lose a considerable quantity of technology-based information just as we have already lost a considerable quantity of manuscript or print-based information. We cannot knowingly take the risk of losing much or all of it. It may seem a far-fetched scenario, especially given recent world events, but we should even give thought to the possibility of a bleak nuclear winter in which access to machine-based information may be impossible. Books, manuscripts, and even microfilm—despite their other flaws—are, at heart, not totally dependent upon technology or even electricity.

Above all, research libraries must continue to give thought to the needs and interests of individual scholars past, present, and future. They will continue to have an obligation to collect and preserve the work of the scholars of the past, to make their collections readily accessible to the scholars of their time, and to collect and preserve materials for the scholars of the future. It is, as Swanson (1979) and Rothstein (1955) remind us, the use of the collections of research libraries to advance scholarship and create new information that remains at the core of their mission. That must continue to be a guiding principle in planning for the future. A library that serves largely or primarily as a means of access to information found elsewhere is not, in the truest sense, a research library. As Radford (1992, p. 418) points out, "In Foucault's conception of scientific knowledge, the library institutionalizes the arrangement of texts that provides appropriate space in which new knowledge claims can be located and given meaning." The research library is far more than a resource for locating bits of information. It is a key component of the processes that lead to the creation, validation, and questioning of knowledge.

The collecting patterns of research libraries will have to continue to change, as they have already begun to do, to take into account the many new ways in which information is being produced and accumulated. Much of that accumulation now appears to be taking place outside the domain of research libraries in response either to commercial interests that are seeking immediate profit, or to the specific needs of individual scholars, or small groups of scholars, who are seeking to meet their own immediate needs. Too seldom, in either case, is any thought given to the needs of future generations of potential users.

The vast range of nonbibliographic numeric and textual information that is now being generated in electronic form represents one specific area of collection development to which American research libraries need to begin to give greater attention. Lesk (1992) provides a list of approximately one hundred substantial computer archives (e.g., the Graveyard Database at York University) in Canada, Great Britain, and the United States that does not include several major resources (e.g., the Roper Center at the University of Connecticut) in those countries and does not include any that undoubtedly already exist in many other countries. That information represents a growing body of potential research material of lasting value that offers unusual challenges for its collection and preservation. It is not easy to identify what the information is and how it is being produced; nor is it easy to identify what steps must be taken to preserve it. Because it involves machine-based systems, there is a need to know not just what the information is but what the programs are that have been generated to access and manipulate the information. If the information is technology dependent, as it generally is, there is a need to preserve not just the information and the programs that provide access to it, but the equipment needed to retrieve the information, or, alternatively, to take steps to convert the information so that it will continue to be accessible through other more readily available and usable equipment. We are only now beginning to contemplate (Lesk, 1992; Kaufman and LeClercq, 1991) the special preservation needs of machine-based information in the hopes that we may somehow avoid the massive problems we now face with books printed on acidic paper that we did not, despite warning, address at the time the information was being produced in a nonpermanent format. One early study (*Preservation of Historical Records*, 1986) estimated, for example, that electronic data will have to be converted to a new generation of media about every twenty years. Lesk (1992) recommends that preservation of such data must be based on regular copying that is budgeted as a cost and on cooperation in the development of conversion technology and standards.

What we now are at least somewhat aware of is, in fact, only the tip of an incredibly large information iceberg. Reports (Gould, 1988, 1989; Gould and Pearce, 1991) indicate that some research libraries and research library organizations are cognizant of, and have begun to work with, scholars within their own communities who need access to massive machine-based numeric and textual files, and who have begun the development of special programs to build and share such files. We need to do more to establish such relationships, but we can, perhaps, at least count on those scholars to share our basic concern about the long-term preservation of, and access to, that body of information.

Some of the print-based collections in research libraries that have proven to be invaluable long-term research sources include such items as pamphlets and other ephemera like, for example, postcards and other material from the world of popular culture. Much of that material traditionally has been produced outside the realm of commercial publishers, research libraries, or scholars. There is already a substantial body of information of that kind being generated through computers. Much of it already is unlikely to end up in printed form and that situation will only intensify in the coming years. How will a scholar of the twenty-first century study the growth, development, and social impact of the numerous bulletin boards and list servers, even those heavily used by librarians in research libraries, that now exist?

The papers of authors, politicians, scholars, and other individuals, including both drafts of manuscripts and correspondence, constitute another important body of materials traditionally collected and preserved by research libraries. Already substantial changes are taking place in the way in which individuals create, generate, produce, and save, or more often do not save, their work. Those changes present a particular challenge for research libraries, since there already are, and will continue to be, substantial differences in the way in which individual creative writers work. To what purpose will it be to collect the correspondence of an author, which she has carefully saved in electronic form, if she worked with an obscure brand of personal computer, or word processor, using hardware, software, or storage devices that have not also been preserved in a usable fashion so that the information is vitually inaccessible?

The staff of research libraries must give particular thought in each of those cases to working more directly with those who are generating information of potential future research value in electronic formats to assist them in developing and adhering to policies, procedures, and techniques that will ensure that the information is retained in a form that will be preserved and accessible over an extended period of time. What must be emphasized, in particular, is that our concern must be not simply with the physical preservation of the format or the content of the information—as is the case with books—but also with the provision of a permanent means of access to the information.

We are now at a transitional point where some scholars, who were trained in the print-based tradition, are uncomfortable with technology-based information, including even microforms. In the not too distant future, we may be at a point where an increasingly large body of scholars, who will have been trained in a technology-based tradition, are uncomfortable or impatient with books and manuscripts. We already see that to some degree in users who disregard the card catalog even when it is clearly posted that the new online public access catalog does not contain as comprehensive a record of a research library's holdings. Since it seems highly unlikely that the vast wealth of "print"-dependent materials in research libraries will ever be totally converted to machine form, we run the risk, if we give no thought to educating future generations of scholars in the value and use of existing collections, that those valuable resources will become obsolete.

Another equally important consideration is how to more carefully tailor mechanisms for access to research collections so that scholars will not simply be overwhelmed, as in many respects they already are, by the vast amounts of information that will be available to them. It is, after all, reasonably certain that, whatever else happens, research libraries wil continue to grow at a rapid rate. There is already evidence in reports like those of Gould (1988, 1989) and Gould and Pearce (1991) that the massive bibliographic compilations of the past are now largely ignored by many scholars. Electronic access to the catalogs of American research libraries, individually and collectively, already provides more than many users want to know. One solution, which I (Stevens, 1980) proposed earlier, may be to devise systems that allow individual scholars to construct strategies that will provide them with individualized catalogs, derived from the catalogs of a multitude of research libraries and other electronic information sources, of the literature of most interest to them. Finally, improved electronic access to the catalogs of research libraries already demonstrates that while collectively research libraries have assembled important scholarly resources, individually they have done so on a basis that appears to have little rhyme or reason to it. I have a scholarly interest in an organized event known as Old Home Week, and sometimes Old Home Day, that began in New Hampshire in 1899, spread rapidly throughout New England and beyond, but largely died out by about 1920, although scattered remnants of it still exist. I have used the Internet to search the online public access catalogs of a considerable number of research libraries in the United States and Canada to locate information about the holdings of the ephemeral programs and other souvenirs of that event. The results have been both productive and instructive. There is a substantial body of such material scattered in the holdings of American and Canadian research libraries. Information about those holdings and the holdings of similar kinds of materials is now readily available to any scholar from a computer terminal at his desk. In some cases the holdings of Old Home Week material reflect an interest in state and local history; it is not surprising, for example, to find that the Dartmouth College Library has an extensive body of such material. Overall, it is abundantly clear, however, that there is little logic to the holdings that exist, and that, in many respects, research libraries have simply stored away whatever material may have come their way. There is, for example, one program from an Old Home Week celebration in a Pennsylvania town that appears regularly in the collections of research libraries across the United States and even in Canada. It is fortunate that so much material exists but in pursuing research on that subject, I will have to track down that material (and I may well be the only person who will want to use it) through still time-consuming interlibrary loan processes if not travel to several research libraries.

Research libraries ought to be less possessive about their holdings and more willing to consider the regular transfer, even if only on a temporary or long-term basis, of collections of material from one library to another to enable scholars with identified research needs to have more ready access to the total body of information they require. We have, in the technology and the personal skills of the research librarians and the scholars with whom they work, the ability to rationalize the collection development policies of the past. By constructing new policies that will eliminate, or at least alleviate, the pack rat tendencies of the past, as valuable as they have been, research libraries can substantially improve the value and utility of their collections.

C. Changing Structures

In whatever fashion research libraries may attempt to deal with those basic issues, it will undoubtedly be in the context of serious financial, institutional, and organizational constraints. Their directions will be shaped, to begin with, in large measure by the fact that their level of financial support will not have undergone any fundamental change. It will continue to be a struggle for research libraries to maintain present levels of financial support, adjusted for inflation, and to secure modest increases to help meet the enlarged demands that will continue to be placed on them. Such changes as do take place will come about, in all likelihood, as a result of local initiatives, not in an overall reordering of institutional priorities or massive increases in federal or other external support. In general, financial support will remain at a level that supports continuity, not dramatic change.

Research libraries are not, especially under those circumstances, any more likely to become the driving force behind developments in information technology in the future than they have been to date. Although, in the coming decades, they may become a more significant component of the marketplace for many segments of the information industry, they will not, for the most part, shape the decisions and directions of that industry. Like other libraries, they will need to continue to adapt to developments but respond cautiously only as those new developments become established. Because of their mission to collect and preserve information, they will continue to be faced with extremely difficult choices in determining their role in the collection and preservation of obsolete information formats and technologies.

With the views, however ill informed or ill conceived, that others, like Frye (1991), in positions of institutional authority hold on the way in which technology may shape the future of research libraries, it seems likely that there will be on one hand few dollars for massive new library buildings. Central or decentralized library facilities are not likely to disappear altogether, as the notion of a physical proximity to learning that brings users to a central place may, indeed, even be reinforced by the isolation that takes place in other aspects of education and information use. Old habits die hard. Older library buildings will be expanded, or renovated, and new facilities will be built gradually, as existing buildings become inadequate not just in accommodating growth in collections and services but, in particular, the more widespread applications of technology. It seems equally likely, on the other hand, that there will be an increased emphasis on alternative means of access to information, including a new emphasis on cooperative storage systems of one kind or another to hold the growing mass of older materials that will be perceived to be of lesser value as well as information in electronic form. That will result in the increased need for improvement in access systems through a variety of techniques. Unless, however, direct document delivery, especially of older physical material, comes about as part of a conscious economic decision to defer the construction of new library space, it will in all likelihood continue to be offered largely on an experimental basis, and with time delays, as educational institutions continue to regard the time of faculty and students as having little or no economic value.

Independent research libraries will remain largely unchanged organizationally, although they may continue to struggle to find new ways to market themselves to secure and improve their financial base. The smaller of those libraries may find it difficult to keep pace technologically with their counterparts in universities who are likely to have greater access to institutional expertise and systems in a setting where there is an increased commitment to technology as a key means of access to information.

Academic research libraries will continue to be swept up in alliances with university computer centers, and other information providers, and subject to greater administrative integration with those functions. Academic research libraries will continue to be, along with computer centers, one of the two major components of those information providers, although both libraries and, perhaps even more so, computer centers will find their role increasingly challenged and altered by the commercialization and decentralization of telecommunications technology and information.

The place and role of research libraries within the administrative hierarchy of academic institutions may vary greatly but they are likely to be based increasingly on an integration, if not a consolidation, with other related information activities and resources rather than independence and isolation. Whether individually or as part of a somewhat greater information whole, most academic research libraries will continue to report to a provost or academic vice president. The library and other information services will continue to be regarded as auxiliary to the primary teaching and research programs of the institution largely because, even in total, those information services will continue in most institutions to constitute less than 10% of the institutional budget. What is now the occasional creation of a position of an associate vice president for information resources, services, or systems is likely to become far more common. In a few universities, perhaps those where the primary focus of the institution is technological, a position of vice president for information resources, services, or systems may be created—as a few already have been—but even such a position inevitably will be subordinate to the chief academic officer of the institution.

Finally, the fate and future of American research libraries will increasingly depend on the quality of their staffs and the commitment of those staffs to service. Some (Lancaster, 1978, 1982) suggest that librarians will become independent of library buildings and even institutions. Others (Campbell, 1992) suggest that the introduction of new information technologies may, and should, make users more independent of librarians and will, in any case, allow users to access a virtual library without human intervention from within and especially from without the library. Others (Anders *et al.*, 1992) describe scenarios in which much of the use of the library involves primarily human-to-human communication via computers.

Most library users are unlikely to become self-sufficient in dealing with the increasingly complex array of available information resources anytime soon. Nor does it seem likely, given the continued rapid growth in the diversity of those information resources, that we will realize anytime soon the dream of a single, or even a few, standardized systems that will allow users to access the total array of information resources from a single workstation, or through a single set of commands. It seems far more likely, as some feel (P. T. Kaufman, personal communication, March 9, 1992), that those who wish to make the maximum use of the resources of a virtual library will, in fact, be more dependent on human specialists. As others (T. Mann, personal communication, December 19, 1991) suggest, librarians make available a whole range of avenues of access to the records of human knowledge and have a distinctive role to play in that regard. Librarians also, as others (S. Plum, personal communication, October 22, 1992) remind us, have an important role, especially in research libraries, in integrating students and other new users into information systems in a way that empowers them and places them into a new relationship with others in the research community. As Radford (1992, p. 420) puts it, "The evolving library environment will not be served by a dominant preconception that characterizes the library as an institution for housing particular texts that contain specific facts and the librarian as an impersonal, source-oriented intermediary whose function is to locate them."

There has been widespread discussion of the particular competencies that should be sought in developing the best possible staff for those libraries, but it seems most likely that adequate compensation to personnel with the broadest possible education will be the key to the development and maintenance of staffs that will be adaptable, flexible, and intelligent. Those staffs will need to maintain an awareness of the rapid changes that are occurring in libraries and in information technology, and to find innovative ways to help a wide variety of users satisfy their information needs. Above all they will need to be able to maintain firm control over the destiny of research libraries. The future of those libraries rests with the quality and wisdom of their staffs.

D. New Visions

What ultimately is required is a new vision of the future of at least some individual research libraries. To develop and put into place that vision will not be easy given the past burdens and continuing constraints that must be taken into account. It will require a great deal more risk than we are used to seeing in research libraries on the part of not just a few individual library directors and their staffs but on the part of others as well.

Swanson (1979, pp. 17–18) argues that "libraries of the future must evolve from present libraries through a step-by-step process of criticism, correction, and improvement. Correctability is more important than the initial plan or design itself. . . . Problems must be attacked one or a few at a time; each attack attempts a specific and identifiable improvement to be tested in the existing system. Unsuccessful changes are eliminated; all problem solving involves trial and error elimination . . . . The user's response to a new kind of library service cannot be reliably predicted, and so an innovative service solves some problems but gives rise to new ones. Far-reaching changes cannot be abruptly effected—not just because of practical difficulties, but also because difficulties in principle arise. Too much change at once forecloses any understanding of the effects of change, for one cannot know to which causes or variables the effects are to be attributed."

At present, research libraries and, in the case of those located in universities, their institutions seem to be locked into a single model. Individually and institutionally all research libraries have pursued the same goals, and research libraries and the universities in which they are largely located are monolithic and comparable institutions. They either wish to maintain their membership in the Association of Research Libraries or the Association of American Universities, or to be invited to join those prestigious associations; to do so requires that they meet established uniform membership criteria that are based almost entirely on measures of size that are held sacred. It might even be better if, for example, the ARL membership criteria reverted to those of an earlier time and consisted largely of a subjective judgment as to the quality of a director's leadership and stature if not the strength and value of her library. The emphasis placed on size of the library in the process for the accreditation and rating of American universities is equally ill conceived. The federal funding that has been available under Title II-C of the Higher Education Act

of 1965, as described in detail by Streit (1991) has led to a stultifying uniformity whereby most applications, and most awards, have for some time been in
support not of innovative ideas but of the cataloging and entry into an
increasingly obsolescent massive national bibliographic database of more and
more obscure and specialized collections of value to a limited number of
scholars. Nor have other associations responsible for library planning or other
funding sources demonstrated any greater vision. The research library community seems to be locked into a pattern of uniformity where a single cause,
even one as noble as preservation, produces a single solution, such as a massive
national microfilming program, that most librarians respond to without
thinking because that is the safer course of action and that is where funds are
being directed.

Large organizations, like universities and their research libraries, are
especially resistant to change and modifications will take place slowly if at all.
The kind of grand digital transformation that some have proposed (Lancaster,
1978) and continue to propose (Seiler and Surprenant, 1991), which would
result in a dramatic transformation of research libraries, seems a most unlikely
future given the history and the nature of those libraries. There are clear signs
of change and evidence that librarians (Buckland, 1992), academic administrators (Frye, 1991), and both together (Dougherty and Hughes, 1991) are
seriously comtemplating a different future for the research library. A new
stultifying uniform approach appears to be emerging that is based on the
concept not entirely of size but, as Dougherty and Hughes (1991, p. 3)
describe it, of "universal access by faculty and students to multiple information sources in all possible media via a single multifunctional workstation." It
is also clear that for many research librarians like Keller (1992) much of the
answer lies in the continued reliance on only a few major research libraries and
on substantial federal support for another set of uniform solutions.

In a democratic and pluralistic society, that approach is increasingly a
mistake, especially at a time of continued rapid change and an environment
that, in fact, may well see increasing differentiation among research universities as they respond to economic and societal changes. Massive solutions may,
as Swanson (1980) pointed out, bring positive results but may also bring
massive failure. Trial-and-error, evolutionary systems that allow for experimentation, local autonomy, and attention to the wide range of variables that
exist are a more intelligent long-term approach to determining how academic
institutions and their research libraries, individually and collectively, might
best adjust to a new information environment. The thoughtful exploration of
alternative approaches to the operation and management of research libraries,
under the right circumstances and with the right leadership, could provide a
valuable view of the different possible futures that research libraries might
elect to follow. Such alternatives, some of which might well turn out to be

nothing more than red herrings, are likely to be pursued only by individuals with courage and vision who are prepared to make difficult choices and who have an environment that is conducive, as a university should be, to experiment and change. Support from ARL, accreditation agencies, the federal government, and granting agencies would be helpful but is probably not essential. Such choices require, however, that hard policy choices be made that could then serve as the underlying basis for individual experimentation.

The role of academic research libraries in support of the basic undergraduate and graduate teaching programs of the institution ultimately requires only limited library collections and services. Since we have little evidence—despite numerous experiments—of the precise nature of the commitment required to support that role, a first step would be to identify the costs of supporting those collections and services and to clarify the nature of the collections and services that are to be provided in a new technological environment. That, in turn, would help identify the larger balance of resources that are dedicated to the support of research and other specialized roles. Since there is not likely to be any major new infusion of institutional and/or external support, that would identify the funds controlled by a research library that might then be available to support experiments and change. A different approach to the use of those funds would require a conscious decision not to be bound by the existing commonly held notions as to the percentage of the library budget to be devoted to materials, staff, and other expenses, the percentage of the materials budget to be devoted to monographs as opposed to serials, or other outmoded rules of thumb.

A second step would be for a research library to carefully examine all of its existing research collections, including those that are regarded as rare and valuable, with a view to transforming some of those into funds to be used for the acquisition of other kinds of research materials and to reducing future obligations for the support of those collections. Historical precedents, donor obligations, national interests, institutional commitments, and research value in relationship to institutional priorities would all need to be taken into account. The ultimate goal of any such experiment would be to direct a research library's limited resources in such a way as to obtain the greatest information return for a defined level of institutional support in respect to meeting both local needs and national obligations. Unfortunately, as Belanger (1993) reminds us, the dismantling of special collections has already begun at some sizable institutions but too often without any careful thought for the consequences of such actions or collective discussion and cooperation.

Such deliberate downsizing would provide the context, and make available the funds, that would allow serious experimentation to occur. There are at least two models that might be pursued by an individual research library director and an institution willing to engage in such experimentation. The risks are great and the opportunity for failure is as great, if not greater, than the chance for success.

The more conventional, and perhaps safer, option would be to concentrate on a largely print-based series of choices radically different from those now typically exercised. This option would not only allow the individual research library to better meet the needs of its users but it would also allow that library to make a more meaningful contribution to the development of significant national or international research collections. It would rely, in part, on the increasingly obvious concept that, for most specialized users, ready access to information they require is their most important requirement. It would be based on a three-stage process. First, the library would identify and acquire those collections needed locally to support the current teaching programs of the institution at all levels. Second, the library would move aggressively to provide access from external sources to the wide range of other common and readily available information needed to meet most of the requirements of graduate students and faculty engaged in research. That would include not simply electronic access, and/or vastly improved document delivery services, but more extensive programs for providing subsidies for the on-site use of research collections at other institutions as well as the trading or loan of collections with other research libraries. Finally, it would include a much more highly concentrated commitment to the building of a true research collection based not on materials widely held by other research libraries, or materials that happen to be donated or otherwise acquired, but on a well-defined, if narrow, collection of unique and specialized materials. Rather than a commitment to building broad-based "research" collections to serve a wide variety of disciplines within the institution, the library would seek to alter its pattern by building and preserving a few specialized collections in a depth not now found in any existing research library. It might, for example, seek to acquire virtually everything published in a country, or a small group of countries, or on a particular subject. Such a program would be a positive way of counteracting the serious decline that Keller (1992), among others, has noted as occurring in the overall strength of research libraries in the United States as financial resources and purchasing power have diminished in recent years.

A second, although more risky, option would be to make a full-scale commitment to an electronic future based on a calculated guess as to the nature of that electronic future. The decision here, however, would be made not simply in terms of meeting the needs of the moment but of developing a permanent research collection built almost exclusively around data in digital or other electronic forms. One difficulty is the likely need to commit, for economic and strategic reasons, to a selected number of formats, such as CD–ROM, that seem to be well established and to avoid experimentation with every prospective new technology that may come along. An essential part of this option would be a decision to build for future generations of scholars a research collection to preserve the data, even as formats and technologies may change, so that their work can involve not only access to data that has not otherwise been preserved but also research into the technology and its applications. While, for example, it now seems convenient to discard or return one CD–ROM disk when an updated or new version is issued, a research library committed to this approach would seek to retain appropriate editions and versions for future use. A research library committed to this electronic alternative would also seriously pursue the development of a variety of specialized collections of unique electronic data. This could well include, for example, a conscious effort to acquire and preserve some of the increasingly large number of information files generated by scholarly researchers, perhaps focusing on those in a particular discipline or field. It could also include a conscious effort to identify authors, other creative artists, politicians, business firms, and other associations, individuals, and organizations whose work is largely electronically based, with a view to acquiring and preserving the electronic records of their work so that they will be available on a long-term basis to future generations of scholars.

Those, in tentative form, are two of several options that individual American research libraries might elect to follow as we struggle to find new directions for the American research library in the twenty-first century. They may, like other visions, turn out to be nothing more than red herrings. They are not easy options to pursue. Fortunately, I am near enough to the end of my career as an academic library administrator that they are not options that I feel I need to implement. I can safely leave my vision for other younger and more daring librarians to pursue.

VI. A Final Comment

Some things never change. Research libraries are most likely to change slowly; they may, as some have suggested, undergo some ambitious transformation; it is even possible that a few research libraries may pursue the different options that I have suggested. If, indeed, library materials are somehow transformed and do become available to a significant extent in machine-readable form, many current research libraries, which have an enormous investment in printed materials, may well be unable to meet the challenge. They could become museums or warehouses. They could well be replaced, as institutions for the support of meaningful research, by smaller and more flexible libraries and information centers of a specialized nature.

It seems certain, based on a tradition that began at the start of this century, that, whatever else may happen by the end of the next century, the presidents of major universities will still refer to the university library as the heart of the university with as much, or as little, conviction and support as they always have. Perhaps, though, there may be one dramatic change as a few bold presidents begin to refer to the library as the brain of the university.

Acknowledgments

This article was originally presented at a colloquium at the Graduate School of Library and Information Science at the University of California at Los Angeles while I was a visiting Professor there in November of 1991. The support of Dean Beverly P. Lynch and the faculty of the GSLIS was an important contribution to its preparation and presentation. This version has benefited from comments and ideas offered by Paula T. Kaufman of the University of Tennessee Libraries, Seymour Lubetzky, Professor Emeritus of the GSLIS at UCLA, Thomas Mann of the Library of Congress, Stephen H. Plum of the Homer Babbidge Library at the University of Connecticut, Sarah Pritchard of the Smith College Library, and David Zeidberg of the University Library at UCLA.

References

Anders, V., Cook, C., and Pitts, R. (1992). A glimpse into a crystal ball: Academic libraries in the year 2000. *Wilson Library Bulletin* **67,** 36–40.

Belanger, T. (1993). *The Future of Rare Book Libraries.* Book Arts Press at the University of Virginia, Charlottesville.

Billings, H. (1991). The bionic library. *Library Journal* **116,** 38–42.

Billington, J. H. (1989). *Building Libraries of the Future.* Institute for Scientific Information, Philadelphia.

Birkerts, S. (1991). Into the electronic millennium. *Boston Review* **16,** 14–15, 18–20.

Brown, R. D. (1989). *Knowledge Is Power: The Diffusion of Information in Early America, 1700–1865.* Oxford, New York.

Buckland, M. (1992). *Redesigning Library Services: A Manifesto.* American Library Association, Chicago.

Bush, V. (1945). As we may think. *Atlantic* **176,** 641–649.

Campbell, J. D. (1992). Shaking the conceptual foundations of reference: A perspective. *Reference Services Review* **20,** 29–35.

Campus of the Future (1987). OCLC, Dublin, Ohio.

Case, D. O. (1991). The collection and use of information by some American historians. *Library Quarterly* **61,** 61–82.

Clapp, V. W. (1964). *The Future of the Research Library.* University of Illinois Press, Urbana.

Cline, H. F. (1983). *The Electronic Library: the Impact of Automation on Academic Libraries.* Lexington Books, Lexington, Massachusetts.

Crooks, S. (1982). *Libraries in the Year 2000.* Arthur D. Little, Cambridge.

Daly, L. W. (1967). *Contributions to a History of Alphabetization in Antiquity and the Middle Ages.* Latomus, Bruxelles.

DeGennaro, O. (1987). *Libraries, Technology, and the Information Marketplace.* G. K. Hall, Boston.

Dougherty, R. M., and Hughes, C. (1991). *Preferred Futures for Libraries.* Research Libraries Group, Palo Alto, California.

Dowlin, K. E. (1984). *The Electronic Library: The Promise and the Process.* Neal-Schuman, New York.

Edelman, H., ed. (1986). *Libraries and Information Science in the Electronic Age*. ISI Press, Philadelphia.

Eliot, C. W. (1902). Division of a library into books in use and books not in use. *Library Journal* **27**, 51–56 (Conference issue).

Flanzraich, G. L. (1990). *The Role of the Library Bureau and Gaylord Brothers in the Development of Library Technology, 1876–1930*. University Microfilms, Ann Arbor, Michigan.

Frye, B. E. (1991). The future of the library: A view from the provost's office. *Library Issues* **12**, 1–2, 4.

Fussler, H. H., and Bryan, H. (1978). *Reflections on the Future of Research Libraries*. Monash University, Clayton, Australia.

Future of Libraries (1982). State University of New York, Albany.

Gellatly, P., ed. (1983). *Beyond "1984": The Future of Library Technical Services,*. Haworth Press, New York.

Gould, C. C. (1988). *Information Needs in the Humanities: An Assessment*. Research Libraries Group, Stanford.

Gould, C. C. (1989). *Information Needs in the Social Sciences: An Assessment*. Research Libraries Group, Mountain View, California.

Gould, C. C., and Pearce, K. (1991). *Information Needs in the Sciences: An Assessment*. Research Libraries Group, Mountain View, California.

Hamlin, A. (1981). *The University Library in the United States: Its Origins and Development*. University of Pennsylvania Press, Philadelphia.

Hayes, R. M., ed. (1981). *Universities, Information Technology, and Academic Libraries: The Next Twenty Years*. University of California, Los Angeles.

Hirsch, R., ed. (1951). *Changing Patterns of Scholarship and the Future of Research Libraries*. University of Pennsylvania Press, Philadelphia.

Holley E. G. (1975). *The Emerging University Library: Lessons from the Sixties*. State University of New York, Stony Brook.

Hubbard, T. E. ed. (1986). *Research Libraries: The Past 25 Years, the Next 25 Years*. Colorado Associated University Press, Boulder.

Hugo, Victor (1958). *The Hunchback of Notre Dame*. Dent, London.

Hyatt, J. A., and Santiago, A. S. (1987). *University Libraries in Transition*. NACUBO, Washington.

Jast, L. S. (1900). Some hindrances to progress in public library work. *Library Association Record* **2**, 82–88.

Kaufman, P., and LeClercq, A. (1991). Archiving electronic journals: Who's responsible for what. *Library Issues* **11**, 1–4.

Keller, M. A. (1992). *Foreign Acquisitions in North Amercian Research Libraries*. Center for Research Libraries, Chicago.

Lancaster, F. W. (1978). *Toward Paperless Information Systems*. Academic Press, New York.

Lancaster, F. W. (1982). *Libraries and Librarians in an Age of Electronics*. Information Resources Press, Arlington, Virginia.

Lathem, E. C., ed. (1978). *American Libraries as Centers of Scholarship*. Dartmouth College, Hanover, New Hampshire.

Lesk, M. (1992). *Preservation of New Technology*. Commission on Preservation and Access, Washington.

Licklider, J. C. R. (1965). *Libraries of the Future*. M.I.T. Press, Cambridge.

Mann, T. (1991). *Cataloging Quality, LC Priorities, and Models of the Library's Future*. Library of Congress, Washington.

Meckler, A. M. (1982). *Micropublishing: A History of Scholarly Micropublishing in America, 1938–1980*. Greenwood, Westport, Connecticut.

Ostrow, S., and Zich, R. (1990). *Research Collections in the Information Age: The Library of Congress Looks to the Future*. Library of Congress, Washington.

Overhage, C. J. F., and Joyce, R. (1965). *Intrex: Report of a Planning Conference*. MIT Press, Cambridge.

Poole, H., ed. (1977). *Academic Libraries in the Year 2000*. Bowker, New York.

Preservation of Historical Records (1986). National Academy Press, Washington.

Radford, G. P. (1992). Positivism, Foucault, and the fantasia of the library: Conceptions of knowledge and the modern library experience. *Library Quarterly* **62**, 408–424.

Riberette, Pierre (1970). *Les Bibliotheques Francaises Pendant la Revolution (1789–1795)*. Bibliotheque Nationale, Paris.

Rider, F. (1944). *The Scholar and the Future of the Research Library*. Hadham Press, New York.

Roberts, K. H. (1987). *The Library in Tomorrow's Society: A Literature Review*. UNESCO, Paris.

Rothstein, S. (1955). *The Development of Reference Services Through Academic Traditions, Public Library Practice and Special Librarianship*. Association of College and Research Libraries, Chicago.

Seiler, L., and Surprenant, T. (1991). When we get the libraries we want, will we want the libraries we get? *Wilson Library Bulletin* **65**, 29–31, 152, 157.

Shaw, R. R. (1953). From fright to Frankenstein. *D. C. Libraries* **24**, 6–10.

Shaw, R. R. (1955). Implications for library services. *Library Quarterly*, **25**, 344–355.

Shaw, R. R. (1965). The form and the substance. *Library Journal* **90**, 567–571.

Shera, J. (1967). What is past is prologue: Beyond 1984. *ALA Bulletin* **61**, 35–47.

Shuman, B. A. (1989). *The Library of the Future: Alternative Scenarios for the Information Profession*. Libraries Unlimited, Boulder, Colorado.

Smith, A. (1980). *Goodbye Gutenburg: The Newpaper Revolution of the 1980s*. Oxford University Press, New York.

Smith, A. (1982). Information technology and the myth of abundance. *Daedalus* **111**, 1–16.

Smith, E. R. (1990). *The Librarian, the Scholar, and the Future of the Research Library*. Greenwood, New York.

Stevens, N. (1980). The catalogs of the future: A speculative essay. *Journal of Library Automation* **13**, 88–95.

Stevens, N. (1984). Cornelia's last information search. *American Libraries* **15**, 84–85.

Stevens, N. (1986). The history of information. *Advances in Librarianship* **14**, 1–44.

Streit, S. A. (1991). *The Higher Education Act, Title II-C Program: Strengthening Research Library Resources*. Association of Research Libraries, Washington.

Swanson, D. R. (1979). Libraries and the growth of knowledge. *Library Quarterly* **49**, 3–25.

Swanson, D. R. (1980). Evolution, libraries, and national information policy. *Library Quarterly* **50**, 76–93.

Taylor, B. W., Mann, E. B., and Munro, R. J. (1988). *The Twenty-First Century: Technology's Impact on Academic Research and Law Libraries*. G. K. Hall, Boston.

Technical Processing in Large Research Libraries: Seeking a New Paradigm. (1992). Research Libraries Group, Palo Alto, California.

Veaner, A. B,. ed. (1976). *Studies in Micropublishing 1853–1976: Documentary Sources*. Microform Review, Westport, Connecticut.

Wasserman, P. (1965). *The Librarian and the Machine*. Gale Research, Detroit.

Weeks, L. (1991). Brave new library. *Washington Post Magazine*, May 26.

Yates, J. (1989). *Control Through Communication: The Rise of System in American Management*. Johns Hopkins University Press, Baltimore.

The Online Catalog: From Technical Services to Access Service

Barbara A. Norgard, Michael G. Berger,
Michael Buckland, and Christian Plaunt
School of Library and Information Studies
University of California, Berkeley
Berkeley, California 94720

I. Introduction

During the last decade, the widespread adoption of the online catalog has launched the library visibly into the computer age and has made the library a center stage for information access in academic institutions and in the communities served by the public library. A whole generation of library users has traveled the path to computer and library literacy through the use of the online catalog. Implementation of online library catalogs has given new impetus to programs for user education, formal bibliographic instruction, and information desks, building, in the process, an infrastructure for electronic access to the resources of the library and the community. Within the profession, the online catalog has led to a host of conference programs, workshops, and professional discussion groups. Not the least of these changes is the gradual redefinition of the "catalog." Ten years ago, most librarians and library users would agree to a definition of the catalog as displaying the bibliographic information for monographs and serial titles physically held in a specific library. Today, it would be harder to find agreement on the definition of a catalog. Present-day online catalogs are beginning to provide access to abstracting and indexing databases, full text, and "pass through" access to catalogs of material housed in physically diverse locations in different institutions. In addition to the simple *find* and *display* functions, online catalogs are providing printing, downloading, electronic mailing of results, requests for document delivery, and access to electronic full text.

Notwithstanding the lack of a clear definition of the online catalog, large libraries now typically have online catalogs or are actively planning to install them. The effort and resources required for adoption are substantial: choosing between numerous different systems; finding funding; installing and connect-

ADVANCES IN LIBRARIANSHIP, VOL. 17

ing terminals; connecting to local area networks and the Internet; training staff and users; and harmonizing the online catalog with other computerized systems. Recent catalog records were generally already in machine-readable form, but the conversion or upgrading of older records has involved and continues to require a major effort.

The widespread adoption of online catalogs is clearly a major advance in library service, and yet, in another sense, there has been relatively little progress in the basic functionality of the online catalog (Hildreth, 1991). The searching functions of the best online catalogs of 1992 were not much better than the best online catalogs of ten years earlier. Online catalogs have evolved through "generations," a categorization proposed by Hildreth (1987, 1991) to differentiate catalogs in terms of the sophistication of their search functions and user interface. A "first-generation" online catalog allows searching in the same manner as a card catalog (searching by main entry, by title, and by subject heading), and typically has one mode of interaction, limited help, and simple displays. A "second-generation" catalog supports, in addition, the searching of individual terms (keywords) within the main entry, title, and subject headings, and allows Boolean searches, two modes of interaction (typically a menu and command mode), multiple display options, and HELP and error recovery facilities. The phrases "third generation" and "next generation" are used to describe the catalogs that do, or will in the future, include advanced functionality and broader access. Over the last ten years, there has been a gradual development from first- to second-generation catalogs facilitated by the increasing awareness of the librarians and users of the potential of online access as well as by the rapid drop in costs of computing.

Almost everything else around the online catalog has changed more substantially: extensive installation of infrastructure (terminals, networks, connectivity); massive conversion of existing catalog records to machine-readable form; the mounting of additional bibliographic databases in conjunction with catalogs or on CD–ROMS; and the mounting of full-text documents online.

During the last ten years there has been a limited relationship between the users and the designers of online catalogs. The origin of both the first- and second-generation online catalogs is deeply rooted in the card catalog. We have often been constrained and our purposes determined, to an extent we often discount, by the types of technological advances currently available (and fashionable) that happen to be more or less useful in the context of an online catalog. With the card catalog as their frame of reference, most of us were not in any better position to provide meaningful input to the design process than the trailblazers who took the first steps. It turned out that online catalogs were easier and more rewarding to use than the card catalog and users responded by expressing high levels of satisfaction with the online catalog and using them more.

The online catalog has brought with it relatively sophisticated tools for automatically gathering data on catalog use. For example, transaction logs, combined with various other kinds of studies, provide a continuous flow of information on the strengths and weaknesses of online catalogs on the basis of patron usage. The information gleaned from these studies has been used to improve the catalog and the library environment of the catalog. Though most of these improvements, such as better HELP messages, new indexes for special functions, orientation programs, and glare-free locations for terminals have been small, the cumulative effect has been a gradual improvement of the catalog and a rapidly broadening perception of its potential. Although the state of the art in functionality of online catalogs has evolved little, numerous constructive proposals have been made, increasingly by researchers interested in, but not responsible for, operational online catalogs.

It is clear, however, from the research reviewed that users are experiencing significant problems in making effective use of online catalogs in spite of expectations. When the users don't go away empty handed, they may feel satisfied even though in reality they have received incomplete search results. Because users may be unaware of what information they are missing, they have been slow to articulate these types of problems. This article examines problems with online catalogs, examines some actual and proposed solutions, and seeks to understand the changing position of the online catalog. Although some of the solutions draw on other kinds of online bibliographic retrieval systems, our focus is on online catalogs, concentrating on recent literature, and is deliberately selective. It is hoped that this analysis will provide not only a convenient summary of recent developments, but also a contribution to the agenda for research, development, and design of future online catalogs.

The review is in five parts: Section I, the introduction, defines the scope of the review and summarizes briefly the present situation. Difficulties encountered by users are examined in Section II. In Section III, opinions and evidence concerning users are noted. Section IV examines solutions (both actual and proposed) for identified difficulties. Finally, conclusions are drawn in Section V. Other recent reviews and broadly based discussions include Van Pulis (1991), Dale (1989), Hildreth (1989), Lancaster, Elliker, and Harkness Connell (1989), Larson (1991a), and Taylor (1992).

II. Problems

A. Formulating a Search

Researchers have been observing users, conducting user surveys, and examining online catalog transaction logs to develop a picture of what is happening when users interact with the system. The results of these studies have been used to improve levels of search effectiveness (Matthews and Associates, Inc.,

1982; Matthews and Matthews 1984). However, recent studies suggest that users continue to experience discouragingly low levels of search effectiveness using online catalogs (Larson, 1986, 1991a,b; Seymour, 1991; Tonta, 1992a,b). Larson (1991b) conducted a transaction log study of the University of California's MELVYL online catalog and concluded that subject searching had declined 2.15% per year over a 6-year period, while title keyword searching increased by a comparable amount. He attributed the likely causes to the high incidence of search failure for subject searches and the problem of "information overload" in successful subject searches as the size of the database grows.

In 1986, Shaw reported that novice searchers choose the wrong database, search several concepts in a single statement, and use unlimited truncation. It has been widely observed that users do not base subject searches on known documents (Shaw, 1986). Hildreth (1992b) reports survey results indicating that 75% of users would be more likely to look up "any publication that may have information on a specific topic or subject area" rather than look up specific books they know about on the topic.

People inevitably make mechanical errors using computers. Seaman (1992) found that 40% of user errors were due to incorrect author or title and 9% were due to unsupported abbreviations. They also make spelling errors and have trouble with conjunctions, ellipses, and missing or incorrect punctuation (Young, Eastman, and Oakman, 1991). A small, but significant, portion of search failures have been attributed to typographical and spelling errors (9.9–15%) and system failure (9.7–18%), but an even larger proportion (29%) arise from the failure to match user terms with controlled vocabularies (Hunter, 1991; Peters, 1989; Seaman, 1992).

Studies are showing that library users still do not find the use of Boolean operators intuitively obvious. Bellardo (1985b) observed that searchers misuse logical operators. Peters (1989) found that 73.5% of Boolean AND searches fail and 84.8% of Boolean AND searches between two subject headings also fail (see also Vigil, 1990). In her recent study of online catalog use, Ensor (1992b) shows that there is still widespread lack of familiarity with Boolean operators. Ensor also found that computer "literacy" affects the degree of facility with which users are using online catalogs. Peters (1991) found that remote users of online catalogs are more sophisticated in terms of search patterns than in-library users. For example, he found that 38% of remote users used right truncation, but user-initiated truncation was almost nonexistent among in-library users.

Users still make errors of basic strategy. Early on, researchers noticed that catalog users were failing to develop successful search strategies. A decade ago, searching on broad single terms that trigger large, unmanageable retrievals, and missing obvious synonyms that could increase results of small retrivals were common user errors (Bates, 1977; Fenichel, 1979). In fact, most subject queries used "whatever [terms] popped into the searcher's mind" (Markey, 1983a). The situation has not improved much a decade later. In a transaction log study of academic library use, Hunter (1991) found that subject searching was used most frequently, but least successfully. In addition to typographical errors and using uncontrolled vocabulary, she attributed this failure to a misunderstanding of how to use the system. Bates (1984b) made the important observation that searchers fail to consider the inverse relationship between recall and precision in searching, that is, that expanding a search to find additional relevant records will also increase the number (and proportion) of nonrelevant records, and refining a search to exclude nonrelevant records will also exclude some relevant ones.

The other side of the coin is search failure. Searches, even in large databases, frequently retrieve sets that are either null (i.e., empty or "zero-hit") or perceived by the user as too small. Ten years ago, between 23 and 45% of searches were reported as resulting in null sets (Markey, 1984; Dickson, 1984). This problem has not changed significantly. Markey (1989) found that 34% of subject keyword searches retrieve no records and 53% of subject keyword searches retrieve only one relevant citation. Peters (1989) reported a 40% zero-hit rate for searches of an online university catalog. Hunter (1991) came to the daunting conclusion that 58% of searches fail.

Of course, not all zero-hit searches are search failures. It is possible that in fact no relevant record in the database matches the search query. Perhaps the user was seeking to confirm the absence of a citation. However, researchers examining zero-hit searches are demonstrating how minor changes in search statements succeed in retrieving the type and quantity of records desired. For example, if a searcher queries a database indexed with Library of Congress Subject Headings (LCSH), a subject word search on "Vietnam War" will fail, although a subject word search on "Vietnamese Conflict" will succeed. An experienced searcher might find this by submitting a title word search on "Vietnam War," look at the subject headings, and discover that the material on this topic is in fact entered under "Vietnamese Conflict." This example reveals the effect of not implementing LCSH cross-references in MELVYL, but it is also characteristic of how LCSH terminology can differ from natural language that people really use. Another example of this type of failure is the perfectly reasonable subject search on "Bayesian statistics," which retrieves no records because LCSH uses "Bayesian statistical decision theory" for this subject category and provides no cross-reference. If these variant phrases were linked, the user would retrieve records on these topics. As these examples clearly demonstrate, zero-hit search results do not necessarily reflect a lack of records in the database. Several researchers have reported that users have difficulty using subject headings. This is discussed in Section II,F.

B. Modifying Searches

Not only do library users have difficulty formulating searches, they also fail to modify them effectively. System features currently available on most online catalog systems for dealing with problematic search results include truncation, Boolean operators, and date, language, and location limits. But users rarely use advanced features even when they are available. Harter (1986) reported that only half of searchers use these system features, usually the "limit" command or a change of output format. Shenouda (1990) found that most changes are related to the deletion and addition of terms and facets. Even many experienced users do not use all system capabilities (Bellardo, 1985b). Are users unaware of the existence of advanced features? Are the advanced features too difficult, too complicated, or too much trouble to use?

That library users rarely base subsequent searches on previous results seems to be a characteristic pattern (Fenichel, 1979, 1981; Seaman, 1992; Walker, 1990, Hildreth, 1992b). Tolle and Hah (1985) found that 15% of users quit immediately after receiving an error message. Both problems are perhaps due to incomplete understanding of how the database is structured.

No satisfactory solution has yet been developed to cope effectively with null and "too small" sets. Novices generally accept null sets unquestioningly (Shaw, 1986). Not only do searchers accept defeat rather quickly when confronted with a zero-hit result, they also flounder when rewarded with a few worthwhile records and want more like them. Ercegovac (1989) reported 46% of users having difficulty increasing results when too little is retrieved. More records on the search topic may exist in the database, but the necessary link that would lead to their successful retrieval has not been made, either on the part of the searcher or the system.

To compound the problem, indexing techniques and retrieval methods that work well with small- and medium-sized catalogs tend to fall short and fail when catalogs become large. An increasing problem is the retrieval of excessively large numbers of records. Factors related to large retrievals include size of the database, keyword indexing, and use of the Boolean OR. Physical limitations of the display screen and inadequate search assistance compound the large retrieval problem, especially for untrained users. When the retrieved set is large, users must decide whether to continue displaying more records, whether to reformulate the search query, and at what point to discontinue the search.

Early studies showed users retrieving large sets 22–53% of the time and 26% of users experiencing problems reducing the result when too much was retrieved (Matthews and Associates, Inc., 1982; Kern-Simerenko, 1983).

Repeated negative experiences with large retrieved sets without adequate online tools to cope with them continue to discourage users from using online catalogs. Kantor (1987) found that the number of positive and negative reinforcements affects when users stop. As the size of the database increases, legitimate types of searches (e.g., subject keyword searches) tend increasingly to retrieve large, unwieldy sets. Even though Bates observed in 1984 that a 30-hit response is considered an optimal search by many searchers, the reality is more often than not "information overload" (Bates, 1984b; Hudson and Walker, 1987). The average subject search by a skilled user in MELVYL in 1987 was yielding over 181 records (Wiberly and Dougherty, 1988). A decade ago, Bates observed that users typically responded to searches that retrieved one hundred or more citations by either walking away from the terminal or displaying all of the citations (Bates, 1984a). Larson (1986) found that the average number of records retrieved by searchers in a large online catalog was 77.5, but users only displayed 9.1 records. In 1992, MELVYL users were still finding many more records than they were willing to display, retrieving an average of 100 records, but only displaying about 15 records per search (Berger, 1992). With a large system like MELVYL, with 7 million records in its catalog database, it has also been necessary during times of peak usage to implement a policy of blocking resource-intensive searches that typically return extremely large sets. Such searches would normally be considered reasonable in smaller databases (Ritch, 1992).

How can methods for modifying a search query be conveyed to users when search results are too large? As of 1992, online search aids provide little strategic help for higher level problem-solving tasks involved in selecting, evaluating, and modifying queries (Oberman, 1991).

C. Handling Retrieved Sets

Having retrieved a set of records, what next? A search on a large database that presents the user with an unmanageably large retrieved set is only accomplishing part of the task. What assistance is available to help the user cope with a large set of records and make decisions about it? How can the user satisfactorily determine if any records in the set are likely to be relevant and where they are within the large set? How can a view of the set be presented so that the user can make reasonably informed decisions about how to proceed? How can the user quickly obtain a summary of features that characterize the set and identify subsets likely to be of interest? Are there functions that can be applied that will sort and display views of the entire set from various perspectives, for example, language, publication date, location, subject headings, title words? Does the average user have, and know about, the tools to reduce the set size in an appropriate, helpful way?

Short of moving on to a new or modified search, the user ordinarily has only one option: to display screen after screen of records that have been sorted into alphabetical order of main entry, a tradition carried over from the card catalog. There may be alternative forms of display (short, long, MARC) for individual records, but, as of 1992, responses to a query on PACS-L indicated that few options were available and that it was still rare for an online catalog to allow the user to choose any other ordering (e.g., reverse chronological) or to provide any tools for understanding anything about the retrieved records other than how many there are. It is, therefore, not surprising that users look at a limited number of items and select a few (Hancock-Beaulieu, 1989; Buchanan, 1992).

D. System Deficiencies

In spite of the aforementioned problems, online catalogs are still proving to be remarkably useful and popular. It is, therefore, fortunate that libraries can benefit from the continuing, dramatic improvements in the power and cost effectiveness of computing, networks, and data storage. Unfortunately, increased speed, memory, and disk space are not enough to cope adequately with the problem of providing effective access to large numbers of records. Searching (as opposed to the mere lookup of already-identified items) is computationally intensive. Second-generation online catalogs consume substantially greater computing resources than those of the first generation because of the need to support keyword indexes, keyword truncation, and Boolean combinations. This results in system slowdowns. In 1989, Farley reported that about 10% of searches on the University of California MELVYL system were resulting in large retrievals that took 60 or more seconds to report back findings (Farley, 1989).

There is also an emerging need to provide high-speed downloading of records. This requirement was not expected a decade ago when the need was to support terminals at relatively low speed, but is now implicit in the expectation that high-speed networks will be used to search and download results from remote catalogs.

E. Data Deficiencies

Data deficiencies affect the quality of search results. Close examination of any large bibliographic database reveals errors in the data. When searching is extended to nonindexed fields, the error rate will probably rise. This will present significant problems when more fields become searchable.

Ballard and Lifshin (1992) have commented on the need to eliminate spelling errors in bibliographic databases. Large database size is an inhibiting factor in tracking down duplicate records (Borgman and Siegfried, 1992). Software designed to analyze retrieved sets will also prove useful in identifying deficient data. The recent achievement of OCLC in correcting up to 30,000 records a day should be an inspiration to all.

F. Topical Access and System Vocabularies

The present review makes no attempt to duplicate Larson's review of subject searching in online catalogs in Volume 15 of *Advances in Librarianship*, to which reference should be made (Larson, 1991a).

In general, users have trouble expressing questions in subject terms and matching terms to information systems (Allen, 1990). Bates (1989) found that there is only a 10–20% likelihood that two people will use the same term for a concept. Peters and Kurth (1991) found that 58% of search sessions begin with terms not used in the system's controlled vocabulary. Several researchers have reported that users have difficulty using LCSH for subject searching. In 1983, Markey found subject searchers did not consult LCSH even when it was easily available (1983b). Bellardo (1985b) noted the failure to use controlled vocabulary. Even when users do attempt to base searches on LCSH, they are confronted with a formidably complicated maze of relationships. Although modifications have been made, the loose structure of LCSH does not fit well into the typical thesaurus organization with highly structured broad, narrow, and related terms. Not only does this present problems in searching, but it also interferes with the presentation of retrieved sets to the user in a coherent fashion. According to McGarry and Svenonius (1991), LCSH phrase headings and inverted syntax disrupt the logical sequencing of subject heading subdivisions. Not surprisingly, Butkovich, Taylor, Dent, and Moore, (1989) concluded that users do not understand the organization and structure of LCSH.

Hancock-Beaulieu (1989) argues that online catalog systems at present do not offer any opportunity for a contextual approach to searching. There are no tools for negotiation or experimentation that the user can call on to further define queries. She also believes that browsing system indexes is of limited value and that alphabetical listings of LCSH do not offer an overview of related subjects. In addition, there is the problem that browsing records ordered by class number fails to convey the structure of the classification scheme to the user. She points out that combining precoordinate subject headings (LCSH) with postcoordinate keyword indexing (the searcher's query) can cause confusion (Hancock-Beaulieu, 1989).

Larson (1989) reported that title word searches are being increasingly favored over subject searches, and Frost (1987) found that, as in a card catalog, faculty do mostly known-item searches. One explanation for this is that faculty do not search for books in their own field by subject because they are already familiar with the books and authors they are investigating. However, this suggests that users are not basing their searches on the indexing system offered by the system. For other criticism of subject access, see Binder, Gustafson, and Merritt (1989) and Peters (1991).

III. Users

A. What Do Library Users Want?

Unquestionably, online catalogs are enjoying high use, and perceived success in service leads to demands for more services. Librarians are becoming familiar with requests that the online catalog be extended to provide access to records for articles held in the library as well as to records for books and, indeed, to the texts themselves. Gradually, many of these additional functions are being put in place. Meanwhile, several comments have been made about the features users want in an online catalog.

Bates (1990b) found that searchers want a sense of control over the search, to know what is going on during the search, and what information is being included and rejected and why. Crawford (1992) thinks that it is important to users to feel in control, but understanding all the mechanics involved is not critical. Ensor (1992a) has found that about two-thirds of library catalog users tend to look at a long list of results rather than take some action to narrow it. She attributes this to two reasons: (1) users have difficulty learning and remembering appropriate actions to take to narrow a search; and (2) users want to maintain control over the whole process.

In her study of keyword and Boolean use in a university online catalog, Ensor (1992b) found that users do use Boolean operators when a search retrieves too much or too little, but faculty and graduate students find Boolean operators easier to learn than undergraduates. She also found that undergraduates use keyword searching more than either graduate students or faculty. Sixty percent of all users felt that keyword searching is easy to learn, but this was affected by possession or lack of computer experience.

Recent literature includes several comments concerning users' preferences. Ercegovac (1989) states that 45% of users want to see related terms. But online catalogs do little to support this. Forty-two percent want to search tables of contents or back-of-book indexes and 24% want to search title words. Fox (1990) and Harman (1990) say searchers prefer document-ranked retrieval, that is, with documents individually ranked according to an estimate of the probability of being relevant, to other methods. Saracevic and others found that precision (not recall) was associated with high satisfaction (Saracevic, Kantor, Chamis, and Trivison, 1988; Saracevic and Kantor, 1988. See also Ankeny, 1991; Markey and Demeyer, 1986). This points to a need on the part of the users for additional points of access and more options to organize result sets that will allow them to judge relevance.

As for how many records are wanted, a 30-record response is widely considered a typical optimal result, and professional searchers view 50–70 references as optimal (Bates, 1986; Wiberly and Dougherty, 1988). Kinnucan (1992) found satisfaction relatively unaffected by retrieval set size but sensitive to precision, though less so as retrieved set size increased.

B. What Do Experienced Searchers Do?

There is good reason to examine what experienced searchers do. What works for experienced searchers could form the basis for redesign of the system to make the strategies adopted by experts more accessible to novice searchers. Experienced searchers tend to adopt stereotyped sequences of tactics that could be embedded, more or less, in the interface. Providing for "strategic commands" that would trigger such a pattern of tactics might empower the novice as well as provide an appreciated labor-saving amenity for the expert (Buckland, Norgard, and Plaunt 1992b). Fidel (1986) has studied the informal, highly intuitive methods used by experienced searchers to select "search keys" and how they can be formalized in a decision tree and incorporated into the knowledge base of an expert system.

Harris (1986) observed that experienced searchers view large sets as intermediary sets, that is, as a basis for a more refined, secondary search. Successful searchers tend to view large sets as being presented with a wider range of choices rather than feeling overwhelmed by information overload. Hancock (1987) noted that searchers who consciously adopt a broad search formulation strategy are more successful than those who take an exact matching approach. Starting with more general terms to gain an overview of the domains they cover can often give a searcher a better idea of how to phrase a narrower search. If novices and successful searchers start their searches in much the same way, does the difference lie more in how they view and continue the search process? If so, how is that "broad view" conveyed? Katzer (1990) sees user interaction with the system as a process of enhancing and refining the original query. In all cases, support for providing tools for analyzing retrieved sets is indicated.

C. Models

Inevitably, any but the most sophisticated design will be based on a set of assumptions concerning the expected users. Similarly, any but the most trivial usage depends on a set of expectations by the user concerning system behavior. Ordinarily, "cognitive model" (or "user model") is used to denote the system's assumptions concerning the user, and "conceptual model" (or "mental model") to denote the user's assumptions concerning the system (Buckland and Florian, 1991).

People do not operate like machines, and some researchers have pointed out that people do not approach problems in a linear, logical fashion. They have memory limitations and tend to organize information idiosyncratically (see Najarian, 1981). Several authors have urged that the development of cognitive models of how users process information ought to lead to the design of better systems (Kieras and Polson, 1985; Daniels, 1986; Saracevic, 1989; Belkin, 1990; Allen, 1991). We still need to look at how people process information when solving problems (Nahl-Jakobovits and Jakobovits, 1988). Belkin (1990) has urged the importance of discovering users' goals, tasks, and behaviors. This has led to attempts to base system design on a conceptual organization of knowledge and human information processing limits. One approach has been to study information-seeking activity at the catalog and at the shelves as an interrelated process (Hancock-Beaulieu, 1989). Another problem with developing concise models of users is that data from user studies is more often qualitative or impressionistic than quantitative (Robertson and Hancock-Beaulieu, 1992). Although Bellardo (1985a) did not find searching performance to be related to cognitive or personality traits, there have been several studies that found observable differences among groups. Horne (1990) found that solvers and nonsolvers use different self-questioning strategies. Harter (1986) reports that researchers in the "hard" scientific and technological disciplines tend to share a common paradigm and agree more on terms than researchers in "soft" literary and sociological disciplines. This makes agreement on terminology outside of narrowly specified domains much more difficult.

For more on user models, see Ellis (1989), who analyzed the search behavior of academic social scientists in terms of six types of procedure: starting, chaining, browsing, differentiating, monitoring, and extracting.

Dickson (1984) concluded that gaps in users' conceptual models were a significant source of errors and several writers have urged the use of metaphor, maps, or models to orient users by providing a conceptual map of the system. Mental models (qualitative methods in the mind of how the system "runs") are effective for complex tasks according to Borgman, who has argued that conceptual training is superior to procedural training, at least for complex tasks (Borgman, 1983, 1986a. See also Allen, 1991; Daniels, 1986). Brown (1990) suggested helping the user develop a search strategy using an outline metaphor. Using a flowchart to create a conceptual map of the search is one way to convey mental models of systems and teach users conceptual models. A flowchart model proposed by Kuhlthau, Belvin, and George (1989) would include six basic steps: initiation, selection, exploration, formulation, collection, and presentation. Rubens (1991) noted that searchers are more successful when they think in categorical terms and concluded that users who have difficulty lack a model of information flow, knowledge of the bibliographic chain, knowledge of relationships between subjects, and an understanding of knowledge creation.

Borgman (1986b) observed that front ends tend more to ease mechanical rather than conceptual problems of use. Shrager and Klahr (1986) made the interesting observation that people who learn to use a complex device without instruction modify their theories with experience, but these changes may be based on limited evidence and can instead reinforce incorrect understanding.

Reviewing the literature on what users want, how experts search, and, especially, cognitive and conceptual models, suggests that it makes little sense to study online catalogs in isolation from other retrieval systems. In the next section, we take a look at some solutions that have been implemented or proposed.

IV. Solutions

A. Formulating a Search

1. Retrieval Techniques

The current state of the art of operational online catalogs is solidly based on the retrieval of sets of records and basic Boolean operations. This is in marked contrast to a quite separate thirty-year tradition in information retrieval experimentation, which is almost as solidly based on probabilistic retrieval models that rank each document by an estimated probability of relevance to each query. Predictably, the dominance of Boolean techniques in on-line catalogs has been challenged. Hildreth (1992c), for example, wrote that "Exact-match Boolean retrieval systems show major performance and user deficiencies" and Larson (1992a) considers partial match techniques and rank-ing of retrieval output to be more useful than Boolean logic. Prabha (1990) has observed that the limitations of keyword indexing and Boolean logic become more pronounced as databases get larger.

Belkin and Croft (1987) concluded in their excellent review of information retrieval techniques that Boolean techniques are widely used but are generally unsatisfactory, that all retrieval techniques perform better for some queries than for others, and that experimental techniques (e.g., probabilistic retrieval where documents are retrieved and ranked based on techniques that predict probability of relevance) perform better than Boolean techniques, but these have not been implemented on any large scale. Fortunately, experimental prototypes, such as Larson's Cheshire (see Section IV,G) are becoming avail-able. At the same time, standard Boolean systems are based on unweighted binary values: to retrieve, every record must have the specified attributes and all other, unspecified attributes are deemed irrelevant. Standard Boolean systems can be considered relatively undeveloped given the possibilities for weighted search terms and for supporting conditional search modifiers that can be invoked heuristically (Buckland *et al.*, 1992b; Buckland, Butler, Norgard, and Plaunt, 1993). As Buchanan (1992) noted, Boolean systems can be used for creating and ranking small subsets. For example, sorting by date in reverse chronological order can provide a useful ranking.

There has been little systematic comparison done, and because probabilistic systems and existing Boolean systems both have the potential to be refined considerably, there is much work to be done in this area.

2. Search Aids and Interfaces

The use of search profiles and searcher profiles has been examined by several writers. Interfaces can be designed to support searching in order of defined priorities (Connell, 1991). The OASIS front end to MELVYL (See Section IV,G) supports a repeating "fewer" command for progressive retrieved set reduction that invokes stored statements of users preferences (Buckland, Norgard, and Plaunt, 1992a; Buckland *et al.*, 1992b, 1993) Myaeng and Korfhage (1990) have examined different information retrieval models that integrate user profiles into the system. SAFIR is an expert system that offers information on search strategies based on information already known about the user and the domain (Reiter, 1989).

One challenging area for research and development is the design of systems that can help searchers formulate a search strategy (Hancock-Beaulieu, 1989; Morris, 1991; Berger, 1992). Slack (1989) points out that most failed searches could be turned into successful ones with minimal guidance by such techniques as limiting searches by date or identifying several relevant records to find subject headings used by the system. It has been suggested that users be offered a variety of tools that they can adapt, mix, and match (Cox, 1992). Markey-Drabenstott and Vizine-Goetz (1990) suggest that systems automatically determine the best search approach based on characteristics of search queries. Such an approach would take into account the number of words in the query and extent to which queries match the controlled vocabulary. Belkin, Chang, Downs, Saracevic, and Zhao (1990) suggest providing online maps, tables of contents, and the capability to browse by genre. Navigation has been suggested as a key concept crucial to building successful systems that empower the user (Newby, 1989, 1991). Among other recommendations, Newby suggests that menus and HELP screens should provide enough information to teach a person to navigate through the system.

A prototype intermediary system called Knowledge-based Intermediary System for Information Retrieval (KISIR) has been under development in Finland since 1986. In the KISIR system, users can request information about the search at any point in the session. The type of information KISIR provides includes (1) current context; (2) status of the search; and (3) instructions on how to do the next step. Current context is indicated by displaying defaults and other parameters in effect. Search status tells the user the stage they have reached in the process and suggests possible next steps. It also offers an option of saving displayed records in either a separate file or marked inside a general session history file (Sormunen, Nurminen, Hamalainen, and Hursalmi, 1987).

There seems to be general agreement that simple functions like automatic spelling and search statement format correction should be implemented (Hildreth, 1987). At first glance, spell-checkers seem simple to implement (Johnson and Peterson, 1992), but the existence of multiple languages poses problems immediately. Although the CITE system was using error-correction techniques, and expert spelling correction systems could identify phonological and sequential errors in the early 1980s, these features have yet to be widely implemented in online catalogs (Doszkocs, 1983a; Yannakoudakis, 1983) and researchers are still reporting the need for automatic spelling and search statement format correction (Hildreth, 1987; Morris, 1991).

Although interface design is out of the scope of this review, work relevant to this review includes looking at functional components of browsing (Kwasnik, 1992) including novel graphical interfaces that offer with direct manipulation approaches to query formulation (Shneiderman, 1990), using forms-type interfaces (Fox, 1990), and weighing the completeness of information against number of screens needed for display (Heustis, 1988).

Berger (1992) has discussed the need to allow the user to configure a number of elements in the interface, such as modifying the interface appearance, location of windows icons, and buttons. Tufte argues against low-density displays: "The more relevant information within the eyespan the better" (Tufte, 1992, p. 15). For a recent review of interface research see Shaw (1991).

Online catalogs are generally hierarchically structured. Searches can be progressively narrowed, but branching is generally unsupported. This means that one typically backs out of one search before entering a new search. Moving sideways or using one feature of a record to browse other records sharing the same feature is not usually an option. Hickey and Prabha (1990) have suggested browsing records and access to more fields, and Larson (1991a) recommended the browsing functionality associated with hypertext. Dynix offers a "related works" option and BLCMP offers a "titles on this subject" option (Walker, 1990).

3. Improved Use of Data

Because of the complexity involved in dealing with subject access, the use of nontopical attributes for searching and, especially, for search modification, may be an effective and easier first step. Searchers typically have basic preferences concerning such nontopical attributes as date, language, and location. Furthermore, the values of such attributes are relatively easy to manipulate in Boolean systems. Harter (1986) discussed the use of identifying such nonsubject search parameters as document type, date of publication, language, author, and corporate source. Databases are often organized by document type (e.g., journal article, conference paper, technical report), making database selection crucial to search success. But this is not always clear to the user. Rubens (1991) has proposed actively soliciting the user for information on format, date, intellectual level, and subject. Borgman and Siegfried (1992) found that although personal name-matching techniques have been developed, they are being applied to databases where no significant name authority work has been done.

There is also considerable scope for improved use of topical data. Most systems offer a limited subject searching approach. This is usually offered in the form of exact LCSH with implicit right truncation and, in second-generation catalogs, keyword searching of terms derived from LCSH, but more should be offered (Markey-Drabenstott and Vizine-Goetz, 1990).

One option is to use more of the existing data. For example, the classification numbers present in catalog records could be used to extend or modify the subject headings to help the searcher make relevance judgments (Geller and Lesk, 1984). According to Connell (1991) keyword matching in the personal name and subject heading fields would increase both precision and recall.

A second option is to make more sophisticated use of existing data, using, for example, probabilistic ranking techniques. Cheshire, an experimental online catalog developed by Larson at the University of California, Berkeley, uses a classification clustering approach. For each Library of Congress Classification (LCC) number, the title and subject keywords of all documents assigned to it are used to increase the number of terms associated with each individual bibliographic record (Larson, 1989, 1991b, 1992a,b). Micco (1991) proposes a term-weighting scheme in which weights are based on the MARC tags the term is drawn from: the first 6*xx* field gets highest weight because it represents aboutness. The lowest ranking goes to natural language keywords from titles, notes, tables of contents. She also suggests extracting and displaying in scrolling windows the x, y, and z subfields containing modifiers of the LCSH. Connell (1991) also recommends searching the subdivisions of LCSH. Warner (1991) recommends the use of surface matching of stems and syntactic phrase types to generate a hierarchical display of phrases showing equivalent, hierarchical, and associative relationships. This category could include almost any nonstandard matching algorithm, such as, for example, Latent Semantic Indexing (LSI), which accepts keywords in any order and returns hits with an index of relevance (Deerwester *et al.*, 1990).

One development of great promise is "entry vocabulary" capability whereby whatever words the searcher uses are converted automatically to the system vocabulary terms (LCSH, LCC numbers, MeSH, etc.) with a high probability of corresponding to what the searcher wants. A simple approach is to use the existing indexes or cross-references of the system vocabulary, possibly enriched with additional cross-references to anticipate use of non-standard terms. A more advanced approach is to use statistical relationships between, say, title words and assigned LCSH. The inferred system vocabulary terms can be presented to the searcher for adoption or rejection. The Cheshire online catalog provides a working example, deriving, from whatever combination of terms the searcher may enter, a ranked listing of the LCC numbers most likely to denote what the searcher is seeking (Larson 1989, 1991b, 1992b). Buckland (1992a) nominated the development of entry vocabularies as the most promising single innovation for online catalogs (see also Connell, 1991).

A third promising line of development is to use additional resources beyond the standard catalog record to improve or modify searches. Bibliographies are an obvious source. Providing access, online, to dictionaries or thesauri could be helpful to the searcher in modifying or extending topical queries (Lesk, 1987). As networked information resources grow, there is also a need for directories of online library catalogs, file archives, online journals, and information servers (Lynch and Preston, 1992). Another suggestion is to give the user more help in finding the most significant literature, the "classics" in a field. Classics could be based on citedness, identification by subject experts, or other indicators (Berger, 1992).

A fourth option is to use the "nearest neighbor" technique: never mind what the specific heading is, what other record(s) resemble this one most closely when all (or several) features are compared? Blair (1986) noted that one of the simplest, but infrequently used, approaches is to begin with a highly useful document. Doszkocs (1983a) suggested using a closest match search strategy along with a dynamic feedback to the user for search refinement.

B. Modifying a Search

1. Mechanisms for Modifying Searches

Successful modification of a search depends heavily on the user's assessment of what has happened in response to a query and ideas about what the best next steps would be. How (and how far) can the system assist with these two tasks? There is no reason why the system's response should not be automatic.

Functionality that would provide the prompt analysis of retrieved sets, although generally a precondition for search modification, has received little attention until recently. There has been more attention to built-in support for automatic search modifications by the system. Borgman (1986b) reviewed user studies and reported that systems should provide such recovery mechanisms as: (1) searching first word of author name (as entered), followed by the first letter of the second word (i.e., truncated); (2) searching unmatched terms in the appropriate index; (3) displaying alphabetically adjacent terms; (4) passing unmatched terms (other than author names) against a spell-checker; and (5) forcing users into a HELP routine after one or more identifiable errors.

Bates suggests monitoring searches at the tactics and strategy levels rather than at the moves level. When there seems to be a need for other terms or the wrong terms seem to have been used, particular tactics should be available to the user as options. When there is a need to revise terms, a different set of tactics could be applied (for details, see Bates, 1990b).

2. Search Expansion

Two fundamental strategies for dealing with zero or too few hits are to widen the scope of the search and process the search against all reasonable information sources (Berger, 1992). Standard practices are to relax Boolean ANDs and to use the Boolean OR to add broader, narrower, and related terms, including synonyms and variant spellings (Chan, 1991; Fidel, 1985; Harter and Rogers Peters, 1985). Other techniques include using LCSH to enhance access, using LCC for subject retrieval, using both Dewey Decimal Classification (DDC) and LCSH, adopting strategies to use LCC, and using LCC for term clustering and ranking (Bates, 1986; Williamson, 1986; Markey and Vizine-Goetz, 1988; Heustis, 1988; Larson, 1989, 1991b). Bates (1990b) has identified a number of tactical responses for query expansion: neighbor, trace, parallel, fix, super, relate, and vary. Connell (1991) suggests manipulating the grammar of LCSH (word sequence, inversion, etc.) and providing access to fields not usually searched. (For further detailed discussion see Morris, Tseng, and Walton, 1989.)

3. Search Reduction

Approaches to dealing with excessive retrieval center around Boolean operations that limit both topical and nontopical parameters. When applicable, Henry, Leigh, Tedd, and Williams (1982) recommended reducing ORed terms. Markey (1983b) thought the user should be prompted to limit his or her search when retrieved sets exceeded 20 records. Bates (1990b) has distinguished a variety of descriptively named search tactics (e.g., specify, exhaust, pinpoint, block, sub). Harter and Rogers Peters (1985) proposed moving truncation characters to the right and limiting the search to a specific subject area by a classification code as effective methods of reducing large retrieved set sizes. Fidel (1985) suggested restricting fields, tightening proximity, limiting by language, or limiting by type of literature to deal with large sets. Morris *et al.* (1989) recommended intersecting with another concept, adding narrower terms, applying more stringent proximity, limiting to one or fewer fields, using NOT and AND NOT, and limiting by language, document type, year, and first few items. Prabha (1989) also supports the traditional approach of managing large retrievals by extending the use of restrictors such as language, format, and date of publication, but she has also suggested using library classification schemes as a limiting feature. Lesk pointed out the benefits of exploring uses of LCC to deal with "too many hits" (Lesk, 1989).

As Prabha (1990) has pointed out, there is much to be learned about the incidence of large retrievals, measures for evaluating retrieval performance, evaluating existing search features for increasing retrieval precision, and using additional data (e.g., the LCC and DDC schemes) for managing large re-trievals. The problem of excessively large retrieved sets does not arise with systems that rank documents, one simply accepts as many as one wishes. Similarly, the problem could be reduced in Boolean systems if they included built-in mechanisms for creating subsets and ranking them.

C. Handling Retrieved Sets

The analysis of retrieved sets to examine the characteristics of what has been retrieved can provide an important basis for search modification decisions. Retrieved set analysis can also be used for database analysis, identifying erroneous data, and collection analysis. Hickey and Prabha (1990) suggest making tools available online that summarize large retrieved sets. These summaries could be presented in the form of tables, pie charts, and bar charts. Several writers have suggested trying new, more compact, approaches to managing browse displays. The size of LCSH displays could be reduced by suppressing the display of geographic and chronological subfield headings (Massicotte, 1988; also McGarry and Svenonius, 1991).

An important new function is now being added to online catalogs for retrieved set analysis. The European Space Agency's Information Retrieval Service (ESA-IRS) offers a command called "zoom." For any retrieved set, zoom provides a frequency analysis of the values for a number of attributes that can be specified by the user. Among the options ESA-IRS provides are arrangements by dates, authors, corporate sources, words, classification codes, molecular formulas, and titles (Raitt, 1992). One good use of a zoom command is to identify the most frequent subject headings in a set, perhaps a set initially defined by use of title keywords (Ingwersen, 1984). Similar capabilities have been included in CITE (Doszkocs, 1983a,b), RUBIKON at Roskilde University Library in Denmark, and OASIS at Berkeley. In OASIS the "summarize" command summarizes subject headings or holding libraries (Buckland *et al.*, 1992b, 1993).

Norway's national online catalog, BIBSYS, offers sorting on the author, title, author and title, publication, and issue fields. The publication and issue fields can be sorted in either ascending or descending order (BIBSYS server, 1992).

D. System Improvements

Fortunately, recent advances in computer technology have made accelerated speeds, massive disk storage capabilities, and expanded memory capacity available at rapidly dropping costs. However, the improvements in hardware are so substantial that new designs are indicated, such as, for example, a shift from traditional line-by-line displays to bit-mapped images and graphical user interfaces. The increasing affordability of more powerful personal computers and workstations facilitates moving some of the processing to the user's desk top, both for the experimental prototyping of enhanced systems and also for routine use. There is a growing recognition that the "intelligence" necessary for aiding the searcher could and, perhaps, should reside in a front-end system (Prabha, 1990). Postprocessing tools can help users refine searches and browse records more easily (Hickey and Prabha, 1990).

Other specific recommendations include adopting a multitasking interface that allows users to download bibliographies while carrying out other searches (Berger, 1992) and providing online catalogs with more user-friendly and adaptive X-Windows graphical interfaces (Needleman, 1992).

E. Data Improvement

Enhanced hardware, software, and searching techniques are still liable to be hampered by deficiencies in the data. Errors and variant forms create the additional problem of duplicate records, often separating records for different copies of the same title. These records need to be consolidated. The OCLC Duplicate Detection Project uses matching algorithms that look for duplicates resulting from typographical errors and cataloging differences (O'Neill and Vizine-Goetz, 1988). Hickey (1981) initiated several techniques for comparing records, of which the "matching trigrams" technique proved to be the most effective.

Another form of improvement is to make records more complete, adding optional fields and/or additional fields. This could include enriched subject vocabulary (Hildreth, 1987; Gomez, Lochbaum, and Landauer, 1990), standard nonroman scripts (Aliprand, 1992), more cross-reference structure for variant forms of names and subject headings (Jamieson, Dolan, and Declerck, 1986), and enhanced use of the LCSH Subject Authority File (Markey-Drabenstott, 1992b).

Cataloging rules, subject headings, classifications, and data format rules change over time. Card catalogs tended to receive rather minimal retrospective modification to bring older records into line with newer practices. With databases, both the need and the means for maintaining standards change over time. (For a report on changing stoplists see Johnson and Peterson, 1992).

The rapid trend toward mounting multiple databases implies the need for support for searching across databases. Since databases overlap in coverage, problems arise in identifying which records are variant representations of the same work and, more generally, in linking works of similar nature across databases (Berger, 1992).

F. Topical Access and System Vocabularies

A thorough discussion of subject searching in the online catalog appeared in a previous volume to which reference should be made (Larson, 1991a; see also Lancaster, Elliker and Harkness Connell, 1989).

As noted above, there are problems and opportunities that arise in the process of moving from the searcher's terms to the catalog's terms. Micco and Smith (1989) suggest guiding the user to select the best search strategy by mapping user's terms to the controlled vocabularies in the database. Bates recommends the provision of a superthesaurus with a large entry vocabulary that includes colloquial terms and spelling variants (Bates, 1986, 1989, 1990b). Warner (1991) advocates showing the user how language is mapped in the system by organizing both natural language and controlled vocabulary into a single display.

According to Matthews and Matthews (1984), online catalogs that force users through a thesaurus lead to more satisfaction with search results than catalogs that do not. Gomez et al. (1990) report that user success is improved when the number of terms indexed is increased (see also Byrne and Micco, 1988). However, larger retrieved sets are also a likely consequence.

Many suggestions have been made to wrestle with the deeply entrenched LCSH. Lester (1989) recommends modifying user input to match LCSH. Markey-Drabenstott and Vizine-Goetz (1990) report that exact matches with LCSH are usually queries for topical subjects, but queries with combinations of topical subjects and names rarely match LCSH.

Markey-Drabenstott et al. (1990) conclude that incorporating subject terms from the DDC and other library classifications into online catalogs would enhance subject access and provide additional subject searching strategies. Possible solutions to the semantic problem include a semantic network approach for generating synonyms and related terms (Sormunen *et al.*, 1987) and a classification knowledge base that could store the semantic components for each LC class or subject heading with which the user would form a query by selecting relevant facets (Soergel, 1990).

Additional problems arise when the catalog provides access through multiple vocabularies (e.g., MeSH, as well as LCSH), or several foreign languages, as is often the case in European systems. Mandel (1991) describes several strategies online catalogs are now using to provide access to multiple vocabularies: segregated files, mixed vocabularies, integrated vocabularies, and front-end navigation.

G. Experimental Systems

A development that deserves special note is the increasing viability of experimental prototypes. It used to be that only those responsible for operational catalogs were in a position to develop them, but now the prevalence of powerful, yet relatively inexpensive, workstations, reduced data storage costs, and increasingly available datasets enable anyone with sufficient expertise to experiment and develop a functioning experimental online catalog. Further, remote access to a wide variety of databases over the Internet offers the opportunity for widespread testing. In this way new techniques can be tried, tested, evaluated, and, perhaps, adopted and developed by others. Experimental systems are beginning to use natural language techniques developed by artificial intelligence researchers. (For an examination of the role of natural language processing in information retrieval systems, see Doszkocs, 1986.)

A good example of a promising experimental system is the Cheshire system developed by Larson (1989, 1991b). For nearly thirty years the advantages of probabilistic retrieval techniques have been advocated. Yet it was not until the Cheshire system was developed on a Unix workstation at Berkeley with little funding, using the MARC records of a nearby library, that one could actually use a probabilistic online catalog with probabilistic document ranking.

Another good example is the Okapi system, developed initially at the Polytechnic of Central London and later at the City University, London. Okapi has been used for numerous interesting studies over the years. Okapi currently develops a query by selecting the best terms from a list of the original query terms as well as terms from records judged relevant by the user (Walker, 1987, 1990).

The OASIS system, also developed at Berkeley, takes low-cost prototyping one stage further. OASIS, running on a Unix workstation, acts as a front end to the massive MELVYL online catalog of the University of California. Ordinarily operating as a terminal connected to MELVYL, additional functionality can be supported through the preprocessing of new commands, and new retrieval results can be achieved through the postprocessing of records downloaded from MELVYL. The result is, in effect, a prototyping of enhanced MELVYL functionality, using the MELVYL database and achieved without any interferences with MELVYL software or service. Although there are limits to what can be done this way, the OASIS system has been successful in developing strategic searches (built-in stereotyped sequences of moves) and performing useful retrieved set analysis (Buckland *et al.*, 1992a,b, 1993). As search and retrieve protocols are adopted (e.g., Z39.50), any workstation could, in principle, develop and demonstrate enhancements to any online catalog supporting a standard protocol (Lynch, 1991).

In Norway, BIBSYS provides access to a 5 million-record database with searching on 33 different fields. BIBSYS also handles e-mail search requests and offers a choice of eight output formats. Records can also be downloaded with FTP or Kermit. Users have a choice of either a simple menu-driven or a command-driven search (BIBSYS server, 1992). In Finland, KISIR provides several browsers, including thesaurus-dictionary browsers, retrieval system description browsers, and database description browsers (Sormunen *et al.*, 1987).

As the online catalog becomes less and less isolated from other retrieval activities, so less cataloglike systems become of potential interest. Also, as the role of libraries expands to include many of the resources provided by the online environment, many new forms of information are falling within the domain of the online catalog. Full-text resources, for example, commonly have little or no human indexing and bring with them a whole new set of problems for both users and the catalogs. Second-generation online catalog techniques, particularly Boolean keyword searching, perform poorly, for many reasons, when applied to full-text documents (Blair and Maron, 1985). Indexing and retrieval techniques new to the catalog world will be needed. Fortunately, there is much interesting research and experimentation going on outside of libraries.

The Information Visualizer is a project at the Xerox Palo Alto Research Center (PARC) where researchers are experimenting with visualizing large amounts of data. The Information Visualizer uses color and interactive real-time three-dimensional animation to depict complex aspects of information. Information is represented as 3D objects. The user is given the sense of moving around the objects to view them from different perspectives (Clarkson, 1991).

Thinking Machines, Inc. has designed a group of applications, known as the Wide Area Information Server (WAIS) that work together to locate and retrieve documents. WAIS accepts queries in natural language and translates them into keywords that are used for a search. A query is entered in the user's own words, which can then be sent out across the Internet, accessing the wide variety of servers and databases now available. Thinking Machines is collaborating with Apple, Dow Jones, and KPMG Peak Marwick to simplify information retrieval from personal files, corporate records, and remote databases. The aim of the project is to develop approaches to the problems presented by the overwhelming surplus of electronic data now confronting large organizations. The long-range goal is to develop technology for a scalable system that will allow users to access a variety of data sources, including large commercial databases, through a common interface. The WAIS system is based on the client server model and consists of server software distributed by Thinking Machines and an open protocol for transmitting queries and responses (Kahle and Medlar, 1991; Norr, 1991; Malamud, 1992).

Thinking Machines has also undertaken a project with Columbia University's Law School. Project Janus is implementing a full-text retrieval system that deals with both text and graphics. This means including full-text documents such as the United Nations library human rights collection. On-line versions of the legal texts like the Maastricht Treaty and the Rio Conference on the Environment are receiving high usage, with the North American Free Trade Agreement getting 200–250 hits per day. The project is aimed at alleviating storage problems in libraries, making fragile items accessible, and providing access to information increasingly only available in electronic form. The system will include user-friendly interfaces, better search methods, and the ability to make scattered databases appear to be a single database. Keyword searches will be replaced by natural language queries, allowing users to search an unknown domain in their own words. The search strategy uses weighting and focuses on uncommon words to direct the search. Portions of full-text documents can be used to form new queries and find more documents on the topic selected. The library is also planning to work with publishers to load copyrighted text onto their system (Project Janus Info Account, 1993).

Apple's Advanced Technology Group has used WAIS to create Rosebud, a personally customizable electronic newspaper based on the metaphor of reporters and newspapers. Basically an Internet search and text-filtering program, Rosebud enables users to create a personal newspaper daily from wire-service reports, arrange documents by priority for action or reading, or locate specific items of correspondence. Rosebud finds information with user-defined keyword lists and provides a statistical content analysis. Aimed at nonexpert information users, Rosebud searches numerous remote databases and presents its findings in a newspaperlike format, prioritizing documents according to user preferences (Erickson and Solomon, 1991; Kahle, Morris, Goldman, Erickson, and Curran, 1992; Cisler, 1991).

A commercially available object-oriented information system called Topic uses a knowledge-based approach centered on the idea of concept retrieval, which uses hierarchically arranged "topics" to search for entire concepts instead of words or phrases. Topic uses typical Boolean retrieval techniques, but allows the user to create topics with rules about relationships to more specific topics. Topic handles data from databases as diverse as news wires, intelligence reporting services, and electronic mail (Appleton, 1992; Schwartz, 1991; Mace, 1989; Tucker, 1988).

AT&T Bell Laboratories is prototyping The RightPages electronic library, the first phase of a plan to create an electronic analog of the traditional library environment. The RightPages library alerts users to incoming scientific and technical journal articles that correspond to their interest profiles. It also allows them to view pages of the articles, browse other articles in the database, and order printed copies (Story, O'Gorman, Fox, Schaper, and Jagadish, 1992).

The United States Defense Advanced Research Projects Agency (DARPA) has specified research on three methods of intelligent document retrieval for investigation under its Tipster intelligent document retrieval project. Keyword searching limitations and inaccurate queries present serious problems for searching documents. DARPA is focusing on context vectors, conceptual graphs, and inference networks as "the most promising technologies" for detecting and retrieving desired documents. Context vectors automatically summarize and compare the meaning of portions of text. Conceptual graphs perform pattern matching to detect the relationships between concepts in multiple bodies of text. Inference networks are used to detect larger patterns in texts using statistical information retrieval and natural language-processing techniques (Johnson, 1992).

The Sloan School of Management at MIT is engaged in a research project called Information Lens, which focuses on ways to handle large quantities of online messages. Information Lens is based on the concept of "intelligent assistants" used in artificial intelligence applications and graphical user interface design. The intelligent assistant in Information Lens can sort, prioritize, and seek out incoming messages (Robinson, 1991).

General Electric Research and Development Center is working on a system called Scisor (System for Conceptual Information Summarization, Organization, and Retrieval) that can handle large input and output of information. Scisor uses artificial intelligence, natural language, and database management to collect relevant financial data from the Dow Jones wire services. To do this, Scisor locates keywords and "reads" them before deciding to keep or discard them. Scisor is able to process news items at the rate of about six stories per minute. The system has also been used to obtain information from other subject areas. Scisor uses information retrieval techniques such as word-based text search and lexical analysis (Puttre, 1989; Jacobs and Rau, 1990).

In addition, special mention should be made of several other experimental "environments" or testbeds being developed for experimental techniques, such as I³R (Croft and Thompson, 1987), CODER (Fox, 1987), and FERRET (Mauldin, 1991).

V. Conclusions

We conclude that, although more popular than the card catalog, the actual effectiveness of the online catalog is lower than has been assumed. Where a searcher's terms coincide with the system's terms, and when the searcher has a specific, definable target in mind, all may be well. But when these conditions do not hold, all is not well.

First- and second-generation catalogs are quite well defined. What of the third generation? It should add the following:

1. Provide an entry vocabulary capability to lead from users' terms to the system's terms
2. Prompt the user at any time in a situationally sensitive manner
3. Have a well-developed toolkit for retrieved set analysis
4. Support "nearest neighbor" searching—Find more like this one!— and, perhaps through "zoom" commands, allow the searcher to browse across the database using any one or more attributes of a record
5. Offer document ranking or a mechanism for converting any retrieved set into small, ranked subsets

More generally, the future catalog should blend harmoniously with other retrieval tools, with the sources to which it provides access, and with the user's personal working environment. Using it should, in itself, be a learning experience. How this functionality will be provided is less clear, but there are numerous options to be explored.

In the preparation of this review we concentrated on identified problems in the use of the online catalog and on actual proposals for its improvement. At the same time, it became increasingly clear that deeper, more fundamental developments were afoot.

1. In the last few years, the online catalog situation has been dominated by the effort of adoption and implementation. There has been gradual

movement from first- to second-generation catalogs despite the substantially greater storage and computing resources required and numerous smaller refinements. These have typically included options to search by call number and limit searches by date of publication, by language, and/or by library in a union catalog. In brief, progress has been more a matter of widespread adoption of existing functionality than of advancing the state of the art. But if the state of the art does not appear to have advanced much in the past several years, there are reasons to expect major changes in the future.

2. Although it has always been accepted that the catalog is the key to the library, it has, in many ways, been determined by the needs of cataloging and technical services. However, since cataloging was in practice limited to the edition of the monograph and the title of the periodical, the extent of bibliographic access was in reality quite limited. This situation is changing radically. Other database files are being mounted alongside the catalog and, increasingly, links are being made from the records in these bibliographies to the library's holding records. This can be seen either as a redefinition of the catalog or as a return to an earlier era when analytical entries could be afforded (Buckland, 1992b). Either way, a significant and popular enhancement of bibliographic access results. Another of the major new growth areas for library catalogs is the linking of the catalog record to the address of full text in electronic form, allowing, in principle, a smoother transition from record to text than with paper documents. Further, as all forms of media are increasingly stored online in digital form, the distinctions between the media become less significant, promising an increasingly unified approach to multiple media. In addition, as ever increasing numbers of electronic journals, books, and texts become available, online catalogs will take on many of the functions of document delivery by enabling the user to inspect, to download, or to request document delivery—all from the catalog terminal. But as more and more of these resources become available, how will they be indexed? A conventional catalog record may enable one to identify and locate a text, but it is of little benefit thereafter in finding material within the text. As the role of libraries expand to include access to many of the resources provided by the online environment, many new forms of information are falling within the domain of (or being associated with) the online catalog, for example, nonbibliographic records of community information and referral and "campus-wide information services" (CWIS). These expanded frontiers bring new challenges. These additional resources, which may have little or no human indexing, bring with them a whole new set of problems for both users and the catalogs. Some significant extension in our view of the catalog and of cataloging practice would appear inevitable following such convergence.

Libraries and other organizations that manage large amounts of information have a great need for increased capacity to deal with the steadily increasing flow of electronic information from a wide variety of sources. Yet this increase is also contributing to the rapid growth in the number, size, and complexity of databases. Much of the original search and display software was not designed for such large size and complexity.

3. Catalogs are becoming less isolated. Librarians and library users are reaching beyond the online catalog and venturing out onto the Internet. Comparison of catalogs has become much easier now that a few hundred online catalogs are accessible over the Internet and "pass-through" connections are making access to multiple online catalogs routinely available to library users. Electronic bulletin boards such as PACS-L greatly enhance the possibilities for discussion and for the rapid dissemination of information and facilitating discussion.

4. After years dominated by implementation, experience in using the systems provides a basis for considering what enhancements are needed. Tools are increasingly available for more evidence-based analysis. In particular, the analysis of transaction logs provides a diagnostic tool not available with card catalogs. The literature has, hitherto, often been impressionistic. It need not stay that way. In effect, we have a new window on the user.

5. Experimental prototypes are increasingly feasible. The increasing power of low-cost workstations, decreasing mass storage costs, and the growing availability of large sets of records for experimental purposes make online catalog experimentation possible for many more people than before. Technology permits greater flexibility and standardized network protocols are making access to a wide variety of information resources increasingly feasible.

We are now at an exciting juncture. There has been a change in the way that online catalogs are perceived. The initial concern was to connect the online catalog to the library's technical services system. Now there is interest in relating the online catalog to online resources everywhere. Online catalogs are now evolving into much more than automated card catalogs for a single library's collection. They are changing how library users interact with the library services. If these interpretations are correct, then examination of the difficulties currently encountered in online catalogs and of proposals for improvement becomes timely as the online catalog shifts from being the end product of technical services to being *the* framework for bibliographic access.

Acknowledgments

We would like to express our thanks to Liv Holm, Clifford Lynch, and Yasar Tonta for their insightful comments, suggestions, and criticism.

References

Aliprand, J. M. (1992). Nonroman scripts in the bibliographic environment. *Information Technology and Libraries* **11**, 105–119.

Allen, G. (1990). Database selection by patrons using CD-ROM. *College and Research Libraries* **51**, 69–75.

Allen, B. L. (1991). Cognitive research in information science—implications for design. *Annual Review of Information Science and Technology* **26**, 3–37.

Ankeny, M. L. Evaluating end-user services—success or satisfaction. *Journal of Academic Librarianship*, (1991). **16 (16)** 352–356.

Appleton, E. L. (1992). Smart document retrieval. *Datamation* **38**, 20–23.

Ballard, T., and Lifshin, A. (1992). Prediction of OPAC spelling errors through a Keyword Inventory. *Information Technology and Libraries* **11**, 139–145.

Bates, M. J. (1977). System meets user: Problems in matching subject terms. *Information Processing and Management* **13**, 367–75.

Bates, M. J. (1984a). Factors affecting subject catalog search success. *Journal of the American Society for Information Science* **28**, 161–169.

Bates, M. J. (1984b). The fallacy of the perfect 30-item online search. *Reference Quarterly* **24**, 43–50.

Bates, M. J. (1986). Subject access in online catalogs: A design model. *Journal of the American Society for Information Science* **37**, 357–376.

Bates, M. J. (1989). Rethinking subject cataloging in the online environment. *Library Resources and Technical Services* **33**, 400–412.

Bates, M. J. (1990a). Design for a subject search interface and online thesaurus for a very large records management database. *ASIS '90. Proceedings of the 53rd ASIS Annual Meeting. Medford, New Jersey. Learned Information* **27**, 20–28.

Bates, M. J. (1990b). Where should the person stop and the information search interface start? *Information Processing and Management* **26**, 575–591.

Belkin, N. J. (1990). The cognitive viewpoint in information science. *Journal of Information Science* **16**, 11–15.

Belkin, N. J., and Croft, W. B. (1987). Retrieval techniques. *Annual Review of Information Science and Technology* **22**, 109–145.

Belkin, N. J., Change, S. J., Downs, T., Saracevic, T., and Zhao, S. (1990). Taking into account of user tasks, goals and behavior for the design of online public access catalogs. ASIS '90. Proceedings of the 53rd Annual Meeting of the American Society for Information Science **27**, 69–79.

Bellardo, T. (1985a). An investigation of online searcher traits and their relationship to search outcome. *Journal of the American Society for Information Science* **36**, 241–250.

Bellardo, T. (1985b). What do we really know about online searchers? *Online Review* **9**, 223–239.

Benson, J., and Maloney, R. K. (1975). Principles of searching. *Reference Quarterly* **14**, 316–320.

Berger, M. G. (1992). The MELVYL system: The next five years and beyond. *Information Technology and Libraries* **11**, 146–157.

BIBSYS server GENSERV. (1992). Users Guide. Available by electronic message to "genserv%nobibsys.bitnet\aun.uninett.no" with the word "info" in the subject line.

Binder, J. E., Gustafson, M., and Merritt, M. (1989). Geological/geographical name subject access. *Information Technology and Libraries* **8**, 408–423.

Blair, D. C. (1986). Indeterminacy in subject access to documents. *Information Processing and Management* **22**, 229–241.

140 Barbara A. Norgard *et al.*

Blair, D. C., and Maron, M. E. (1985). An evaluation of retrieval effectiveness for a full-text document-retrieval system. *Communications of the Association for Computing Machinery* **28**, 289–299.

Borgman, C. L. (1983). Performance effects of a user's mental model of an information retrieval system. In *Proceedings of the 46th ASIS Annual Meeting, 1983*. American Society for Information Sciences, 121–124.

Borgman, C. L. (1986a). The user's mental model of an information retrieval system: An experiment on a prototype online catalog. *International Journal of Man-Machine Studies* **24**, 47–64.

Borgman, C. L. (1986b). Why are online catalogs hard to use? Lesson learned from information retrieval studies. *Journal of the Society for Information Science* **40**, 153–157.

Borgman, C. L., and Siegfried, S. L. (1992). Getty's Synoname™ and its cousins: A survey of applications of personal name-matching algorithms. *Journal of the Society for Information Science* **43**, 459–476.

Brown, M. (1990). Design for a bibliographic database for non-professional users. *ASIS '90. Proceedings of the 53rd Annual Meeting of the American Society for Information Science* **28**, 276–282.

Buchanan, P. (1992). RE: CLR OPAC Study. E-mail message sent by PACS-L, August 7, 1992.

Buckland, M. K. (1992a). Agenda for online catalog designers. *Information Technology and Libraries* **11**, 157–163.

Buckland, M. K. (1992b). *Redesigning Library Services: A Manifesto*. American Library Association, Chicago.

Buckland, M. K., and Florian, D. (1991). Expertise, task complexity, and the role of intelligent information systems. *Journal of the American Society for Information Science* **42**, 635–643.

Buckland, M. K., Norgard, B. A., and Plaunt, C. (1992a). Design of an adaptive library catalog. In *Networks, Telecommunications, and the Networked Information Revolution: Proceedings of the ASIS 1992 Mid-Year Meeting, May 27–30, 1992*, pp. 165–171. American Society for Information Science, Silver Springs, Maryland.

Buckland, M. K., Norgard, B. A., and Plaunt, C. (1992b). Making a library catalog adaptive. In *American Society for Information Science. Proceedings of the 55th Annual Meeting, 1992*, pp. 260–263. Learned Information, Medford, New Jersey.

Buckland, M. K., Butler, M. H., Norgard, B. A., and Plaunt, C. (1992). OASIS: A front-end for prototyping catalog enhancements. *Library Hi Tech* **46**, 7–22.

Butkovich, N. J., Taylor, K. L., Dent, S. H., and Moore, A. S. (1989). An expert system at the reference desk: Impressions from users. *Reference Librarian: Expert Systems in Reference Services* **23**, 61–74.

Byrne, A., and Micco, M. (1988). Improving OPAC subject access. *College and Research Libraries* **49**, 432–441.

Chan, L. M. (1991). Subject analysis tools online: The challenge ahead. *Information Technology and Libraries* **9**, 258–262.

Cisler, S. (1991). Mac monitor: Future visions. *Online*, **15**, 90–92.

Clarkson, M. A. (1991). An easier interface. Xerox PARC, originator of the computer desktop, unveils a vision for the future of user interfaces. *Byte* **16**, 277–282.

Connell, T. H. (1991). Techniques to improve subject retrieval in online catalogs: Flexible access to elements in the bibliographic record. *Information Technology and Libraries* **10**, 87–98.

Cox, B. B. (1992). The assumption of rationality in information systems. *Bulletin of the American Society for Information Science* **19**, 20–21.

Crawford, W. (1992). Re: Boolean, bread and nonsense. E-mail message sent by PACS-L, August 11, 1992.

Croft, W. B., and Thompson, R. H. (1987). I³R: A new approach to the design of document retrieval systems. *Journal of the American Society for Information Science,* **38,** 389–404.

Culkin, P. B. (1989). Rethinking OPACs: The design of assertive information systems. *Information Technology and Libraries* **8,** 172–177.

Dale, D. C. (1989). Subject access in online catalogs: An overview. *Cataloging and Classification Quarterly* **10,** 225–251.

Daniels, P. J. (1986). Cognitive models in information retrieval—An evaluative review. *Journal of Documentation* **42,** 272–304.

Deerwester, S., Dumais, S. T., Furnas, G. W., Landauer, T. K., and Harshsman, R. (1990). Indexing by latent semantic analysis. *Journal of the American Society for Information Science* **41,** 391–407.

Dickson, J. (1984). An analysis of user errors in searching an online catalog. *Cataloging and Classification Quarterly* **4,** 19–38.

Doszkocs, T. E. (1983a). CITE NLM: Natural language searching in an online catalog. *Information Technology and Libraries* **2,** 364–80.

Doszkocs, T. E. (1983b). From research to applications: The CITE natural language information retrieval system. In *Research and Development in Information Retrieval* (Springer lecture notes in Computer Science No. 146). pp. 251–262, Springer-Verlag, Berlin.

Doszkocs, T. E. (1986). Language processing in information retrieval. *Journal of the American Society for Information Science* **37,** 506–513.

Drewett, B. (1988). Reports and working papers: Report on the LITA screen design preconference. *Information Technology and Libraries* **7,** 430–438.

Ellis, D. (1989). A behavioural approach to information retrieval systems design. *Journal of Documentation* **45,** 171–212.

Ensor, P. (1992a). Re: Boolean, bread and nonsense. E-mail message sent by PACS-L, August 12, 1992.

Ensor, P. (1992b). User practices in keyword and boolean searching on an online public access catalog. *Information Technology and Libraries* **11,** 210–219.

Ercegovac, Z. (1989). Augmented assistance in online catalog subject searching. *Reference Librarian: Expert Systems in Reference Services* **23,** 21–40.

Erickson, T., and Solomon, G. (1991). Designing a desktop information system: Observations and issues. *Human Factors in Computing Systems, CHI '91 Conference Proceedings, April 1991, New Orleans,* pp. 49–54, ACM, New York.

Farley, L. (1989). Dissecting slow searches. *DLA Bulletin* **9,** 1–6.

Fenichel, C. H. (1979). Online information retrieval: Identification of measures that discriminate among users with different levels and types of experience. Dissertation, Drexel University, Philadelphia, Pennsylvania.

Fenichel, C. H. (1981). Online searching measures that discriminate among users with different types of experience. *Journal of the American Society for Information Science* **32,** 23–32.

Fidel, R. (1985). Moves in online searching. *Online Review* **9,** 61–74.

Fidel, R. (1986). Towards expert systems for the selection of keys. *Journal of the American Society for Information Science* **37,** 37–44.

Fox, E. A. (1987). Development of the CODER system: A testbed for artificial intelligence methods in information retrieval. *Information Processing & Management* **33,** 341–366.

Fox, E. A. (1990). Advanced retrieval methods for online catalogs. *Annual Review of OCLC Research, July 1989–June 1990,* pp. 32–34. Online Computer Library Center, Dublin, Ohio.

Frost, C. O. (1987). Faculty use of subject searching in card and online catalogs. *Journal of Academic Librarianship* **13,** 86–92.

Geller, V., and Lesk, M. (1984). An on-line library catalog offering menu and keyword user interfaces. In *Fourth National Online Meeting Proceedings. Learned Information,* 159–165. Medford, New Jersey.

Gomez, L. M., Lochbaum, C. C., and Landauer, T. K. (1990). All the right words: Finding what you want as a function of richness of indexing vocabulary. *Journal of the American Society for Information Science* **41**, 547–559.

Hancock, M. (1987). Subject searching behaviour at the library catalogue and at the shelves: Implications for online interactive catalogues. *Journal of Documentation* **43**, 303–321.

Hancock-Beaulieu, M. (1989). Online catalogues: A case for the user. In *The Online Catalogue: Developments and Directions* (Charles R. Hildreth, ed.), pp. 25–46. Library Association Publishing, London.

Harman, D., and Candela, G. (1990). Retrieving records from a gigabyte of text on a mini-computer using statistical ranking. *Journal of the American Society for Information Science* **41**, 581–589.

Harris, M. A. (1986). Sequence analysis of moves in online searching. *The Canadian Journal of Information Science* **11**, 35–56.

Harter, S. P. (1986). *Online Information Retrieval: Concepts, Principles, and Techniques.* Library and Information Science Series. Academic Press, Orlando.

Harter, S. P., and Rogers Peters, A. (1985). Heuristics for online information retrieval: A typology and preliminary listing. *Online Review* **9**, 407–424.

Henry, W., Leigh, J. A., Tedd, L. A., and Williams, P. W. (1982). *Online Searching—An Introduction.* Butterworth, London.

Hert, C. A., and Nilan, M. S. (1991). User-based information retrieval system interface evaluation: An examination of an on-line public access catalog. *Proceedings of the ASIS annual meeting* **28**, 170–177.

Heustis, J. (1988). Clustering LC classification numbers in an online catalog for improved browsability. *Information Technology and Libraries* **7**, 381–393.

Hickey, T. B. (1981). *Development of a Probabilistic Author Search and Matching Technique for Retrieval and Creation of Bibliographic Records.* (Rep. No. OCLC/OPR/RR-81/2). OCLC Office of Planning and Research, Dublin, Ohio.

Hickey, T. B. (1989). The Experimental Library System (XLS). *Annual Review of OCLC Research, July 1988–June 1989*, pp. 18–20. Online Computer Library Center, Dublin, Ohio.

Hickey, T. B., and Prabha, C. (1990). Online public catalogs and large retrievals: Methods for organizing, reducing and displaying. *ASIS '90. Proceedings of the 53rd Annual Meeting of the American Society for Information Science* **27**, 110–116.

Hildreth, C. R. (1987). Beyond boolean: Design the next generation of online catalogs. *Library Trends* **35**, 647–667.

Hildreth, C. R. (1989). *Intelligent Interfaces and Retrieval Methods: For Subject Searching in Bibliographical Retrieval Systems.* Cataloging Distribution Service, Library of Congress, Washington, D.C.

Hildreth, C. R. (1991). Advancing toward the E30PAC: The imperative and the path. In ALA Midwinter Meeting, Chicago, Illinois. *Think Tank on the Present and Future of the Online Catalog: Proceedings.* N. Van Pulis, ed. (RASD Occasional Papers, 9). American Library Association, Reference and Adult Services Division, Chicago.

Hildreth, C. R. (1992b). RE: Third Generation OPAC. E-mail message sent by PACS-L, July 1, 1991.

Hildreth, C. R. (1992c). CLR OPAC Study. E-mail message sent by PACS-L, July 29, 1992.

Horne, E. (1990). An investigation into self-questioning behavior during problem solving. *ASIS '90. Proceedings of the 53rd Annual Meeting of the American Society for Information Science* **28**, 86–97.

Hudson, J., and Walker, G. (1987). The Year's work in technical services research, 1986. *Library Resources and Technical Services*, **31**, 275–286.

Hunter, R. (1991). Successes and failures of patrons searching the online catalog at a large academic library: A transaction log analysis. *Reference Quarterly* **30**, 395–402.

Ingwersen, P. (1984). A cognitive view of three selected online search facilities. *Online Review* **8,** 465–492.

Jacobs, P. S., and Rau, L. F. (1990). SCISOR: Extracting information from on-line news. *Communications of the ACM* **33,** 88.

Jamieson, A. J., Dolan, E., and Declerck, L. (1986). Keyword searching vs. authority control in an online catalog. *Journal of Academic Librarianship* **12,** 277–283.

Johnson, B., and Peterson, E. (1992). Reviewing initial stopword selection. *Information and Technology in Libraries* **11,** 136–139.

Johnson, P. (1987). Specification of expertise. *International Journal of Man-Machine Studies* **26,** 161–181.

Johnson, R. C. (1992). Tipster requires new document-search methods. *Electronic Engineering Times* **680,** 35.

Kahle, B., and Medlar, A. (1991). An information system for corporate users: Wide area information servers. *Online* **15,** 56–60.

Kahle, B., Morris, H., Goldman, J., Erickson, T., and Curran, J. (1992). Interfaces for distributed systems of information servers. In *Proceedings of the ASIS Mid-Year Meeting, May 28–30, 1992.*

Kantor, P. B. (1987). A model for the stopping behavior of users of online systems. *Journal of the American Society for Information Science* **38,** 211–214.

Katzer, J. (1990). Toward a more realistic assessment of information retrieval performance. *ASIS '90. Proceedings of the 53rd Annual Meeting of the American Society for Information Science* **27,** 80–85.

Kern-Simerenko, C. (1983). OPAC user logs: Implications for bibliographic instruction. *Library Hi Tech,* **1,** 27–35.

Kieras, D., and Polson, P. G. (1985). An approach to formal analysis of user complexity. *International Journal of Man-Machine Studies* **22,** 365–394.

Kinnucan, M. T. (1992). The size of retrieved sets. *Journal of the American Society for Information Science* **43,** 72–79.

Knutson, G. (1990). A comparison of online and card catalog accuracy. *Library Resources and Technical Services* **34,** 24–35.

Kuhlthau, C. C., Belvin, R. J., and George, M. W. (1989). Flowcharting the information search: A method for eliciting users' mental maps. *ASIS '89. Proceedings of the 52nd ASIS Annual Meeting,* **26,** 162–164. Learned Information, Medford, New Jersey.

Kwasnik, B. (1992). A Descriptive Study of the Functional Components of Browsing. *Annual Review of OCLC Research, July 1990–June 1991,* p. 38. Online Computer Library Center, Dublin, Ohio

Lancaster, F. W., Elliker, C., and Harkness Connell, T. (1989). Subject analysis. In *Annual Review on Information Science and Technology* **24** (M. E. Williams, ed.), pp. 35–84. Elsevier Science Publishers, Amsterdam.

Larson, R. R. (1986). Workload characteristics and computer system utilization in online library catalogs. Doctoral dissertation, University of California at Berkeley (University Microfilms No. 8624828).

Larson, R. R. (1989). Managing information overload in online catalog subject searching. In *Managing Information and Technology: Proceedings of the 52nd Annual Meeting of the American Society for Information Science* (J. Katzer and G. B. Newby, eds.), **26,** pp. 129–135. Learned Information, Medford, New Jersey.

Larson, R. R. (1991a). Between Scylla and Charybdis: Subject searching in the online catalog. *Advances in Librarianship* **15,** 175–236.

Larson, R. R. (1991b). Classification clustering, probabilistic information retrieval, and the online catalog. *Library Quarterly* **61,** 133–173.

Larson, R. R. (1991c). The decline of subject searching: Long-term trends and patterns of index use in an online catalog. *Journal of the American Society for Information Science* **42,** 197–215.

Larson, R. R. (1992a). Evaluation of advanced retrieval techniques in an experimental online catalog. *Journal of the American Society for Information Science* **43**, 34–53.

Larson, R. R. (1992b). Experiments in automatic Library of Congress classification. *Journal of the American Society for Information Science* **43**, 130–148.

Lesk, M. (1987). Can machine-readable dictionaries replace a thesaurus for searchers in online catalogs? In *The Uses of Large Text Databases, Proceedings of the 3rd Annual Conference of the University of Waterloo Centre for the New Oxford English Dictionary*, pp. 65–74. Waterloo.

Lesk, M. (1989). What to do when there's too much information. *Hypertext '89 Proceedings, Pittsburg SIGCHI Bulletin, Special Issue*, 305–318.

Lester, M. A. (1989). Coincidence of user vocabulary and Library of Congress Subject Headings: Experiments to improve subject access in academic library online catalogs. Dissertation. University of Illinois at Urbana-Champaign.

Lynch, C. A. (1991). The Z39.50 information retrieval protocol: an overview and status report. *Computer Communications Review* **21**, 58–70.

Lynch, C. A., and Preston, C. M. (1992). Describing and classifying networked information resources. *Electronic networking: Research, Applications and Policy* **2**, 13–23.

Mace, S. (1989). Topic upgrade to include hypertext, query builder, real-time integration. *InfoWorld* **11**, June 26, 1989: 14.

Malamud, C. (1992). WAIS: Is it the Lotus 1-2-3 of the Internet? *Communications Week* **394**, 17.

Mandel, C. (1991). Multiple vocabularies in subject authority control In *Subject Authorities in the Online Environment: Papers from a Conference Program held in San Francisco*, June 29, 1987. (Karen Markey Drabenstott, ed.). American Library Association, Chicago.

Markey, K. (1983a). *The Process of Subject Searching in the Online Catalog: Final Report of the Subject Access Research Project* (OCLC Research Report Number OCLC/OPR/RR-83/1). OCLC, Inc., Dublin, Ohio.

Markey, K. (1983b). *Online Catalog Use: Results of Surveys and Focus Group Interviews in Several Libraries. Technical Report.* OCLC, Inc., Dublin, Ohio.

Markey, K. (1984). *Subject Searching in Library Catalogs: Before and After the Introduction of Online Catalogs.* OCLC, Inc., Dublin, Ohio.

Markey, K. (1989). Integrating the machine-readable LCSH into online catalogs. *Information Technology and Libraries* **33**, 299–312.

Markey, K., and Demeyer, A. (1986). Dewey decimal classification online project: Evaluation of a library schedule and index integrated into the subject searching capabilities of an online catalog. Dublin, Ohio: OCLC Online Computer Library Center, Inc., Office of Research.

Markey, K., and Vizine-Goetz, D. (1988). Characteristics of subject authority records in the machine-readable Library of Congress subject headings. Dublin, Ohio: OCLC Online Computer Library Center.

Markey-Drabenstott, K. (1992a). Determining the Content of Machine-Readable Subdivision Records. *Annual Review of OCLC Research, July 1990–June 1991*, pp. 40–43. Online Computer Library Center, Dublin, Ohio.

Markey-Drabenstott, K. (1992b). The need for machine-readable authority records for topical subdivisions. *Information Technology and Libraries* **11**, 91–104.

Markey-Drabenstott, K., and Vizine-Goetz, D. (1990). Improving Subject Searching in Online Catalogs. *Annual Review of OCLC Research, July 1989–June 1990.* pp. 42–43. Online Computer Library Center, Dublin, Ohio.

Markey-Drabenstott, K., Demeyer, A. N., Gerckens, J., and Poe, D. T. (1990). Analysis of a bibliographic database enhanced with a library classification. *Library Resources and Technical Services* **34**, 179–198.

Massicotte, M. (1988). Improved browsable displays for online subject access. *Information Technology and Libraries* **7**, 373–380.

Matthews, G. S., and Matthews, J. R. (1984). *Detailed Data Analysis of the CLR Online Catalog Project.* Final report for the Council on Library Resources, (ED 242 332). Council on Library Resources, Washington, D.C.

Matthews, J., and Associates, Inc. (1982). *A Study of Six Online Public Access Catalogs: A Review of Findings.* Final report for the Council on Library Resources (ED 231 389). Council on Library Resources, Washington, D.C.

Mauldin, M. L. (1991). *Conceptual Information Retrieval: A Case Study in Adaptive Partial Parsing.* Kluwer, Boston.

McGarry, D., and Svenonius, E. (1991). More on improved browsable displays for online subject access. *Information Technology and Libraries* **10**, 185–191.

Micco, M. (1991). Dealing with the problem of very large retrieved sets. Alternatives to 'Brute Force' keyword searching. *ASIS '91. Proceedings of the 54th Annual Meeting of the American Society for Information Science.* October 27–31, 1991. Learned Information, Medford, New Jersey.

Micco, M., and Smith, I. (1989). Designing a workstation for information seekers. *Reference Librarian: Expert Systems In Reference Services* **23**, 135–152.

Mischo, W. H. (1979). Expanded subject access to reference collection materials. *Journal of Library Automation* **12**, 338–354.

Mischo, W. H., and Lee, J. (1987). End-user searching of bibliographic databases. In *Annual Review of Information Science and Technology* **22**, 227–263.

Morris, A. (1991). Expert systems for library and information services—A review. *Information Processing and Management* **27**, 713–724.

Morris, A., Tseng, G. M., and Walton, K. P. (1989). MOSS: A prototype expert system for modifying online search strategies. *Online Information* **89**, 415–434.

Myaeng, S. H., and Korfhage, R. R. (1990). Integration of user profiles: Models and experiments in information retrieval. *Information Processing and Management* **26**, 719–738.

Nahl-Jakovovits, D., and Jakobovits, L. A. (1988). Problem solving, creative librarianship, and search behavior. *College and Research Libraries* **49**, 400–408.

Najarian, S. E. (1981). Organizational factors in human memory: Implications for library organization and access systems. *Library Quarterly* **51**, 269–291.

Needleman, M. (1992). Computing resources for an online catalog: Ten years later. *Information Technology and Libraries* **11**, 168–172.

Newby, G. B. (1989). User models in information retrieval: Applying knowledge about human communication to computer interface design. *Proceedings of the ASIS Annual Meeting* **26**, 71—74.

Newby, G. B. (1991). Navigation: A fundamental concept for information systems in implications for information retrieval. *Proceedings of the ASIS Annual Meeting* **28**, 111–117.

Norr, H. (1991). WAIS promises easy text retrieval; prototype links Mac, Connection Machine. *MacWeek* **5**, 22–23.

Oberman, C. (1991). Avoiding the cereal syndrome, or critical thinking in the electronic environment. *Library Trends* **39**, 189–202.

O.Neill, E. T., and Vizine-Goetz, F. (1988). Quality control in online databases. *Annual Review of Information Sciene and Technology* **23**, 125–156.

Peters, T. A. (1989). When smart people fail: An analysis of the transaction log of an online public access catalog. *Journal of Academic Librarianship* **15**, 267–273.

Peters, T. A. (1991). *The Online Catalog: A Critical Examination of Public Use.* McFarland & Co., Jefferson, North Carlina.

Peters, T. A., and Kurth, M. (1991). Controlled and uncontrolled vocabulary subject searching in an academic library online catalog. *Information Technolgoy and Libraries*, **27**, 201–211.

Potter, W. G. (1989). Expanding the online catalog. *Information Technology and Libraries* **8**, 99–104.

Prabha, C. G. (1989). Managing Large Retrievals. *Annual Review of OCLC Research*, pp. 21–23. July 1988–June 1989. Online Computer Library Center, Dublin, Ohio.

Prabha, C. G. (1990). Managing Large Retrievals. *Annual Review of OCLC Research*, pp. 24–26, July 1989–June 1990. Online Computer Library Center, Dublin, Ohio.

Project Janus Info Account. (1993). Announcement of Virtual Library Project. Newsgroup news release sent by comp.text.sgml from janus@sparc-1.law.columbia.edu, February 1, 1993.

Puttre, M. (1989). GE brings software to life. *Information Week* **213**, 15.

Raitt, D. (1992). Computer and information science technology. In *Manual of Online Search Strategies* (2nd ed.). (C.J. Armstrong and J. A. Large, eds.), pp. 308–356. G. K. Hall, New York.

Reiter, M. (1989). Improving online information retrieval with an intelligent front-end system. *Online 12–14 Information 89*, 597–604.

Ritch, A. (1992). Ten years of monitoring MELVYL: A librarian's view. *Information Technology and Libraries*, **11**, 172–179.

Roberston, S. E., and Hancock-Beaulieu, M. (1992). On the evaluation of IR systems. *Information Processing & Management* **28**, 457–466.

Robinson, M. (1991). Through a lens smartly. *Byte* **16**, 177.

Rubens, D. (1991). Formulation rules for posing good subject questions: Empowerment for the end user. *Library Trends* **39**, 217–98.

Saracevic, T. (1989). Modeling and measuring user-intermediary-computer interaction in online searching: Design of a study. In *Managing Information and Technology: Proceedings of the 52nd Annual Meeting of the American Society for Information Science* **26**, 75–80.

Saracevic, T. (1991). Individual differences in organizing, searching and retrieving information. *Proceedings of the ASIS annual meeting* **28**, 82–86.

Saracevic, T., and Kantor, P. (1988). A study of information seeking and retrieving. II. Users, questions, and effectiveness. *Journal of the American Society for Information Science* **39**, 177–196.

Saracevic, T., Kantor, P. Chamis, Y., and Trivison, D. (1988). A study of information seeking and retrieving. I. Background and methodology. *Journal of the American Society for Information Science* **39**, 177–196.

Schwartz, K. D. (1991); AMHS spies messages for intelligence analysts. *Government Computer News* **10**, 57(2).

Seaman, S. (1992). Online catalog failure as reflected through interlibrary loan error requests. *College and Research Libraries* **53**, 113–120.

Seymour, S. (1991). Online public access catalog user studies. *Library and Information Science Research* **13**, 89–102.

Shaw, D. (1986). Nine sources of problems for novice online searchers. *Online Review* **10**, 295–303.

Shaw, D. (1991). The human-computer interface for information retrieval. *Annual Review of Information Science and Technology* **26**, 155–195.

Shenouda, W. (1990). Online bibliographic searching: How end-users modify their search strategies. *ASIS '90. Proceedings of the 53rd Annual Meeting of the American Society for Information Science* **27**, 117–128.

Shneiderman, B. (1990). Visual user interface for information exploration. *ASIS '90* **28**, 379–383.

Shrager, J., and Klahr, D. (1986). Instructionless learning about a complex device: the paradigm and observations. *International Journal of Man-Machine Studies* **25**, 153–189.

Slack, F. E. (1989). Transaction logging as a method of evaluation for help and instruction facilities on online information retrieval systems. *Online Information 89, 13th International Online Information Meeting Proceedings*. 23–32. Learned Information, Oxford, England.

Soergel, D. (1990). Investigating the Structure of LCC and LCSH: Developing a Knowledge Base. *Annual Review of OCLC Research*, pp 54–55. July 1989–June 1990. Online Computer Library Center, Doublin, Ohio.

Sormunen, E., Nurminen, R., Hamalainen, M., and Hursalmi, M. (1987). *Knowledge-Based Intermediary System for Information Retrieval. Requirements Specification.* Laboratory for Information Processing, Espoo, Finland.

Srinivasan, P. (1992). Expert System Interface to Library of Congress Subject Headings. *Annual Review of OCLC Research*, p. 43. July 1990–June 1991. Online Computer Library Center, Dublin, Ohio.

Story, G., O'Gorman, L., Fox, D., Schaper, L., and Jagadish, H. V.. (1992). The RightPages image-based electronic library for alerting and browsing. *Computer* 25, 17.

Taylor, A. G. (1992). Enhancing subject access in online systems: The year's work in subject analysis, 1991. *Library Resources and Technical Services* 36, 316–332.

Thompson, R. (1992). Information Retrieval Research Laboratory. *Annual Review of OCLC Research*, p. 43. July 1990–June 1991. Online Computer Library Center, Dublin, Ohio.

Tolle, J. E., and Hah, S. (1985). Online Search Patterns: NLM CATLINE Database. *Journal of the American Society for Information Science* 36, 82–93.

Tonta, Y. A. (1992a). Analysis of search failure in document retrieval systems: A review. *Public-Access Computer Systems Review* 3, 4–53.

Tonta, Y. A. (1992b). An analysis of search failures in online catalogs. Dissertation, School of Library and Information Studies, University of California, Berkeley.

Tucker, M. (1988). Object-oriented text management debuts. *Computerworld* 22, 37.

Tufte, E. (1992). The user interface: The point of competition. *Bulletin of the American Society for Information Science* 18, 15–17.

Van Pulis, N., ed. (1991). "Think Tank on the Present and Future of the Online Catalog: Proceedings." ALA Midwinter Meeting, Chicago, Illinois. (RASD Occasional Papers, 9). American Library Association, Reference and Adult Services Division, Chicago.

Vigil, P. J. (1990). A model expert system for online bibliographic database searching. *Online Information 90*, 269–276.

Walker, S. (1987). OKAPI: Evaluating and Enhancing an Experimental Online Catalog. *Library Trends* 35, 631–45.

Walker, S. (1990). Interactional aspect of a reference retrieval system using semi-automatic query expansion. In *Informatics 10: Prospects for Intelligent Retrieval*, pp. 119–136. Aslib, London.

Warner, A. J. (1991). Automatic Hierarchical Organization of Phrases Using Machine-Readable Dictionary Information. *Annual Review of OCLC Research*, pp. 38–39. July 1990–June 1991. Online Computer Library Center, Dublin, Ohio.

Wiberly, S. E., and Dougherty, R. A. (1988). Users' persistence in scanning lists of references. *College and Research Libraries* 49, 149–156.

Wilbur, W. J. (1992). Retrieval testing by the comparison of statistically independent retrieval methods. *Journal of the American Society for Information Science* 43, 358–370.

Wildemuth, B., Jacob, E. K., Fullington, A., and Deblick, R. (1991). A detailed analysis of end-user search behaviors. *American Society for Information Science. Proceedings of the ASIS Annual Meeting, 1991* 29, 302–312.

Wilkinson, M. A., Burt, P. V., and Kinnucan, M. T. (1988). The effects of entry arrangement on search times: A cross-generational study. *Information Technology and Libraries* 7, 253–262.

Williamson, N. J. (1986). Classification in online systems—Research and progress. In *Librarianship in Japan: [Proceedings of the] International Federation of Library Associations and Institutions 52nd General Conference*, 1986 August, Toyko, Japan. Japan Organizing Committee of IFLA, Tokyo, Japan.

Yannakoudakis, E. J. (1983). Expert spelling error analysis and correction. *Intelligent Information Retrieval: Informatics 7. Proceedings of a Conference held by the Aslib Informatics Group and the Information Retrieval Group of the British Computer Society* (Kevin P. Jones, ed.), pp. 39–52. Cambridge, 22–23 March 1983. Aslib, London.

Yee, M. M. (1992). *Headings for Tomorrow: Public Access Display of Subject Headings:* ALCTS Subjects Analysis Committee, Cataloging and Classification, Association for Library Collections and Technical Services. American Library Association, Chicago.

Yee, M. M., and Soto, R. (1991). User problems with access to fictional characters and personal names in online public access catalogs. *Information Technology and Libraries*, **10**, 3–13.

Young, C. W., Easstman, C. M., and Oakman, R. L. (1991). An analysis of ill-formed input in natural language queries to document retrieval systems. *Information Processing and Management* **27–6**, 615–622.

Electronic Journals: A Formidable Challenge for Libraries

Margo Sassé and B. Jean Winkler
University Libraries
Colorado State University
Fort Collins, Colorado 80523

I. Introduction

Greater specialization accompanied by tremendous increases in research and publishing output has made staying current an intellectual challenge as well as a financial burden. Scholarly journal prices have increased far more rapidly than inflation and currency fluctuations so that fewer individuals subscribe to these journals. Thus, academic libraries have become the primary market for scholarly journals (Urbach, 1984). Concurrent with the "information explosion" has been the development and growth of more sophisticated publishing and communication technology. All these factors have contributed to the hope that electronic publications, specifically electronic journals, will answer the problems of time, cost, and relevance in scholarly communication (Garson and Howard, 1984).

The notion of an electronic journal was first described in 1945, long before the information explosion and the full development of computing and communications networks. The attraction of the idea lies in the presumed advantages of electronic journals: (1) the time between acceptance of a paper and its publication would be shorter than for conventional journals; (2) long papers could be more easily published; and (3) the costs of printing and mailing would be eliminated (Senders, 1976). Skeptics have countered that paper scholarly journals play a strong social role; they are the records of scholarship, and the technology has not easily accommodated formulas, graphs, and other special characters used in scientific writing (Turoff and Hiltz, 1982). Librarians have a special interest in the progress of electronic journals; one expectation is that they may provide an answer to the high cost of scholarly journals. On the darker side, this technology also has the potential of altering the library's role if not bypassing it altogether. One role for librarians could be as consultants and surrogate users of information technology for users who lack the skills; another would be as creators and managers of local information systems (Schultz, 1992).

Electronic publishing and electronic distribution raise a new set of problems for publishers and authors that includes intellectual rights, file integrity, standards, preservation, and worldwide access. Libraries must contend with another level of challenges related to access, and those libraries that have subscribed to electronic journals are coping with bibliographic access as well as physical access for users. While only a few academic libraries are experimenting with electronic journals, nearly all are considering how they will contend with this new mode of publication. In the future, electronic publications "May span the entire range of resources now handled by libraries—from textbooks to instructional manuals to novels to poetry to children's picture 'books'—and they may be available in a wide variety of formats. This will create a formidable challenge for the profession" (Lancaster, 1989).

II. Definitions

Standard nomenclature and definitions in electronic publishing are absent. Besides publishers and librarians, other participants in the discussion include computer center managers, analysts, imformation managers, and scholars, with each group having a different interpretation of "publish" or "author" (Kassirer, 1992). The fact that these terms have no common meaning for the groups involved in electronic publishing can become a source of conflict. For example, participants at a meeting of three workgroups of the Coalition for Networked Information found that there was not even a common use of "electronic publishing" and decided to proceed without establishing agreement on usage of shared terms (Grycz, 1992).

The concept and definition have evolved as the technology has changed. Before there were any examples, electronic journals were described as "virtual journals," and Roistacher (1978) proposed the dissemination of virtual journals over computer networks. Basic to virtual journals was an editor, and editorial board, a theoretical focus, and articles monitored for quality.

Commonly, writers have referred to electronic journals in terms of what they were not, for example, as "paperless journals." "Paperless journal" was also used by proponents of computer output microform journals. These microform journals could be written, edited, refereed, and finalized in electronic format but distributed in microfiche (Sondak and Schwartz, 1973). The term "online journal" has also been used for journals in electronic format and has been most commonly applied to parallel publishing such as the

IRCS *Medical Science* journal, which was available online via BRS as well as print format (Biomedicine gets, 1983; IRCS moves, 1982). Piternick (1989a) reinforced the distinction between "electronic" and "online" journals. In the case of the former, the contents are produced and stored only in electronic forms. She noted the growth of parallel or online journal publication in both paper and electronic formats and that some journals are scanned into databases so they can be retrieved online.

The distinction has also been made between "electronic journals"—a network of computers being used to exchange, evaluate, and store information—and "journal in electronic format," the text of a print journal made accessible online (Electronic publishing, 1992). Others have used "electronic journal" to refer to publications in a digital format available via phone lines or distributed on magnetic media that could be processed and used in an onsite computer. Besides online journals, this would include materials distributed on tape, CD–ROM, or diskette. "Electronic journal" has also been applied to video text and radio and television broadcast data (Garson and Howard, 1984).

For the EIES experiment in scholarly electronic communication, the form described as an electronic journal was designed to be similar to the classic print journal, that is, it was edited, refereed, and copyrighted. One difference was that the articles were distributed singly as each was ready (Turoff and Hiltz, 1982). Some scholars welcomed this mode of distribution because the immediate publication of an article once it has been accepted in final form would mean that "journal" would once again exist in its etymological sense of daily or publication that is carried out every day (Senders, 1976). However, in the BLEND project, a counterpart to EIES, all the electronic communication was described as "electronic journals" even though only one form was refereed (Katzen, 1986). Concurring with this usage, Okerson (1991a) makes a case for computer conferences to be included in the concept.

Perhaps the most restrictive use of "electronic journal" was in the plans developed by Learned Information for its publications. Under its criteria, not only should the articles be available exclusively online, but they should contain no references to sources published in paper (Collier, 1984).

Currently, there are ongoing discussions on definitions and usage of terms in electronic publishing at many computer conferences with no consensus. Therefore, for purposes of this discussion, we will use "electronic journal" to indicate a "scholarly electronic journal" or a serial publication that issues the results of intellectual, technical, or scientific investigations. The journal publisher's goal is to contribute to the advance of scholarship and to provide a record of the results of scientific investigation, advances in technology, or scholarly inquiry. These journals often originate in academic institutions. They are edited, refereed, and distributed to the readers in electronic format, generally over a network such as BITNET or Internet (Langschied, 1991). Some may provide alternative formats for readers not on networks or for libraries for archival purposes, but the primary mode of publishing is electronic.

For libraries, access is the basic problem they face today when dealing with scholarly electronic journals. Access encompasses much more than a reader logging into a network to retrieve an article. It includes bibliographic description of the journal itself, creation of a means for readers to obtain the contents of the journals both now and in the future, links between the reader's options for access and the bibliographic information, and the inclusion of the articles in standard indexing and abstracting services. For these reasons, this article will focus on three aspects of access: bibliographic records, direct patron access, and citation references in indexing services.

Certainly, librarians need to be concerned with a host of other issues raised by electronic publishing that relate to access including the future of NREN, copyright, costs, and rapidly shifting technology (Lerner, 1984). However, these and other problems lie outside of the library's control, and, while libraries may influence the outcome of these larger issues, there are many other interests to consider.

It must be noted that for the present and immediate future, if scholarly electronic journals are to find general acceptance, they need to be produced in ways that make it easy for libraries to accept, collect, and preserve them (Bailey, 1991a). Many do take on the general attributes of a print journal; they have issues that are published on a regular basis, carry volume and number designations, and are paginated. Many have also created mastheads and obtained ISSN numbers. Even so, publishers need to work with librarians to make these journals more palatable (Blixrud, 1992).

To insure their future, publishers also need to develop a more powerful vision of the scholarly electronic journal. The notion of an electronic journal was first described by Vannevar Bush (1967) as part of the memex proposal. Memex would contain electronic books, pictures, current journals, and newspapers. Bush developed memex when computers were still in their infancy and before networks existed. Unlike other writers who have predicted the future of electronic communications, he was not hampered by the known limits of the technology; rather, his depiction was based on an intuition of the computer's possibilities and knowledge of the scholar's needs. Memex would contain information obtained from commercial publishers, and scholars would add notes, photographs, or other materials with a scanner. Memex would be the quintessence of the researchers' dreams; all the information they need would be literally at their fingertips. Thus, Bush places the contemporary wizardry of the scholar's workstation into a self-contained center of knowledge, or Prospero's cell. Perhaps the most exciting part of his vision was his description of associative indexing, an alternative means of access that is individualized to the user in a more poetic or even Freudian system rather than the formal Aristotelian subject structures or free-form keyword index more commonly used. Associative indexing allows scholars to build access points based on the relationship of the information to their research trails and habits of mind. Nearly fifty years later, this vision still has considerable power to attract readers.

What appears to be lacking in much of electronic publishing is a compelling vision. Because researchers, readers, and publishers are generally a conservative group, it will take more than superior technology to bring about the behavioral and social changes that are an integral part of the scholarly journal publishing system.

III. History

Critiques of traditional scholarly journal publishing that include proposals to use new communications and computer technologies to resolve the problems date back to a UNESCO report published in 1960. The first scholarly electronic journals were created as part of two pilot projects to test networking computers as a means of improving scientific communications (Piternick, 1989a). What was arguably the first electronic journal (scholarly intent, no print counterpart, planned to publish indefinitely) was *Mental Workload*, produced in 1980 as part of a National Science Foundation experiment. It was published via an NSF-funded computer conferencing system, EIES, at the New Jersey Institute of Technology. It was produced by one component of the project and was to be a form of electronic communication that would replicate the functions of a print scholarly journal in an electronic format; it was intended to test assumptions of increased efficiency in production and of reduced costs of publishing (Freeman, 1987).

Mental Workload was focused on person–machine interfaces in the operation of complex systems; there was no print-based journal devoted to this specialty. The editors were to follow the same protocols for advertising the journal, refereeing and editing articles, copyrighting, and distributing as traditional journals. One difference was that an article was to be "published" as soon as it was in final form; at that point an abstract was placed in an online "Bulletin" and readers downloaded the article to a printer. Readers could also search an index of the journal by author or title and could retrieve abstracts online. The editors planned to link readers' comments and responses to the original articles. The subscribers could be members of the pilot communication study discussion groups or one of up to 1000 others who could use a public member address. While the technology, both hardware and software, were not ideal, the biggest stumbling block was getting authors to submit articles. The effort of publishing in an unknown journal with an uncertain readership was perceived as too high a risk. The journal received few submissions because the authors could not be assured of general scholarly acceptance, that is, that their work would be read and cited (Piternick, 1989a; Turoff and Hiltz, 1982).

In his survey of why *Mental Workload* failed, Freeman (1987) described the human–machine interface problems including unfriendly software; since it was hard to do things, they did not get done. A second reason was that researchers gave other projects a higher priority. This appears to relate to the social role of scholarly journal that is, because publication in *Mental Workload* offered no change in status nor increase in prestige for the author, it became a low priority. Finally, because of a conflict between EIES and the British Post Office over transatlantic telecommunication rights, the journal was only available in the United States. The scientific community is an international one and the parochial nature of the project again reflected back on prestige and visibility factors.

However, the unrefereed computer conferences were judged a success; users like the interactive features. Authors would submit drafts or summaries of papers being prepared for professional meetings or journals and they served as a means for preprint or gray literature distribution. This open communication also encouraged coauthoring of proposals (Turoff and Hiltz, 1982).

A nearly parallel project in the United Kingdom also failed. After the Post Office prevented transatlantic cooperation in the EIES project, the British Library Research and Development approved BLEND, a three-year research project to access the usefulness of electronic communication networks among scientists. The journal, *Computer Human Factors* was designed to accept, referee, edit, and archive articles electronically. The journal held the copyright on articles for only three months; after that, the author could seek republication elsewhere. To assure a certain level of activity, 40–50 participants active in the field were recruited. Each had access to suitable equipment and agreed to submit at least one paper and one shorter piece during each of the three years of the experiment (Shackel, 1983).

Again, the technology was not powerful, fast, or friendly enough, and similar to the EIES project, participants perceived a lack of benefits in learning to use the system. However, two issues of *Computer Human Factors* with four refereed articles were distributed. Corresponding to the EIES project, the informal options received the most use. In addition, the project pointed out the need for more research on how people read computer screens compared with print (Freeman, 1987). BLEND also demonstrated the potency of social factors. There have to be incentives and rewards for researchers to submit articles, and authors need predictable deadlines to work against to provide the necessary motivation to complete the manuscript. This holds true for editors and referees as well as authors (Piternick, 1991).

Another view on why these two projects failed to demonstrate the effectiveness of electronic journals was that the interest came from the possibilities offered by the technology rather than from user demand. Because these journals received no mandate from the reader or the author, the result was the generation of unrefereed material of generally poor quality. For electronic publications to gain user acceptance, they must offer added dimensions over print journals. The only dimension open to experiments in the early 1980s was speed of publication (Gurnsey, 1982).

Parallel but separate breakthroughs in publishing automation led scholars to propose electronic distribution as a logical extension of shared electronic processing (Rhodes and Bamford, 1976). Gardner (1990) took a more conservative view of these publishers' databases; he proposed that they become the basis for centralized electronic archives. Fox (1990) responded that the networks could accommodate a distributed system for archiving, while Harnad (1990) noted that these archives could be extended into electronic journal and could included prepublication ideas and findings.

Improvement in computers and electronic networks along with a greater proliferation of electronic communication in university and research centers has encouraged the development of a second wave of electronic journals. These new titles have much in common with the BLEND and EIES prototypes.

IV. Current State of Scholarly Electronic Journals

There are over thirty publications available in 1992 that could be considered scholarly electronic journals. Some follow the models established by the EIES or BLEND projects, but the form, format, and access points are unique for each journal. As one electronic journal editor pointed out, the nature and social practices of the discipline will shape communication so that no one model of electronic journal may be suitable for all applications (Harrison, Stephen, and Winter, 1991). Printed serials present endless variations in form and format, but most printed scholarly journals fall into familiar and predictable patterns that allow libraries to set up standard procedures for acquiring, cataloging, and archiving. The existing and potential mutations in electronic publishing make it risky for libraries to commit to a networking system, to order hardware, or even to establish policies and procedures. Thus, in spite of the fact that most electronic journals are free or charge only a minimal price for subscriptions, other factors may make them extremely expensive.

The similarities and differences among the electronic journals currently available point up some of the problems for libraries. Most journal editors are confronted with the same problems the EIES and BLEND editors faced—securing contributors and gaining legitimacy. Many of these publications were created to explore the potential of the medium, for example, *Electronic Journal of Communication/La revue electronique de communication*, which is distributed on Comserve. The editors selected Comserve because they hoped the network's successful track record would give some measure of legitimacy to their publication. They also hoped Comserve would make the journal more visible because the network was supported by professional organizations and departments of communication, the intended audience. This journal, which originates in Canada, has articles in either French or English; the editorial comments, article titles, and abstracts are in both languages. The publishers are conscious of the library market and will also distribute the journal in diskette form (Harrison *et al.*, 1991).

Public Access Computer Systems Review uses BITNET to distribute the journal to subscribers of the discussion group Public Access Computer Systems Forum (PACS-L). The editors send PACS-L members and other subscribers a table of contents with the file addresses of the articles; readers then download the articles they want to read. Articles are copyrighted but there are generous access and reproduction provisions similar to the EIES project. There is also a newsletter distributed on PACS-L (Bailey, 1991b, 1992). The Library and Information Technology Association will publish the 1990 and 1991 volumes of the journal in hard copy (For immediate, 1992).

E-Journal is distributed an article at a time, similar to the EIES projects. The editor, Edward M. Jennings (1991) developed the concept of the journal in part through BITNET discussion groups. Similar to the EIES difficult obtaining manuscripts, Jennings has found that it is easier to gain subscribers than contributors.

Psycoloquy distributes articles gathered in issues and follows the EIES practice of including commentaries and authors' responses with the articles. The refereed contents are brief reports of ideas and findings at the prepublication stage. Steven Harnad (1991), the editor, calls this "scholarly skywriting." Harnad was most interested in exploring the interactive qualities of electronic publishing, and this journal provides content control for the form that was most successful in the EIES and BLEND projects, the preprint conference. The refereeing ensures that the quality of discussion will be consistent.

Postmodern Culture is also gathered into issues and distributed three times a year. It has the formal attributes of a scholarly humanities journal including book reviews and columns. There is an open discussion group, *PMC-Talk*, that takes advantage of the interactive quality valued by Harnad. The publisher provides microfiche and diskette alternatives for a nominal fee to readers without online access or for library archives (Amiran and Unsworth, 1991).

Journal of Reproductive Technology now provides articles in both electronic and paper format because indexing services did not cite the journal when it existed only in electronic format. Subscribers pay $400 annually for dial access to the text, which included reviewers' comments of the articles. The online version does not contain graphics; these are distributed separately in photomicrographs (Sexton, 1991).

New Horizons in Adult Education was developed by graduate students participating in the Syracuse University Kellogg Project. The journal is run by graduate students who serve as editors and on the editorial board. *New Horizons* is distributed over AEDNET (Adult Education Network), which is linked to other networks including BITNET and Internet. Because network access is not universal and because some countries charge for network access, the journal is also distributed in paper (Hugo and Newell, 1991). *New Horizons* originally gathered articles into issues, but beginning in 1992 articles will be released as soon as they are in final form (Langschied, 1992).

The Journal of the International Academy of Hospitality Research was also developed as part of a project, the Scholarly Communication Project of Virginia Polytechnic Institute and State University (VPI-SU). The project selected hospitality research for the focus of an electronic journal because (1) no comparable print journal existed; (2) the field was new and the small community of researchers was open to a new form of scholarly communication; and (3) the small numbers of researchers meant that development would be easier to manage. The committee that developed *JIAHR* decided to charge for subsriptions because it felt that readers would give it more serious consideration than they would a free publication. Moreover, libraries would follow through on obtaining articles for a journal for which they had paid, and the committee wanted to market to libraries in a way similar to printed journals. The editors of *JIAHR* are working with subscribing libraries in part because individuals are less likely to have network access or technical expertise, while libraries have been successful in obtaining the journal and in distributing to faculty and student. Subscription income was only $1,5000 in the first year, a fraction of the actual publication costs. Because the journal contained fewer articles than promised, subscription charges were dropped in 1992. As with other electronic journals, subscribers appear to be more easily found than contributors. The editors plan to add a moderated discussion capability. The journal is archived on the mainframe computer at VPI-SU (Savage, 1991).

Current Clinical Trials (*CCT*) is the result of a joint venture between the American Association for the Advancement of Science (AAAS) and OCLC Online Computer Library Center. *CCT* publishes the results of medical research as soon as the data has been reviewed, one article at a time. Readers can search the *CCT* database by subject, title, author, keyword, date, as well as by Boolean and proximity operators. (OCLC and, 1991; Online journal, 1992). Most electronic journals cannot reproduce scientific notation or graphics; however, *CCT* readers with special equipment can see figures, graphs, tables, and equations. The special equipment also provides high-quality screen resolution. Subscribers without special equipment receive the journal minus the graphics (New science, 1992).

Some of the *CCT* articles are published simultaneously in *Lancet*; authors who want dual publication submit papers to *CCT*, which forwards them to *Lancet* where they are reviewed. If accepted, the authors then reduce the *CCT* version of the article by less than half (More brevity, 1992). This arrangement may give a boost to *CCT*, which has not had as many submissions as the editors would have liked (Holden, 1992).

These examples of the variations among electronic journals demonstrate the difficulties facing libraries that want to acquire them. There is no dominant pattern of distribution; patrons may not want to read lengthy articles on computer screens (Standera, 1985) and instead ask for printouts. Alternative modes of publication more friendly to libraries may exist. These journals are continually changing in form, format, and mode of dissemination.

V. Bibliographic and Patron Access

There are pros and cons about whether librarians should provide bibliographic access for electronic journals. Some detractors feel it is too great a burden to assume as library budgets and staffing continue to shrink. Others feel that electronic journals will never "catch on," so why bother? Of course, these same people probably expressed similar pessimistic concern about microform, CD–ROMs, and OPACs (Fecko and Langschied, 1991; Langschied, 1991). Electronic journals are changing the face of scholarly communication and greatly influencing how libraries do business (Manoff, Dorschner, Geller, Morgan, and Snowden, 1992). Libraries have traditionally been "conveyors of academically relevant information" and they have never discriminated against scholarly information because of format (Dougherty, Hanson, Litchfield, McMillan, Metz, Nicol, and Queijo, 1991). However, journals in electronic format promise to change the role of the

technical services staff dramatically. The following case studies of two libraries currently struggling to implement this new format into their existing
collections illustrate some of the issues and concerns confronting libraries as
they cope with this new technology.

Virginia Polytechnic Institute and State University established a task
force in the Fall of 1990 to investigate and recommend how electronic journals
should be integrated into their library processes and procedures. The first
problem they addressed was where to store electronic journals. The general
consensus was that they should not be printed and bound as traditional paper
journals but rather stored electronically. Four options were explored: the
VTLS mainframe computer, the VM/University mainframe, the PC-based
Local Area Network (LAN), and a PC-based Bulletin Board System. The
ideal option would be the VTLS mainframe computer, as patrons would then
have direct access to electronic journals through the library's online catalog
and the library would be able to retain complete control over data management, storage, and access. However, this would necessitate a commitment of
programming staff, time, and money that the University did not have at the
present time. Another option, the LAN (CD–ROM network), was already in
existence but if electronic journal subscriptions continued to increase, this
would probably present problems in access response time and increased
storage capacity. The University mainframe seemed to be the next choice in
terms of cost and access. Electronic journals at VPI-SU would be accessible to
anyone using a terminal in the library, which was dedicated to receiving
electronic journals. Otherwise, a user ID and ready access to the university
mainframe would be a requirement for access. Direct costs associated with
downloading or printing would be passed on to the user. These kinds of
decisions would vary from institution to institution, depending on available
resources and the type of access the library wanted to provide.

Other recommendations of the Task Force stated that electronic journals
should receive the same full MARC catalog records, following CONSER
guidelines, as serials in other formats including LC call numbers, subject
headings, linking entries, and name authority. The holdings screen should list
the full extent of the library's holdings of full-text journals and articles available online. It should also direct the patron to the files where the electronic
journals reside and identify the sites of the dedicated terminals. The bibliographic record should describe the means of access in a general note (MARC
500) and in a local note (MARC 590). A HELP screen should be designed to
facilitate access through proper search commands.

The Task Force felt that electronic journals should be processed along the
same lines as printed serials, for example, the process would begin with the
subject specialist, and billing would go through accounting/acquisitions, with
instructions directing the publisher to send the text to the account maintained

by acquisitions and dedicated to ordering and receiving electronic journals. After the electronic journals were checked in, the text would be forwarded to the serials cataloging department. Acquisitions would also be responsible for checking in new issues, claiming and notifying the serials cataloging department of title changes, or frequency or numbering irregularities.

Public service personnel must also become familiar with the journals by learning new search strategies and commands as well as recognizing the files and fields contained in a variety of databases, since electronic journals are transmitted in various ways. They must keep up to date with copyright laws and how they would affect copying and/or downloading by the staff and/or the users.

All of these additional services would require equipment, supplies, and a trained staff. The library administration must be committed to providing additional resources and staffing if necessary to implement this new technology but yet allow the current level of service to be maintained. In addition to training the technical and public services staff, the public must also be informed of these new services through ongoing publicity and hands-on training provided for patrons as needed.

The Task force suggested five e-journals that might be used to test these new procedures: *Newsletter of Serials Pricing Issues; Postmodern Culture; Journal of the International Academy of Hospitality Research; Electronic Journal of Communications*, and *New Horizons in Adult Education*. These journals cover a wide variety of subjects, demonstrate various means of receipt, and are currently free to subscribers.

The Task Force would evolve into an advisory committee for implementation issues and perhaps assist in drafting policies. If the Task Force was representative of the library departments involved, they could possibly carry out implementation without the necessity of creating another team (Dougherty *et al.*, 1991; McMillan, 1991a, 1992).

The MIT approach also demonstrated the importance of involving all sections of the library in adding electronic journals to the collection. In July 1991, MIT appointed an Electronic Journals Task Force to examine the nature of electronic journals and evaluate their role in traditional library collections. Their rationale was that since electronic journals have the potential of becoming a valuable resource for libraries and their patrons, it is essential that libraries gain expertise in this emerging field of technology in order to participate in developing standards, procedures, and policies to deal with this new medium.

The MIT Task Force also felt that the introduction of electronic journals into the library collection should begin with the subject specialist. This would necessitate their becoming familiar with the Internet since this is where information about available electronic journals is most often found. The acquisitions department could use many of their same routines in ordering electronic journals as they did with print materials, but some new procedures would have to be implemented and staff would have to become familiar with the technology involved in receiving and transferring electronic files. MIT plans to catalog electronic journals with full MARC records in serial format with the addition of local notes about types of text, graphic files, and means of access. They are hoping to provide electronic journals in the Athena environment through WAIS, taking advantage of the availability of such enhancements as keyword, full-text searching, and direct access to specific files (Geller, 1992; Manoff et al., 1992).

The recommendations and suggestions put forth by the two task forces at VPI-SU and MIT portray a common theme: electronic journals are a potentially valuable resource for libraries but there are many technical issues and concerns that must be addressed before they can successfully be integrated into existing library collections.

CONSER is also attempting to provide answers in implementing bibliographic control of electronic journals. Whether or not to include electronic journals in the CONSER database is a moot point, as over two hundred records that could be considered electronic serials already reside in their database. Many electronic formats are unfamiliar and difficult to process physically, but most electronic journals are being assigned an ISSN number, have specific issues usually with volume and number designation, but may or may not be paged. Description is relatively straightforward but can sometimes be difficult, depending on how the text is transmitted and received. It is essential to include a general mode of access note and an online address, with individual libraries adding a local mode of access note (Blixrud, 1992).

Even though most electronic journals are being cataloged in the serials format, OCLC is cataloging some in the computer data file. The Library of Congress has identified MARC fields that could be used to include information unique to the electronic format such as log-on/subscription instructions, network addresses, and type and size of file (Library of Congress, 1991). OCLC recently completed a research project designed to test the cataloging format and rules over a wide variety of electronic files residing in the Internet (Leahy and Smith, 1992). Thirty volunteer catalogers were selected to receive thirty randomly selected records from a total of 300 computer files assembled by OCLC for the experiment. The files were received and transmitted using the File Transfer Protocol (FTP). Participants were charged with cataloging these records using "any means at hand" but within the limits of the USMARC Computer Files Format and the rules for computer files contained in Chapter 9 of AACRII. The resulting catalog records and a log file for each item recording actual time spent in cataloging, problems encountered, and comments and suggestions were then transmitted via FTP to OCLC for review and analysis. OCLC plans to publish its findings and prepare recommendations based on this experiment for presentations to appropriate standards groups such as MABRI in early 1993. Preliminary results seem to indicate that the USMARC Format can generally accommodate the description of electronically published information. However, clear guidelines are needed to assist catalogers in dealing with these unique formats (Jul, 1992a). There is little doubt that the cataloger's role will need to adjust to the idiosyncracies of the medium as we change from a print-based environment to an electronic information publishing format. The dilemma catalogers face in deciding whether to catalog electronic journals in the serials or computer data format will become a moot point with implementation of the final components for format integration in late 1993 or early 1994 (Caplan, 1992; Sheblé and Sheblé, 1991).

VI. Issues and Concerns

A. Patron Access

Even though the current generation is growing up in a world of computer technology, there are many library patrons who are not computer literate or do not have ready access to the equipment necessary to access electronic publications. The Internet still remains unavigable by many who would both contribute and benefit from its communication and publication capabilities (Jul, 1992b). Access can also be a problem where disciplines are dependent on contributions from and visibility to participants residing in less developed countries. Politics, reliability, and cost are other factors influencing ease of network access in some foreign countries (Piternick, 1991). The profusion of incompatible hardware and software along with the lack of standards for format also present access problems for both libraries and users.

B. Abstracting and Indexing

Even though most electronic journals are receiving full bibliographic access, few are listed in any indexing or abstracting services thereby presenting a problem in patron access. Basic for general acceptance of electronic journals is their inclusion in standard indexing and abstracting services, but they must be considered both important and numerous enough before these services will justify the added effort of adding them (Manoff et al., 1992). ERIC is one of the first major indexing and abstracting services to experiment with citations for electronic journals. *New Horizons in Adult Education* appears in the Resources in Education (RIE) portion of the ERIC index. The decision to index *New Horizons* in the RIE section resulted from their desire to make the journal more accessible and it was felt that it would be better accessed at the issue level rather than at the article level. For those who might argue that individual articles should be indexed in the Current Index to Journals in Education (CJE) portion of ERIC like any other journal it is worth noting that *New Horizons* is not like any other journal on ERIC. Indexing in RIE also gives the patron an alternative to electronic access through the ability to acquire hard copy in fiche or paper and provides a means of preserving back issues until a more viable standard of archiving is developed.

For reader access the abstract refers to information given in the ERIC document for joining AEDNET, the electronic mail network through which the journal is available, but nowhere else in the citation is it evident that this is an electronic journal. The indexing does not include the descriptor portion "electronic publishing" or the identifier (ID) of "electronic journals"; ERIC plans to correct these oversights in a later update. A new PUB-TYPE code will eventually be created for electronic journals, which would be another source of identification and, when combined with the descriptor and identifier, provide for more effective searching (Kerka, 1992).

MLA Bibliography is now indexing *Postmodern Culture*, but it is cited as *PMC*, making it difficult to access through a title search, which leads the unsuspecting searcher to believe it is not indexed. The file name under which a particular article can be found is provided as well as instructions on how it can be accessed through the listserve on BITNET, Internet, and others. *Gestus; The Electronic Journal of Brechtian Studies, Dover* is also cited, but the required mode of access is not included anywhere in the citation!

In a less traditional mode, Comserve is indexing *The Electronic Journal of Communication/La revue electronique de communication* along with nine print journals. The citations do not distinguish between the two formats, but do include instructions for retrieving the articles via electronic mail messages to Comserve. Meckler has also started a network-accessible database, which includes its new electronic journal, *Meckjournal*, along with two of its print journals. Articles from the electronic journal can be located and downloaded (Manoff *et al.*, 1992).

As electronic journals become more "respectable" and thus more readily accepted by the scholarly community, we will probably begin to see citations appearing in more of the traditional sources. The examples given above highlight the lack of standards in indexing electronic journals and the access problems that presents for the user. Dwyer (1986) suggested the need to link indexing, abstracting, and cataloging. The user could then "search for citations, read the abstracts to decide whether he or she would like to read the whole article, and determine whether the material was locally available in one unified process. . . ." Years later, however, integrated cataloging, indexing, and abstracting services, for the most part, still do not exist, so retrieval capabilities are hindered and it becomes difficult to determine what electronic journals exist, what their contents might be, and, often, even how to access them (Jul, 1992b).

C. Archiving

Libraries have traditionally played a role in archiving published materials because most publishers have focused on production for the present audience. One exception has been some scholarly societies that maintain extensive archives. Because so much scholarly publication is now in the hands of commercial publishers who are notorious for going out of business, merging with conglomerates, or otherwise changing their identity, libraries are justifiably concerned with electronic journals' future access. Another concern is centralization. Libraries depend on multiple copies of publications existing in other institutions so that damaged or missing issues in one library can still be accessed by patrons in another library. However, electronic publishing is much less tangible. If there is only one "copy" accessible exclusively through the Internet, how long will it be available and who is responsible for preserving it? The unique features of electronic journals—speed of publication, potential for continuous publication, ability to update or add original data—raise questions about their integrity and stability, which are key points in facilitating preservation over time and space. The lack of widely used communication standards and protocols also hinders preserving electronic output (Kaufman, 1991).

There are several methods of preserving the backfiles of electronic journals: CD–ROMs, video CD–ROMs, magnetic tapes, disks, and storing online. Storing online is still quite expensive, tape or disks often develop "noise" that may result in degradation from heat, sunlight, humidity, magnetism, or dirt, and there is still considerable controversy over the life of magnetic and digital storage media. The issue of compatible hardware and software becomes important as we move from DOS or ASCII files to more complex databases with embedded smart codes. Uniform standards for transmission and preservation of digitally encoded data are essential in dealing with technological obsolescence of electronic data and will provide easy migration from a known system to an unknown one (Blake, 1989).

Libraries are not alone in this concern. The National Academy of Public Administration (NAPA) contracted for a study of criteria to approve the value of electronic databases. Among the recommendations were the need to develop standards for ownership, documentation, access, and preservation. While electronic journals were not singled out, serials available in electronic and paper formats were noted as an area for further consideration. If NAPA is successful in developing standards for preservation, these may have a broad influence on electronic publishing (National Academy of Public Administration, 1991).

Libraries also need to be concerned with government databases because of GPO's trend to make considerable amounts of information available online only in the form of bulletin boards. In some cases the bulletin board has replaced a print journal (GPO/2001, 1991). One NAPA report did note the need to establish a position on the preservation of electronic mail and bulletin boards.

D. Acceptance

Electronic publishing has many advantages over the print media as a means of scholarly communication. It offers the capability of disseminating information almost immediately; it is flexible and interactive, allowing correspondents to respond and converse electronically about changes or additions to their text (Smith, 1991). Schrage (1991) states "that just as technology has transformed the way people communicate, it will reshape the way people collaborate." One-on-one collaboration between researchers would allow them to share and critique ongoing experiments or scholarly communication regardless of their proximity to each other. Traditional relationships between author, reviewer, and reader will be reshaped as coauthors simultaneously work with the same material while chitchatting onscreen as the article progresses (Pullinger, 1986; Schrage, 1991). However, these very advantages are often the reason authors are reluctant to use electronic journals for their scholarly research. They are concerned about the lack of control over what will appear on the computer screen as some formats and search software make it easy to scan portions of an online text, making it possible to read excerpts of the article out of context. They are also concerned about security and the integrity of their text. Files can be lost or wiped out by viruses, articles can be easily altered or appended, and who is going to archive or preserve his/her articles so future scholars can have access to the contributions he/she made today? As long as academia uses publication in "particular prestigious" journals as criteria for tenure and promotion, authors are going to be reluctant to trust their work to an unknown technology producing journals that lack credibility in their eyes (Anderson, 1991; Maddox, 1992). How often a scholarly work is cited is another aspect of publishing tied to tenure and promotion. How do you cite an electronic journal if it has not appeared in any indexing services, or if it has disappeared from the database because no one has archived it? Perhaps the number of times an article is accessed could be used rather than the number of times it was cited, but what if it was not accessed because the author's name was misspelled or because of a simple inputting error? How long will the user keep looking if it is not accessed on the first couple of searches?— probably not very long (Anderson, 1991; Piternick, 1991)! Electronic journals still suffer from a lack of acceptance as a means of professional or scholarly communication because authors are often reluctant to submit their articles because of perceived lack of audience, lack of reward, or a fear of transience. However, electronic journals need articles from researchers and scholars in order to survive and to gain acceptance in the eyes of the people responsible for granting or denying tenure and promotion, thus creating a vicious circle (Jul, 1992b).

E. Readability

Many computer systems today offer poor readability and often lack appropriate formats for screen reading. Staring at a computer screen for minutes or hours is somewhat like reading documents on microfiche or microfilm. It is difficult to move from screen to screen and still retain perspective and continuity of thought. Hypertext structures may be one answer. Perhaps authors could be asked to provide abstracts or synopses and to apply formats using modular structures with clearly defined sections, making it easier to move from place to place (Getz, 1992; Piternick, 1991). Some electronic journals are difficult to page through. Some lack pagination, making it harder to reference certain portions or to go back and reread a certain paragraph that sticks in your mind as relevant—but where was it? Using the analogy of reading microform, which has never been a pleasant experience for patrons and eventually led to the invention of the microfilm and microfiche reader/printer, do you spend considerable time trying to find the section you are looking for or print out the entire document so you can study it and reread it and makr relevant passages for more leisurely reading? At the present time, however, output formats for electronic information vary dramatically, so even printing out the document may or may not make it more readable (Alley, 1991; Dillon, 1991). Reading from paper is still generally preferred to reading from a computer screen, so how quickly acceptable display technologies and user interfaces can be developed will play a key role in the acceptance of electronically published information (Jul, 1992c).

F. University Publishing

Academia may become a more active participant in publishing electronically as commercial publishers continue to shun entering this new arena of communication. The electronic journal adds speed and spontaneity through interactive discourse that is lacking in the paper journal. Electronic journals cannot be monitored as closely or use cannot be restricted as effectively as in paper journals, so as long as commercial publishers continue to base price on costs rather than value or need, they are going to be reluctant to venture into this new medium. Academia can become more easily involved in the electronic journal environment because they have less to lose. Scholars already give their information away to commercial publishers and have lost control through copyright laws. Rather than allowing commercial publishers to transform this information into a commodity and then sell it back to academia at exorbitant prices, why not keep it within the realm of academia where it can be shared with colleagues far and wide at a nominal price? This would also allow the smaller and less resourceful libraries to have the same access to scholarly communications as the more wealthy libraries for a one-time investment in developing telecommunication and computing infrastructure (Metz and Gherman, 1991; Okerson, 1991b).

VII. Projects in Progress

There are a number of relevant projects and publications in process. *Access to Electronic Journals in Libraries* by Dennis Benamati and Dave Tyckoson will be published by Meckler in 1993. This book will contain at least three working policies accompanied by discussions on the decision-making process used to develop the policy, on the effectiveness of the policy, and on any subsequent changes (Tyckoson, 1992). The format of the book is quite novel; it will have the look of an electronically generated publication and will include "hypertex" buttons in the margins to aid readers in finding similar sections across chapters. Chapter authors will use side bars for different perspectives on the topics. The intent is to show that electronic information blurs the lines among what were formerly thought of as discrete issues (Benamati, 1992).

The Global Online Information Project received a grant from IBM to study how and why readers use the same information differently when it is in print and electronic format. For example, people use an index differently online; frequently they browse it for vocabulary to use in keyword searches. The researchers will use IBM technical manuals (Technology update, 1992), so their results may not be directly applicable to the design of online journals.

Computer conferences will be used to discuss principles, policies, and practice related to scholarly communication in a networked environment. Sponsored by the Science, Technology, and Public Policy Program of Harvard's John F. Kennedy School of Government and the Coalition for Networked Information, the project's goal is to aid groups ranging from research teams to academic and professional societies developing appropriate policies and priorities. Issues being discussed include collaboration, control of dissemination, site licensing, and international access (Kahin, 1991).

Creating a consortium for networked refereed research journals is the goal of a conference being organized by Larry W. Hurtado (1992) at the University of Manitoba. The goals of the project are to see that the scholarly community is included in the development of computer network publication projects; to make academic merit, not commercial consideration, become the criteria for publication; to offer an outlet for research publication, especially in less commercially attractive fields; and to make use of the technological and cost advantage of network publications.

Besides the sponsored research listed above, developments in software, computer screen resolution, and communication networks may also encourage evolution of electronic journals.

VIII. Future

King (1991) predicts that little will change in the delivery of scholarly information before the turn of the century. By the year 2006, he feels we will see dramatic changes in how we search for information and how that information will be delivered to libraries. He also feels that the print media will continue to exist but play a different role in our society. King does not feel the reviewing process will be greatly enhanced through the electronic medium or that scholars will submit articles any faster after the novelty of working in this medium wears off. Researchers will, however, spend less time in the library as access becomes available through remote workstations and a standard set of search protocols becomes a reality. It will no longer be necessary to locate the materials, make photocopies, and then return the materials to their original location.

King's predictions on the rate of change in scholarly information delivery are echoed in the recommendations of the Report of the American Physical Society Task Force on Electronic Information (Report, 1991). The Task Force projected that the dominant mode for information delivery will be via a single electronic physics library that will contain all published books, papers, conference proceedings, numerical data, and computer programs. This database would be continually updated and the entire contents would be searchable. Users could download information and the system would monitor usage and assess charges. This database could be developed under the auspices of a government agency, a consortium of not-for-profit institutions, a consortium of publishers, or a combination of all these. Ultimately, all science databases would be interconnected and researchers would have access to the Science Database. To achieve this, the Task Force recommended that the Society take the lead in developing standards so that the scientific information systems are compatible.

The Task Force recognized that at present libraries are the dominant consumers of physics information in journal form, but because libraries' influence is diffuse, journal publishers have the most economic power. The Physics Information System would replace the library and may also replace some publishers. The report noted that paper publication would continue to exist but the special enhancements of electronic information—options for display including multimedia features, access to data, resources to solve equations and evaluate expressions in the document, ability to check citations on line, and ability to append readers' comments to the original document—will make print less desirable.

The Task Force also noted that users could employ hypertext to construct user-based complex, multibranched paths through the information. This plan for individualizing indexing certainly echoes Bush's (1967) proposal for memex. While the Task Force does not cite Bush, his vision of memex anticipates this information system and hypertext access the report describes. The Task Force noted the many obstacles including technical, sociopsychological, administrative, and financial must be resolved if they are to realize this vision. To this end, the Task Force exhorted the Society to keep its eye on the vision and take the appropriate leadership to move the world scientific community toward the vision.

A detailed scenario of the evolution of the electronic journal was developed by Ann Okerson (1991a). She noted that if present trends continue through 1995 the likely result will be bibliographic confusion and chaos for utilities, libraries, and scholars. Near the turn of the century, she predicted that the markets for paper and for electronic journals would be divided equally, single article distribution would dominate over journal subscriptions, and collaboration would increase as would copyright law tensions and economic stratification of information users.

What is unclear in these new models for article distribution is how they would accommodate the social role of scholarly journals. The point has been made repeatedly that the scholarly journal imparts prestige and exerts a high level of social control; any new journal must also take on that role (Turoff and Hiltz, 1982). The electronic journal has the potential to meet this social role; therefore, libraries must continue to consider them as a potentially important medium. Finally, articles-on-demand services do not require libraries, so the future success of electronic journals could be viewed as being in the libraries' best interest.

IX. Library Trends

Most libraries are considering adding electronic journals to their collections because they represent a less costly, faster means of collecting scholarly information. However, it is a common feeling that electronic journals will not replace the traditional print format but rather compliment it as a new means of communication. Whether the e-journal succeeds depends on many factors. Editors, publishers, and readers need to make a clear distinction between an electronic journal and unedited list servers, bulletin boards, and electronic discussion groups. If potential authors are satisfied that their work has passed strict editorial standards and these standards are acceptable to the powers that control their advancement in their respective fields, then they will be more willing to submit their work to this new medium of publication (McMillan, 1991b).

Authors also need assurance that their work will be accessible; for this format to succeed, libraries need to integrate electronic journals into their OPACs, insist that they become a part of commercial indexing services, and initiate and implement a plan for preserving and archiving these texts so access is readily available to users. Taking these steps would most certainly assist in making electronic journals more readily accepted as a means of scholarly communication.

Libraries must decide what role they are to play in the network information environment. If the potential of the electronic journal is to become a reality, libraries need to collaborate with the authors, editors, and scholarly societies who are currently advocating this new form of scholarly communication (Langschied, 1992). They also need to be cultivating strong alliances with their computer center. By combining the libraries' expertise in solving problems of access with the computer centers' expertise in networking electronic journals, the library can play a pivotal role in the success of this new mode of disseminating scholarly information.

References

Alley, B. (1991). The electronic scholar vs. the electronic reader. *Technicalities* **11**,1.
Amiran, E., and Unsworth, J. (1991). Postmodern Culture: Publishing in the electronic medium. *Public-Access Computer Systems Review* **2**, 67–76. (To retrieve send to LISTSERV@UHUPVM1 or LISTSERV@UHUPVM1.EDU--message Get AMIRAN PRV1N1 F=MAIL).
Anderson, J. (1991). Beyond journals: There's going to be a better way. *The Serials Librarian* **19**, 163–167.
Bailey, C. W. (1991a). Electronic (online) publishing in action. . . . *Online* **15**, 28–35.
Bailey, C. W. (1991b). Electronic serials on BITNET. *Computers in Libraries* **11**, 50–51.
Bailey, C. W. (1992). Electronic message on "Serials in Libraries Discussion Forum" (SERIALST%UMVM.BITNET) dated 3 March.

Benamati, D. (1992). Electronic message to the author dated 15 December.

Biomedicine gets its first electronic journal (1983). *Outlook on Research Libraries* **5**, 6–7.

Blake, M. (1989). Archiving of electronic publications. *The Electronic Library* **7**, 376–386.

Blixrud, J. C. (1992). CONSER and electronic serials. *CONSER* **22**, 3–5.

Bush, V. (1967). Memex revisited. In *Science is Not Enough*, pp. 75–101. Morrow, New York.

Caplan, P. (1992). E-mail to (LISTSERV@MAINE.maine.edu) in response to "Providing Access to Online Information Resources: A Paper for Discussion" (MABRI Discussion Paper No. 54) dated 1 November.

Collier, H. R. (1984). The Concept of Learned Information's electronic journal. *Electronic Publishing Review* **4**, 179–188.

Dillon, Andrew (1991). New technology and the reading process. *Computers in Libraries* **11**, 23–26.

Dougherty, W., Hanson, B., Litchfield, C., McMillan, G., Metz, P., Nicol, J., and Queijo, K. (1991). *Report of the Task Force on the Electronic Journal*. Virginia Polytechnic Institute and State University, Blacksburg, Virginia.

Dwyer, J. R. (1986). Evolving serials, evolving access: Bibliographic control of serial literature. *Serials Review* **12**, 59–64.

Electronic publishing. (1992). *Communication and Technology Impact* **4**, 1–3.

Fecko, M. B., and Langschied, L. (1991). The impact of electronic journals on traditional library services. *The Serials Librarian* **21**, 185–187.

For immediate release: *PACS Review* from LITA. (1992). *Technicalities* **12**, 2–3.

Fox, E. A. (1990). How to proceed toward electronic archives and publishing. *Psychological Science* **1**, 355–358.

Freeman, D. T. (1987). The false start of the electronic journal: A look at human factors and automation. *ASIS Proceedings* **24**, 79–82.

Gardner, W. (1990). The electronic archive: Scientific publishing for the 1990's. *Psychological Science* **1**, 333–341.

Garson, L. R., and Howard, J. G. (1984). Electronic publishing: Potential benefits and problems for authors, publishers and libraries. *Journal of Chemical Information and Computer Sciences* **24**, 119–123.

Geller, M. (1992). "Handling Electronic Journals in the Academic Library: The MIT Experience." Paper presented at the Third National LITA Conference, Denver, Colorado, September 13–16.

Getz, M. (1992). Electronic publishing: An economic view. *Serials Review* **18**, 26–31.

GPO/2001: Vision for a New Millennium (1991). U.S. Government Printing Office, Washington, D.C.

Grycz, C. J. (1992). Economic models for networked information. *Serials Review* **18**, 11–18.

Gurnsey, J. (1982). *Electronic Document delivery—III: Electronic Publishing Trends in the United States and Europe*. Learned Information, Medford, New Jersey.

Harnad, S. (1990). Scholarly skywriting and the pre-publication continuum of scientific inquiry. *Psychological Science* **6**, 342–344.

Harnad, S. (1991). Post-Gutenberg Galaxy: The fourth evaluation in the means of production of knowledge. *The Public-Access Computer Systems Review* **2**, 39–53. (To retrieve, send to LISTSERV@UHUPVM1 or LISTSERV@UHUPVM1.UH.EDU--message GET HARNAD PV12N1 F=MAIL).

Harrison, T. M., Stephen, T., and Winter, J. (1991). Online journals: Disciplinary designs for electronic scholarship. *Public-Access Computer systems Review* **2**, 25–38. (To retrieve, send to LISTSERV@UHUPVM1 or LISTSERV@UHUPVM1.UH.EDU--message GET HARRISON PRV2N1 F=MAIL).

Holden, C. (1992). Online journal joins forces with *Lancet*. Science **257**, 1341.

Hugo, J., and Newell, L. (1991). *New Horizons in Adult Education*, the first five years (1987–1991). *Public-Access Computer Systems Review* **2**, 77–90. (To retrieve, send to LISTSERV@UHUPVM1 or LISTSERV@UHUPVM1.UH.EDU--message GET HUGO PRV2N1 F=MAIL).

Hurtado, L. W. (1992). Electronic message on PACS-L(PACS-L@UHUPVM1) dated 6 May.

IRCS moves into electronic publishing, (1982). *Communication Technology Impact* **4**, 1–3.

Jennings, E. M. (1991). *EJournal*: An account of the first two years. *Public-Access Computer Systems Review* **2**, 91–110. (To retrieve, send to LISTSERV@UHUPVM1 or LISTSERV@UHUPVM1.UH.EDU--message GET JENNINGS PRV2N1 F=MAIL).

Jul, E. (1992a). Internet Resources Project volunteers provide critical support. *OCLC Newsletter* **198**, 18–19.

Jul, E. (1992b). Of barriers and breakthroughs. *Computers in Libraries* **12**, 20–21.

Jul, E. (1992c). Present at the beginning. *Computers in Libraries* **12**, 44–45.

Kahin, B. (1991). Electronic Message on PACS-L (PACS-L@UHUPVM1) dated 26 September.

Kassirer, J. (1992). Journals in bits and bytes: Electronic medical journals. *The New England Journal of Medicine* **326**, 195–197.

Katzen, M. (1986). Electronic publishing in the humanities. *Scholarly Publishing* **18**, 5–16.

Kaufman, P. (1991). Archiving electronic journals: Who's responsible for what. *Library Issues*, **11**, (July).

Kerka, S. (1992). Sidebar: Indexing an E-journal in a print index. *Serials Review* **18**, 132–133.

King, T. B. (1991). The impact of electronic and networking technologies on the delivery of scholarly information. *The Serials Librarian* **21**, 5–13.

Lancaster, F. W. (1989). Electronic publishing. *Library Trends* **37**, 317–325.

Langschied, L. (1991). The changing shape of the electronic journal. *Serials Review* **17**, 7–14.

Langschied, L. (1992). Electronic journal forum. *Serials Review* **17**, 131–136.

Leahy, S., and Smith, R. J. (1992). A suggested guide and comments for cataloging electronic files. *Technicalities* **12**, 8–11.

Lerner, R. G. (1984). The professional society in a changing world. *Library Quarterly* **54**, 36–47.

Library of Congress (1991). *Discussion paper no. 49*. LC, Washington, D.C.

Maddox, J. (1992). Electronic journals have a future. *Nature* (*London*) **356**, 559.

McMillan, G. (1991a). Embracing the electronic journal: One library's plan. *The Serials Librarian* **21**, 97–108.

McMillan, G. (1991b). Electronic journals: Considerations for the present and the future. *Serials Review* **17**, 77–86.

McMillan, G. (1992). Technical processing of electronic journals. *Library Resources & Technical Services* **36**, 470–477.

Manoff, M., Dorschner, E., Geller, M., Morgan, K., and Snowden, C. (1992). Report of the Electronic Journals Task Force MIT Libraries. *Serials Review* **18**, 113–129.

Metz, P., and Gherman, P. M. (1991). Serials pricing and the role of the electronic journal. *College & Research Libraries* **52**, 315–327.

More brevity in *The Lancet*. (1992). *The Lancet* **340**, 519.

National Academy of Public Administration (1991). *The Archives of the future: Archival strategies for the treatment of electronic database*. Washington, D.C.

New science journal goes online. (1992). *OCLC Reference News* July/August, **5**, 8.

OCLC and the American Association for the Advancement of Science develop new online journal. (1991). *The Third Indicator* **6**, 5–6.

Okerson, A. (1991a). The electronic journal: What, whence, and when? *The Public Access Computer Systems Review* **2**, 5–24. (To retrieve, send to LISTSERV@UHUPVM1 or LISTSERV@UHUPVM1.UH.EDU--message GET OKERSONPDV1N1 F=MAIL).

Okerson, A. (1991b). Back to academia? The case for American universities to publish their own research. *Logos* **2,** 106–112.

Online journal is *Database* magazine's product of the year. (1992). Electronic message *OCLC News* (OCLC-News@FSSUN09.DEV.OCLC.ORG) dated 29 October.

Piternick, A. B. (1989a). Attempts to find alternatives to the scientific journal: A brief review. *Journal of Academic Librarianship* **15,** 260–266.

Piternick, A. B. (1989b). Serials and new technology: The state of the 'electronic journal.' *Canadian Library Journal* **46,** 93–97.

Piternick, A. B. (19991). Electronic serials: Realistic or unrealistic solution to the journal "crisis?" *Serials Librarian* **21,** 15–31.

Pullinger, D. J. (1986). Chit-chat to electronic journals: Computer conferencing supports scientific communication. *IEEE Transactions on Professional Communications* **PC29,** 23–29.

Reich, V. (1992). Discipline-specific literature bases: A view of the APS model. *Serials Review* **18,** 52–54, 65.

Report of the APS Task Force on Electronic Information Systems (1991). *Bulletin of the American Physical Society* **36,** 1119–1151.

Rhodes, S. N., and Bamford, H. E., Jr. (1976). Editorial processing centers: A progress report. *American Sociologist* **11,** 153–159.

Roistacher, R.C. (1978). The virtual journal. *Computer Networks* **2,** 18–24.

Savage, L. (1991). *The Journal of the International Academy of Hospitality Research. Public-Access Computer Systems Review* **2,** 54–66.

Schrage, M. (1991). Computer tools for thinking in tandem. *Science* **253,** 505–507.

Schultz, T. D. (1992). A world physics information system: An online highly interactive discipline-oriented facility. *Serials Review* **18,** 45–48.

Senders, J. (1976). The scientific journal of the future. *American Sociologist* **11,** 160–164.

Sexton, M. (1991). No room for troglodytes at scholarly publishers' meeting. *Publishers Weekly* **238,** 44–45.

Shackel, B. (1983). The BLEND system: Programme for the study of some "electronic journals." *Journal of the American Society for Information Science* **34,** 22–30.

Sheblé, M. A., and Sheblé, G. B. (1991). Cataloging in the "paperless information" age. *Cataloging Classification Quarterly* **13,** 3–29.

Smith, E. (1991). Resolving the acquisitions dilemma: Into the electronic information environment. *College & Research Libraries* **52,** 231–240.

Sondak, N. E., and Schwartz, R. J. (1973). The paperless journal. *Chemical Engineering Progress* **69,** 82–83.

Standera, O. L. (1985). Electronic publishing: Some notes on reader responses and costs. *Scholarly Publishing* **16,** 291–305.

Technology update. (1992). *Chronicle of Higher Education* **38,** 32.

Turoff, M., and Hiltz, S. R. (1982). The electronic journal: A progress report. *Journal of the American Society for Information Science* **33,** 195–202.

Tyckoson, D. (1992). Electronic message on library administration and management (LIBADMIN%UMAB.BITNET) dated 10 July.

Urbach, P. F. (1984). The view of a for-profit scientific publisher. *Library Quarterly* **54,** 30–35.

Output Measures for Evaluating the Performance of Community College Learning Resources Programs: A California Case Study

Tobin de Leon Clarke
San Joaquin Delta Community College
Stockton, California 95207

Elmer U. Clawson
School of Education
University of the Pacific
Stockton, California 95207

I. Introduction

The need for some form of measure to evaluate library programs in the community colleges has been recognized by librarians since 1930 (Homer, 1930). Even in the early years of the development of these measures, program administrators recognized that having a model against which a particular program could be evaluated might be influential in assuring adequate support for their libraries. These standards related only to aspects of a program necessary for the program to be judged up to standard, such as, for example, size of staff, amount of budget, and numbers of books. They are considered *input measures*.

These first input measures were called *standards*. Standards are considered to be rules and, when adopted by a governing body, enforceable (Wallace, 1972). They are generally set high and are considered by some to be unrealistic. Because of this they are not often adopted by governing bodies.

During the 1960s, it became politically more realistic to call the measures *guidelines* rather than standards, because standards were considered by some to be too inflexible and unrealistic to be adopted, and therefore, ineffective. Guidelines are typically more descriptive of a model program, rather than prescriptive. They are not considered rules and are, therefore, not enforceable; or, as Matthews and Associates (1985) suggest, guidelines are optional measures, whereas standards are fixed measures.

Because of the increased interest in accountability in the 1970s, it became apparent that input measures by themselves were no longer an appropriate means of evaluating library programs. In order to assist libraries to become more accountable, library *output measures* were developed. Output measures can relate to the number of materials circulated, the number of reference questions answered, the number of students receiving instruction, the number of productions, the amount of equipment used, and so on. The first such output measures were developed for public libraries.

Libraries and other service providers need to have meaningful ways to express their requirements or "inputs," but they also need to have meaningful ways to measure their "outputs" or achievements (Bommer and Chorba, 1982; Hamburg, Ramist, and Bommer, 1972; Lancaster, 1977). As Herbert Goldhor states in the forward to (Lancaster, 1977, p. vii), "As more and better measures of performance are devised and used, the difference between an effective and ineffective library will become more obvious and more easily documented." Libraries and learning resources programs in the community colleges have this same need.

A. Comprehensive Community College Learning Resources Programs

The development of the comprehensive learning resources program parallels that of the development of the comprehensive community college. Because of the complex nature of the mission of the colleges and the nontraditional nature of the student body, new ways were sought to provide library services that would more appropriately meet the needs of the students and faculty in the colleges. The result was the evolution of the traditional library program into the comprehensive learning resources program (Allen and Allen, 1973; Wallace, 1976).

The definition of a learning resources program selected in this article is closely modeled after that developed by the joint committee for standards (American Library Association [ALA]; American Association of Community and Junior Colleges [AACJC]; Association of Educational Communication and Technology [AECT], 1990). A learning resources program is an organizational structure that primarily provides library and audiovisual services to students, faculty, and staff in a two-year college program. The library includes print as well as nonprint materials. Audiovisual services are provided for students and faculty in classrooms as well as in centralized facilities.

A number of special services may be provided such as: campuswide reprographics, teleconferencing, community cable channel operation, on-campus closed circuit cable television, television and other types of audiovisual production, and operation of Instructional Television Fixed Service (ITFS) broadcast systems.

The program may also include additional instructional responsibilities. Typical of these additional instructional responsibilities are telecourse and other independent study program coordination, tutorial programs, microcomputer labs, instructional development, and other staff-development programs (ALA, ACRL, AECT, 1990).

The history and development of the community college library from traditional library to learning resources program have been covered in the literature (Veit, 1975). The junior college movement and the development of the library within that context up to 1976 is covered by Wallace (1976). The several distinctions between traditional library services or programs and learning resources services and programs have also been identified and discussed. Chief among these are involvment in instruction, access to print and nonprint information resources, equipment distribution, television production, language laboratories, and all the traditional library services as well (Accrediting Commission for Community and Junior Colleges, 1987; Bender, 1980; Dale, 1977; Reeves, 1973; Wallace, 1976).

It should be mentioned here that there is some confusion associated with the names learning resources, learning resource center (LRC), and libraries. This is due in part to the terms being used interchangeably in some sources (Dale, 1977; Genung and Wallace, 1972; Veit, 1975; Wallace, 1976). Others have been careful to distinguish among them (Bender, 1980; Peterson, 1975). Some professionals in the field refuse to use the term "learning resources" because, as is often said, "No one knows what a learning resource center is, and a learning resources program is even more difficult to explain, so it is just easier to call it a library." Some also refuse to accept the idea that the role of audiovisual services in the community colleges is as important as traditional library services. There seems to be no adequate solution to end this confusion or conflict, since it apparently revolves around a basic phiosophical difference among librarians (Bierbaum, 1990). Regardless of this discussion, however, the phrase, comprehensive learning resources program, was selected for this study because it is the most inclusive descriptor of the breadth of services provided by the community colleges (Dennison, 1978). Much of the information presented here relates equally well, however, to libraries, learning resource centers, or other subsets within the learning resources program.

B. Rationale for the Evaluation of Learning Resources Programs

The literature relating to the evaluation of community college libraries, learning resource centers, or learning resources programs is limited. Most of what is available in the area of learning resources programs are descriptions of operations or discussions of standards or guidelines. Apparently, most evaluation of learning resources programs is done informally, if at all, and therefore not reported in the literature (Bender, 1980; Bierbaum, 1990; Dennison, 1978; Reeves, 1973).

Three reports or studies that evaluate or describe an evaluation process for learning resources programs have been identified. Apple (1978) describes an evaluation for the LRC at Elgin Community College in Illinois, in which four measures are used to evaluate use of the facility. An article describing an evaluation process for learning resource centers provides some measures and sample instruments for the evaluation (Terwilliger, 1983). The Cuesta College Library in California used the evaluation process developed by the Learning Resources Association of the California Community Colleges in an institutional self-study for accreditation (Wilhelm, 1986).

Because of the scarcity of material, the majority of the literature related to evaluation and measurement reviewed for the purposes of this article is related to libraries. Even though the scope of learning resources programs is different from that of the traditional library (Accrediting Commission for Community and Junior Colleges, 1987; ALA, ACRL, AECT, 1990; Bender, 1980), the goal of each is to provide service to users.

It is generally agreed, however, that the library is the major component of a learning resources program. The other components provide services of a different type, for example, distribution of audiovisual equipment to the classroom and production of instuctional materials. Also, sometimes the services are provided to different users, that is, faculty and not students (Dennison, 1978). However, it is worthwhile to note at this point that public service providers have similar rationale for evaluating and measuring their services, regardless of the type of service provided (Cronin, 1985; Drucker, 1973; Lancaster, 1988). For these reasons, the assumption is made that generalizations and inferences can be drawn for learning resources programs from the types of evaluation and measurement discussion in the library literature.

Within the context of the learning resources program, discussion on the value of evaluation to the library is most significant in the literature. This discussion can be grouped around particular questions: Why should one evaluate? How should one evaluate? What problems are associated with library evaluation?

The focus of the following discussion is on why a library or any public service agency should evaluate itself. Since the process of evaluation is time consuming and expensive, many libraries have been reluctant to do it. Since most libraries do not have adequate resources, either human or fiscal, it is understandable why they do not evaluate. Also, unlike private businesses, an evaluation component is not typically built in to the budgets of service organizations (Cronin, 1985). Often, too, data are collected for no apparent reason, and then librarians are left to wonder about the value of data collection at all. As Lancaster (1988) points out, evaluation must be done with specific objectives in mind or it is a "sterile exercise."

In the same work, Lancaster identifies four reasons to evaluate. They are: (1) to establish a base or "benchmark" for evaluating performance in order to establish comparative data for evaluating change; (2) to establish a database for comparison across libraries using an established standard; (3) as a justification of the service; and (4) to find out where improvements can be made in existing services (Lancaster, 1988, p. 7).

Most authors mention accountability and competition for funds as the purpose of evaluation (Apple, 1978; Cronin, 1985; Daniel, 1976; DeProspo, 1975; Hamburg *et al.*, 1972; House, 1978). Others mention justification or feedback for change as the rationale for evaluation (Daniel, 1976; DeProspo and Liesner, 1975; Feldman, 1974).

Generally speaking, while there is agreement regarding the value of evaluation to public service agencies, there is not agreement on how one should evaluate library services. Partially, this is because of problems associated with the nature of the service, the difficulty of establishing appropriate measures, and the difficulty of determining what the expected results should be. But, regardless of the difficulties, there is agreement that evaluation should be done.

II. Standards and Guidelines for Evaluating the Performance of Community College Libraries and Learning Resources Centers in California: A Historical Perspective

The development of the comprehensive community college in California followed the national norms, as did the development of comprehensive learning resources programs to augment the instructional program. The movement toward standards or guidelines that would be more representative of the services and staff found in learning resources programs was also operative in California.

Since separating from K–12 Districts in 1963, two-year college library administrators in California have been proactive in support of standards, and have worked through their professional associations for the adoption of either quantitative or qualitative standards as valid measures for library programs. One indication of this is that the Junior College Round Table of the California Library Association voted to accept the new national standards for California Community College Libraries in 1963 (Learning Resources Association of the California Community Colleges [LRACCC], 1978).

While library administrators are supportive of the development and adoption of standards, other community college administrators generally have not been. This is because standards are often considered either threatening to local autonomy or self-serving professional documents. Unless it can be shown that what is currently operational is not too different from what is suggested in the standards, they are not likely to be adopted by a governing body. For the first time, however, in 1969, the Standards Committee of the Junior College Round Table, California Library Association, collected enough data to convince the California Junior College Association that the ALA standards should be accepted as guidelines for the California Community Colleges (LRACCC, 1978).

Following the lead of ALA in including other than library representatives on the standards committee for community colleges, the Standards Committee of the Community College Librarians Chapter of the California Library Association (formerly the Junior College Round Table) was expanded to include representatives of the media associations in California. Then, in 1974, this committee combined with the Standards Committee of the Learning Resources Association of the California Community Colleges. Significantly, the expanded committee included not only representatives from professional associations, but also representatives of the California Community College Chancellor's Office and the California Postsecondary Education Commission [CPEC] (LRACCC, 1978). The participation of representatives from these state agencies lent authority to a group previously comprised of librarians and other learning resources directors from the field.

This new committee, the Learning Resources Center Guidelines Committee, served to provide a broad base of interest for the development of standards for California community college learning resources programs. The goal of this committee was to develop quantitative standards that would provide specific measures by which to evaluate learning resources program quality.

By using as a base both the qualitative standards presented in *Guidelines for Two-Year College Learning Resources Programs* (ALA, ACRL, AACJC, AECT, 1972), and the results of a quantitative study of library space by CPEC (1974), the committee was able to develop the first standards specifically related to California learning resources programs. These standards were published as the *Facilities Guidelines for Learning Resources Center: Print, Non-Print and Related Instructional Services* (LRACCC, 1978).

Because of the success of the previous committee in developing the facilities standards, LRACCC appointed an ad hoc committee to develop recommendations for quantitative quidelines for personnel and materials for learning resources programs in California community colleges. The guideline were to be developed as a complement to the facilities guidelines.

At the time this committee was beginning its work, however, a national document of quantitative standards for learning resources programs was adopted and published in final form (ALA, ACRL, 1979). The quantitative standards set forth in this document were then used as the basis for the development of the publication, *Personnel and Materials Guidelines for California Learning Resources Programs* (LRACCC, 1980).

However, even with all the input and cooperation between and among the professional organizations and the state agencies in the development of the standards, the only standards incorporated into California law were space standards for library facilities (Title 5, CA). The adoption of the space standards was welcomed by California Community College library administrators. While they are useful as guidelines for designing new buildings or justifying building modifications, they provide no guidance for program development, nor do they provide any measures by which to evaluate the level of success of the services provided by a learning resources program. The most recent review of the space standards pointed out clearly that even the best space standard will not provide any indication of how well a learning resources program is serving its users (Matthews and Associates, 1985).

Library adminstrators, library faculty, and other learning resources professionals have continued to urge the State of California to legislate minimum prescriptive standards for learning resources programs. To date, however, with the exception of space standards, no other standards have been developed for California. Some possible reasons for this include the following: the diversity of the California community colleges themselves; the lack of baseline data upon which to develop standards; and resistance on the part of local administration when outside sources, whether governmental agencies or professional associations, seek to tell individual districts how much money to allocate and in which areas to concentrate allocation.

Meanwhile, because standards are helpful to adminstrators when bargaining for fiscal support from their institutions and for measuring the quality of a program, the pursuit of legislated standards continued. For example, in 1984, LRACCC, working with the Faculty Association of California Community Colleges (FACCC), succeeded in gaining enough influence with the Board of Governors to effect some change in the status quo regarding the adoption of minimum standards. The Board agreed to adopt the standards and guidelines developed for learning resource programs by the American Library Association (ALA, ACRL, 1979; ALA, ACRL, AECT, 1982a,b) as incorporated in the program assessment document published by LRACCC (Simans, 1983). However, this decision was overturned after review by the State Office of Administrative Law (California Community Colleges Board of Governors, 1984).

This was not an altogether unsuccessful attempt to make changes in the area of standards. It did result in the Board of Governors authorizing the Chancellor's Office to hire a consultant to review the library space standards and to broaden the study to include some proposed guidelines for the effective operation of community college libraries/learning resources centers (T. de Leon Clarke representing LRACCC, Statement to the Board of Governor's Education Policy Committee, July 12, 1984).

In the report, *A Review of Library Space Standards for the California Community Colleges* (Matthews and Associates, 1985), the second part of which discusses standards and guidelines are requested by LRACCC, a recommendation was made that, in the event of the development of specific standards or guidelines for community college library or learning resources programs, provision be made for both input measures and output measures by which to evaluate how well the programs were doing. This report was accepted by the Chancellor's Office, but neither the recommendations made in the report regarding the space standards nor those regarding the guidelines for measuring the operation of libraries or other components of learning resources programs have been adopted or implemented.

The suggestion that both input and output measures be used for evaluating programs came as a surprise to many administrators and faculty in California community college library and learning resources programs. There was considerable discussion during the meeting of the Community College Librarians Chapter at the California Library Association Conference in November, 1985, regarding the impact the potential inclusion of output measures would have on learning resources and library programs. In view of the constant struggle for financial support, many library and learning resources administrators did not agree that output measures rather than standards would be helpful to the field.

Related to the desire of California librarians for the development and adoption of standards was a perceived lack of understanding and leadership on the part of the Community College Chancellor's Office of either learning resources programs or libraries. Since there was no specialist in this area in the Chancellor's Office, there was no one to articulate the needs of library and learning resources programs at the state level. Most leadership in the struggle toward the adoption of standards had been coming from library professionals in the field. Some administrators of library and learning resources programs thought that the Chancellor's Office should provide more leadership in regard to their programs. An illustration of this lack of leadership is that none of the recommendations made in the Matthews and Associates (1985) report, neither those related to changes in the existing space standards nor those related to the establishment of guidelines for measuring program input or output, have been inplemented by the Chancellor's Office.

In 1985, a selected group of administrators of California community college libraries and learning resource programs were called together at the California State Library to address the issue of lack of leadership at the state level. The solution proposed at this time was the establishment of a position for a specialist in the area of libraries and learning resources on the Chancellor's staff. It was thought that a knowledgeable person could provide the leadership necessary to help develop and maintain quality programs in the state. It was also thought that this person would enhance the visibility of libraries and learning resources programs in the Chancellor's Office, as well as increase communication between the state's library and learning resources program directors.

That same year, based on a proposal developed through the work of this committee, a Library Services and Construction Act Grant (LSCA) was awarded by the California State Library to the California Community College Chancellor's Office to fund such a position. After a grant period of three years, the position, Library Services Coordinator, became permanent in the Chancellor's Office. In addition to the establishment of a permanent position in the Chancellor's Office, there were two significant achievements accomplished through the leadership of the Library Services Coordinator during the grant years. The first was related to funding for library materials. The second was related to the development of standards for measuring learning resources programs.

In 1978, funding shifted from local districts to the state level, caused by the passage of a state law, known as Proposition 13, which limited the ability of cities, counties, and special districts to levy and collect property taxes, and severely impacted all aspects of learning resources programs. Some components were cut altogether, particularly television, graphic and audiovisual production, and instructional development. These areas have yet to fully recover. Library budgets for staffing and materials were seriously curtailed as well (Fisher, 1986; Hicks, 1984).

It is only recently that materials budgets have shown some improvement brought about by a one-time infusion of state bond money specifically earmarked for library materials. This special augmentation of funds was the result of a successful strategy developed by the library specialist in the

Chancellor's Office with input from the field. Fortunately, some local districts have continued this increased level of funding support. However, others have not, even though encouraged to do so by the Community College Chancellor's Office. Thus, because of the lack of statewide standards, there are still large discrepancies among materials budget allocations to individual college libraries. In fact, in 1988, the allocations ranged from $0.00 to $22.34 per student (Fisher, 1989, p. 2). This difference between the various colleges' level of support for learning resources once again highlighted, for library and learning resources administrators in the field, the need for some enforceable standard by which to measure programs in order to maintain quality in California community college library and learning resources programs.

III. Developing Output Measures for California Community Colleges: The Present Study

Because of the perceived need for enforceable standards to measure programs, a small committee of library and learning resources program administrators, working with the Library Services Coordinator, produced a proposal to hire a consultant to develop standards that could be adopted at the state level. As a result, in 1987, using funds from the LSCA grant, a consultant was hired to study if this would be feasible.

Specifically the contract stated the following objectives:

1) Propose performance standards and output measures on a phased in basis over a two year period that would address provision and use of services, print and non-print collections, staffing and access. This tool will measure performance and excellence in library services in support of the academic and instructional programs in the colleges. 2) List the criteria and rationale for minimum standards as provided for in Section 1801 of the State Education Code, and demonstrate the relation between the library function and the scope of instructional programs. 3) Discuss the appropriateness of adopting systemwide library standards in the event that a Statewide community college system is established in the future and propose types of performance measurements which would be useful or effective for the libraries in such a system. (Sherwood and Associates, 1987, p. 3)

Subsequently, another committee of library and learning resources program administrators was appointed by the Library Services Coordinator to work with the consulting firm, Sherwood and Associates. The Study Review Committee was charged with the responsibility of assisting the consultant with feedback and direction. Regular contact was maintained with the consultant by the committee chair and the coordinator at the Chancellor's Office in order to make sure that the report addressed all the issues identified in the contract.

The completed report to the Chancellor discussed all three objectives specified in the contract. Most were covered in a relatively cursory fashion, except for the major part of the report, which dealt with the development of the output measures to be used as a tool for measuring performance in the california community college learning resources programs. Table I lists the thirteen original output measures developed as a result of the work of Sherwood and Associates.

Ultimately, the consultant recommended that the thirteen output measures identified in the report be field tested by a sample group of colleges for a one-year period. After the test, the measures should be reevaluated and refined, if necessary, for statewide adoption.

This report, *Performance Measurement in California Community College Libraries and Learning Resources Centers* (Sherwood and Associates, 1987), was accepted by the Chancellor's Office. The output measures were pilot tested by 16 community colleges in Spring 1988. This test was organized by a committee established by the Library Services Coordinator. The results of the test were tabulated, and a meeting of program administrators was held to discuss the results.

Although several inadequacies were identified within the measures themselves, such as a need for clarifying the definitions and the directions,

Table I   The Thirteen Original Output Measures for California Community College Learning Resources Programs

---

1. Circulation per FTE[a] User
2. In-House Use per FTE User
3. Facilities Use per FTE User
4. Reference Transactions per FTE User
5. Library/LRC Orientation Participation Rate
6. Library Skills Course Completion Rate
7. Faculty Audiovisual Services (Hardware)
8. Faculty Audiovisual Services (Software)
9. Media Production per FTE Faculty
10. Title Fill Rate
11. Subject Fill Rate
12. Turnover Rate
13. Interlibrary Loan and Delayed Fill Rate

---

[a] FTE, Full-time equivalent.

the overall result of the pilot test was positive. The data collected during the pilot test were not analyzed, and no effort was made to summarize the written recommendations of the pilot group regarding the measures.

The initial process in the research for this study consisted of a review and analysis of the results of the pilot test to ascertain what changes needed to be made, if any, to the output measures. During this review and analysis, it was determined that three of the four measures reported as not being valuable were the same as those reported as having directions that were not clear. Because of this congruence, it was decided that the validity of these measures could most likely be established if the directions were made clear. On reviewing the responses to the open-ended questions, it was found that the problem with the remaining measure described as not being valuable was related to the sample size suggested to be collected in the measure, not to the measure itself. Most of the other suggestions for changes or modifications to the measures had to do with making the data collection easier.

After this initial review and analysis, a meeting was held in Spring 1990, with the members of the Library/Learning Resources Sub-Committee on Output Measures. This committee, appointed by the California Community College Chancellor's Office, was made up of a group of five professional librarians familiar with and interested in continuing the development of the output measures. It was composed of two learning resources program directors, one library dean, one library faculty member, and a representative from the Chancellor's Office. Two of the members of the committee represented Northern California, one, Central California, and two, Southern California.

At this initial meeting, the committee reviewed the pilot test summary data. As a result of this review, a major modification was made. Two of the output measures, 10 (Title Fill Rate) and 11 (Subject Fill Rate), had caused problems for a significant number of those who had participated in the pilot test. The pilot test data indicated that 33% of the respondents thought these output measures not valuable, 35% thought the data were too difficult to gather, and 20% thought the directions were confusing.

Since the committee thought the information intended to be gathered by these two output measures was important to learning resources and library program evaluation, a new output measure was developed to take the place of those that had been a problem. This new output measure 10 (User Success/Satisfaction Rate) is a survey designed to find out how well the collections are meeting the needs of the users by asking more specific questions regarding those needs.

In addition to a number of minor modifications suggested to make the output measures manual more useful, it was agreed that, since the original manual included forms for only some of the measures, data collection forms should be developed for all the measures and included in the survey.

A new survey instrument was developed to elicit responses to the revised manual. The colleges were surveyed regarding the usefulness and clarity of the output measures, if and how the measures would be used for evaluating learning resources programs in California community colleges, and whether there was still a need for the State of California to adopt standards for the community college library and learning resources programs.

The sample for the survey was the same group of 24 colleges selected to participate in the pilot test. A second group of 24 colleges was randomly selected by the Output Measures Committee from the remaining 3 groupings developed by the California Community College Chancellor's Office as being representative of California community colleges as a whole.

These groups are composed of all of the community colleges in California. At the time of the survey there were 107 community colleges. The Chancellor's groupings are arranged so that all types of the colleges are represented in each group: large, small, urban, rural, single-campus, and multi-campus.

The rationale for using the original group in the survey was that they had used the output measures manual, they were familiar with the process, and they had made the suggestions for most of the modifications of the instrument. The second group was added to help insure that the results of the survey were unbiased and to see if the manual and measures were perceived to be understandable and useful to a group that had not used them previously.

In all, 37 colleges out of a possible 48 participated in the survey. This gave a total participation rate of 77%. A breakdown of the two groups of participating colleges resulted in the following statistics. Of the pilot test group, 18 of the 22 colleges that agreed to participate actually returned the survey, a return rate of 82%. Of the new group, 19 of the 20 colleges that agreed to participate actually returned the survey, a return rate of 95%.

IV. Analysis of the Data

The data are analyzed and discussed in three parts. The first part discusses the responses of the two groups to the survey on the output measures themselves. The second part discusses the responses to the questions regarding whether the output measures would be used and how they would be used. The third discusses the responses to the question of whether the State still needs to adopt minimum standards for learning resources programs.

A. Survey Part One: Perceived Usefulness and Clarity of the Output Measures

For each of the twelve output measures (see Table II) the participants were asked to respond to the following statements:

1. I think this measure (no. _____) is/is not a useful one.
2. Gathering the data will be: a. Too difficult, b. Difficult but possible, or c. Not difficult.
3. The directions are clear/confusing.
4. The definitions are clear/confusing.
5. The directions for calculating the statistics are clear/confusing.
6. The sample size is appropriate for this measure: yes/no.

A brief description of each of the twelve output measures is included in the Appendix.

The responses of both groups to statements 1–6 for each of the output measures were tabulated and analyzed using *StatView SE+Graphics* (Feldman, Gagnon, Hofmann, and Simpson, 1988) software on a Macintosh SE. A frequency distribution was computed to determine the percent of responses to the various elements in the survey.

The Output Measures Subcommittee accepted an 80% and above positive response to each of the elements in the survey as an indicator that the output measure did not need to be revised. The reason for this decision was the committee's understanding that because of variations in experience, size,

Table II The Twelve Output Measures for California Community College Learning Resources Programs

1. Circulation per FTE[a] User
2. In-House Use per FTE User
3. Facilities Use per FTE User
4. Reference Transactions per FTE User
5. Library/LRC Orientation Participation Rate
6. Library Skills Course Completion Rate
7. Faculty Audiovisual Services (Hardware)
8. Faculty Audiovisual Services (Software)
9. Media Production per FTE Faculty
10. User Success/Satisfaction Rate
11. Turnover Rate
12. Interlibrary Loan and Delayed Fill Rate

[a] FTE, Full-time equivalent.

and organization in the California community colleges, not every responder would approve of or could use each output measure, and that differences in individual responses did not necessarily mean that the measure needed revision. Based on this consideration, it seemed reasonable that if 80% or more of those responding thought positively about the various elements of the survey, there was no need to revise the output measure.

Table III shows the total percentage of responses to each element of the survey for each of the output measures. It also shows the number of responses to each. These data were used to determine which elements in each output measure needed to be revised.

The following six statements relate to the usefulness and clarity of the twelve output measures:

Statement 1. I think this measure (no.) is/is not a useful one. Only one of the output measures was judged to be useful by less than 80% of those responding. Output Measure 6 (Library Skills Course Completion Rate), received a positive response from 27 (79%) of the colleges. Seven (21%) of the colleges judged this measure not useful to them.

The reasons given in the comment section of the survey for Measure 6 not being useful were mixed. Apparently, three of the colleges did not have a formal library course similar to that described in the output measure, one thought that the statistics gathered would be too small a number to be meaningful, another thought the wrong population was measured, one thought the course description should be enough, as the course was not mandatory, and one thought there were too many variables among courses to provide meaningful statistics.

If the three colleges that judged this output measure not useful because they did not offer such a course are removed from the sample, the percent useful response is increased to 87%, well within the 80% guideline set by the subcommittee for not revising the output measures. It was therefore decided that this measure did not need to be revised.

Statement 2. Gathering the data will be: a. Too difficult, b. Difficult but possible, or c. Not difficult. Because this item in the survey offered three choices rather than two, the percentage responses were analyzed as follows. Two of the three available choices were judged to be positive, and one negative. In analyzing the percent responses, therefore, the two responses considered positive, "not difficult" and "difficult but possible," were added together to determine the total percent positive response. As an example, for Output Measure 1, the respondents selected "difficult but possible" 19% of the time and "not difficult" 81% of the time. When these responses were totaled, the positive response was 100%. None of the measures received less than 80% positive response when these calculations were completed for all the measures.

Table III   Percent Responses to Question Regarding the Usefulness and Clarity of the Output Measures

Output measure	1	2	3	4	5	6
This measure						
is useful	97	92	86	92	91	79
is not useful	3	8	13	8	11	21
$n =$	37	37	37	37	35	34
Gathering data is						
too difficult	—	11	11	3	—	—
difficult but possible	19	51	32	27	6	—
not difficult	81	38	57	70	94	100
$n =$	37	37	37	37	36	33
Directions are						
clear	97	100	97	100	97	100
confusing	3	—	3	—	3	—
$n =$	37	36	37	37	36	33
Definitions are						
clear	92	100	97	95	100	97
confusing	8	—	3	5	—	3
$n =$	37	36	37	37	36	33
Directions for calculating statistics are						
clear	91	100	95	100	97	100
confusing	9	—	5	—	3	—
$n =$	35	36	37	36	36	33
Sample size is						
appropriate	78	78	78	85	97	91
not appropriate	22	22	22	15	3	9
$n =$	36	36	37	34	35	32

Statement 3. The directions are clear/confusing. Eighty-eight percent or more of the respondents judged the directions clear for all of the measures.

Statement 4. The definitions are clear/confusing. All of the measures were judged to have clear definitions by more than 82% of the respondents.

Statement 5. The directions for calculating the statistics are clear/confusing. All of the measures were judged to have clear directions for calculating the statistics.

Statement 6. The sample size is appropriate for this measure: yes/no. Even though it was suggested throughout the manual that a college that collected annual data should use this data in computing the statistics, the question relating to the sampling method used in the output measures manual was a problem for four of the measures. The sample sizes for Output Measure 1 (Circulation per FTE [full-time equivalent] User), Output Measure 2 (In-

Output measure	7	8	9	10	11	12
This measure						
is useful	90	85	84	94	88	82
is not useful	9	15	16	6	12	18
$n =$	33	33	32	35	33	34
Gathering data is						
too difficult	—	6	19	8	6	10
difficult but possible	9	13	53	70	19	23
not difficult	91	81	28	22	75	68
$n =$	33	32	32	37	36	31
Directions are						
clear	100	100	88	94	89	97
confusing	—	—	12	6	11	3
$n =$	33	33	33	35	36	33
Definitions are						
clear	94	88	82	94	86	97
confusing	6	12	18	6	14	3
$n =$	33	33	33	36	36	33
Directions for calculating statistics are						
clear	100	94	85	92	86	97
confusing	—	6	15	8	14	3
$n =$	33	33	33	37	35	33
Sample size is						
appropriate	88	91	79	91	91	94
not appropriate	12	9	21	9	9	6
$n =$	32	32	33	35	33	31

house Use per FTE User), and Output Measure 3 (Facilities Use per FTE User), were judged not appropriate by 22% of the responders.

The suggested sampling technique is the same method suggested for use by both academic and public libraries in Van House, Weil, and McClure, (1990) and Van House, Lynch, McClure, Zweizig, and Rodger (1987). Because the sampling technique has been validated by use over time, and because the sample is a recommended minimum number, the subcommittee decided that rather than change the suggested sample size, more emphasis should be given in the manual to the fact that the suggested sample is the minimum recommended size. The colleges could collect more data if they felt the need. Most of the comments made indicated that those who did not think the sample size appropriate either collected annual data or would like to use two or more sampling periods rather than one.

The sample size for Output Measure 9 (Media Production per FTE Faculty) was deemed not appropriate by 21% of the respondents. Of the six colleges that thought the sample inappropriate, only two suggested another sample size. Both suggested the data be collected over an entire semester rather than for a one-month period as suggested in the manual. Since the same suggested is the minimum recommended size and because the other four colleges did not comment on why the suggested sample was not appropriate, the subcommittee decided not to change the minimum sampling method suggested for this output measure, but decided to emphasize in the manual the fact that the suggested sampling size is a minimum.

Of the remaining measures, six were judged to have appropriate sample sized by 91% and above. The remaining two were judged appropriate by 88% and 85%, respectively.

B. Survey Part Two: Potential Uses of the Output Measures

In addition to the survey regarding the individual measures, two questions were asked. The first question related to the willingness of the colleges to use the output measures in order to evaluate their programs. The second question asked the respondents to place in rank order five possible uses for the output measures in program evaluation.

Question 1. Will you use these output measures if it is not mandated by the Chancellor's Office? The responses were tabulated and a frequency distribution computed to obtain the percent response to the question. Thirty-six colleges, 97% of the sample, responded to the question. Of those, 61% responded yes, 22% responded no, and 17% responded that they would use some of the output measures.

Question 2. How will you use the results obtained from the output measures? The respondents were asked to place in rank order the five possible responses identified in the survey by numbering them from 1 through 5, 1 being the highest. To determine the rank order of the five possible responses to the question regarding use of the output measures, the mean for each use was computed. The rank order and mean of the five possible choices is presented in Table IV.

Table IV   Rank Order for Use of Output Measures with Computed Means

Use	Mean
1 Developing baseline data for comparing performance over several years	2.333
2 Program or service justification	2.469
3 To find out where improvements in existing program or services can be made	2.515
4 Accreditation self-study	3.375
5 To develop data for comparing across libraries of similar size and program	4.312

C. Survey Part Three: Perceived Value of State-Adopted Standards for Learning Resources Programs

This question was asked because of the long-term interest of California Community College Library and Learning Resources Program administrators in standards. It was also asked because the contract of the consultant originally called for the development of standards rather than output measures. Because standards were not developed, it seemed appropriate to ask whether there was still a perceived need for California to adopt standards for library and learning resources programs.

Question 1. Do you still think that the State needs to adopt minimum standards for learning resources programs in order to maintain quality programs? All 37 colleges responded to this question. Of those, 33 (89%) responded yes. Only four (11%) responded no. Overall, the data show that most learning resources program administrators still think that the only way to ensure quality programs is to have minimum standards adopted by the State.

V. Discussion of the Data

The usefulness and clarity of the revised output measures were validated by this study. No further revisions were made to them as a result of the survey. Some minor editorial revisions were made to the data collection manual based on suggestions written in the manual or in the comment section by the responders. These suggestions made the manual more clear or consistent. Most of the other written comments were related to the differences among learning resources programs at the colleges and how this would affect the use and validity of the data.

A. Willingness to Use the Output Measures

Of the total responses, 61% indicated that they would use the output measures to evaluate their programs on a voluntary basis. An additional 17% responded that they would use some of the measures voluntarily, and 22% responded that they would not use the measures to evaluate their programs unless they were mandated to do so. Even though the literature on program evaluation documents the need for data to be collected for a variety of reasons (Daniel, 1976; DeProspo and Liesner, 1975; Feldman, 1974; Lancaster, 1988), 22% of California community college learning resources program administrators surveyed are not convinced of the value of using the output measures. This is somewhat surprising in light of the fact that the California Community College System has recognized the need for an ongoing program review of all instructional programs. It is also surprising because the responses regarding the usefulness of the measures ranged above 80% for all but one of the measures.

Whether the reluctance to use the measures is because the responding administrators do not believe in the need to evaluate or document the quality of their programs, or whether it is related to the staff time and expense involved, or to the difficulties inherent in collecting and analyzing data, was not answered by this study.

B. Possible Uses for the Output Measures

Of the five possible purposes identified in the survey for evaluating programs, four are identified in Lancaster (1988, p. 7). They are: (1) to establish a base or "benchmark" for evaluating performance in order to establish comparative data for evaluating change; (2) to establish a database for comparison across libraries, using an established standard; (3) as a justification of the service; and (4) to find out where improvements can be made in existing services. A fifth purpose, accreditation self-study, was added because accreditation is a regularly occurring activity in the colleges for which data are collected.

The discussion of the rank order of uses for the output measures is organized around each of the possible uses. The possible uses of the output measures are not necessarily mutually exclusive, but once the data are collected and analyzed, they can be used for a variety of purposes, including each of the five selected to be ranked in this study. Collecting data for comparing across institutions, the least favored use, presents the most interesting opportunity for discussion. It is, therefore, discussed first.

Collecting data for comparing across institutions was ranked last. Some indication of why this was the least popular use was evidenced in the comments of the responders. There were concerns expressed about using comparative data, which would be like comparing "apples to oranges" because of differing interpretations of the manual, and differing organizational structures at the colleges, or size, or location. This concern is evident even though the majority of responders judged the directions clear, the definitions clear, and the directions for calculating the statistics clear for all the output measures. The fear of misinterpretation of data is apparently strong for some library administrators, especially if the data are expected to be reported outside of individual programs or institutions.

This concern or fear probably contributed in one way or another to the ranking of the purposes identified for using the data. The top four rankings were given to either in-house or within-institution use of the data. These uses can be presented and controlled by the collector. There is a fear that raw data reported to an outside agency can be manipulated and/or misinterpreted. There is also a fear that reported data could be potentially dangerous, if used for the wrong purpose.

Because of these results, it seems unlikely that the data collected when using the output measures manual would be used for comparing across libraries of similar size and program. It is possible, however, that if there were an established standard of comparative output data for community college learning resources and library programs, as there is for input data, this fear would likely be eliminated. Both Matthews and Associates (1985) and Sherwood and Associates (1987) discussed the need to collect data over time in order to develop standards. While their discussion related to input standards, output standards could be just as valuable to administrators of learning resources and library programs.

The possible use ranked first was developing baseline data for comparing performance over several years. This use could be viewed as similar but potentially less threatening than comparison across institutions. Baseline data of this type can be used to show how well or how poorly a particular program is doing in relation to a number of variables including input measures relating to budget and staffing. For instance, if the budget is reduced and the outputs go down, then there is documentation to show the effects of budget reductions on the level of service.

Program or service justification was ranked second in order of importance of use. This reason for evaluating is mentioned frequently in the literature on evaluation, particularly in regard to accountability and competition for funds (Apple, 1978; Cronin, 1985; Daniel, 1976; DeProspo, 1973; Hamburg et al., 1972). Given the experience of California Community College Library and Learning Resources program funding, it is not difficult to see why this reason ranked high in importance among the program administrators surveyed.

Ranked third in order of importance in the survey was to find out where improvements in existing program or services could be made. These reasons are also mentioned frequently in the literature (Daniel, 1976; DeProspo and Leisner, 1975; Feldman, 1974). A program administrator who was not sure of the quality of a particular component of service, such as Reference Service, could use output data on reference to see if and how much the service was being used. A treatment intended to improve the service could then be devised, and new output data could be collected to determine if improvement in the use of the service resulted from the treatment.

Accreditation self-study was selected next to last in the ranking of the possible uses for the output measures. Since all Community College Learning Resources programs are evaluated during accreditation self-study, it is somewhat surprising that this ranked low. Possible only those colleges preparing for self-study saw the value of the output measures for this purpose. Another possibility is that the other uses ranked higher by the responders were more compelling than institutional self-study because accreditation is not necessarily seen as a vehicle for making change.

In any case, the fact that 78% of the administrators responding to this survey will use some or all of the output measures to evaluate their programs is indicative of the perceived value of the output measures. The rank order of the five possible uses is indicative of the reasons these same administrators see for using the output measures to evaluate their programs.

C. Perceived Value of State-Adopted Standards for Learning Resource Programs

Standards and guidelines have been considered appropriate measures for evaluating community and junior college libraries since the 1930s (Wallace, 1972). Traditionally, libraries gathered and reported data related to a variety of resources or inputs that the library had, such as the amount of budget, the size of the collection, and numbers of staff. Because there are a number of problems associated with this type of data, including number inflation (DeProspo, 1975) and the lack of data that measure performance (Bommer and Chorba, 1982; Hamburg et al., 1972; Lancaster, 1977), there has been a movement in the library profession to develop means to measure the output or achievements of the services provided in libraries (Van House et al., 1987, 1990).

This movement from standards for input measurement to output measurement led to the development of the output measures for the California Community Colleges. The question regarding standards was asked to determine whether community college library and learning resources program administrators perceived that there was a need for standards to ensure quality programs. From the responses of the sample groups of program administrators to this survey question, it is apparent that standards are still thought to be valuable. Only four (11%) of the total 37 responded no.

No comments were made that clarified why the need for standards is still perceived to be there, but given the past experience of library and learning resources program administrators, particularly in regard to funding (Fisher, 1986; Hicks, 1984), it is not surprising that this is the case. Even given the fact that a new funding mechanism based on programs, of which learning resources is one, has been adopted by the State of California for the community colleges, and that the funding for libraries is now driven by the ALA (ALA, ACRL, AECT, 1990) standards for community college learning resources programs, most think that there needs to be some guarantee of a basic level of support for their programs at the local level. That the need is perceived to be there is most likely because there is no mandate or enforcement mechanism in the law to ensure that the colleges support learning resources or library programs at the same level the state funds them. Clearly, library and learning resources program administrators think that in order to receive the necessary funding for their programs, there needs to be some help at the state level.

VI. Summary and Conclusions

The usefulness and clarity of the revised output measures were validated by this study. No major revisions were made to them as a result of the survey. Some minor editorial revisions were made to the data-collection manual based on suggestions written in the manual or in the comment section on the survey form by the responders. These suggestions made the manual more clear or consistent. Most of the other written comments were related to the differences among learning resources programs at the colleges and how this would affect the use and validity of the data.

The purpose of the study reported in this chapter was to develop output measures and a data-collection manual for California Community College Learning Resources Programs. Two groups of community colleges in California were surveyed regarding the usefulness and clarity of the output measures. Additionally, two questions were asked regarding whether the colleges would use the measures to evaluate their programs and how they would use them. A third question regarding whether there was a need for the adoption of statewide standards was also asked.

It is possible to formulate conclusions from the data collected from the sample of colleges surveyed. The following conclusions are drawn:

1. The usefulness and clarity of the output measures manual was validated by this study.

2. The data indicate that 78% of community college learning resources program administrators will use all or some of the output measures to evaluate their programs whether it is mandated or not.

3. Most community college library and learning resources program administrators in California think that it is more valuable to use data in-house or within the institution, than to use it for comparing across libraries of similar size and program.

4. Community college learning resources and library program administrators agree strongly that California needs to adopt minimum standards for learning resources programs in order to maintain quality programs.

Appendix: A Brief Description of the Twelve Output Measures[1]

1. Circulation per Full-Time Equivalent User. This output measure determines the average number of circulation transactions per full-time equiva-

[1]The Output Measures Manual has been published and is available for purchase through the Learning Resources Association of the California Community Colleges, 4000 Suisun Valley Road, Suisun, California 94585-14341.

alent (FTE) user per academic year (i.e., 35 weeks, if your institution has 175 instructional days). Circulation transactions include all items charged out for use within or outside the Library/LRC (books, periodicals, microforms, reserve materials, audiovisual programs disseminated to student stations within the Library/LRC, etc.). The exception is media hardware and software checked out to faculty for classroom use, which is measured elsewhere (see Output Measures 7 and 8).

"Full-time equivalent user" includes all the students, faculty, and staff who make up the college population. The term is used here as a standard unit of measure to allow for more precise measurement of collection utilization over time within the institution and, in addition, to allow for cross-comparison with other Library/LRCs, if desired.

2. In-House Use per FTE User. The in-house use measure estimates the number of items used in the Library/LRC that are not checked out in relation to the college population. Examples of items used in-house include books, periodicals, microforms, and AV materials available directly to the user. Items counted in Output Measure 1. Circulation per FTE User are, of course, not counted here.

3. Facilities Use per FTE User. This output measure estimates the number of users who come into the facility to make use of one or more of the services provided by the Library/LRC. Users may enter the facility to complete an assignment, view a telecourse, or other instructional purposes, seek reference assistance, or simply to find a quiet place to study or relax. When considered along with the other output measures in this group, the facilities utilization output measure provides useful information when evaluating the total learning resources program.

4. Reference Transactions per FTE User. This output measure determines the average number of reference transactions per full-time equivalent user for the academic year (35 weeks). The definition of reference transaction for use in this output measure is taken from the *Library Data Collection Handbook*, Mary Jo Lynch, editor (Chicago, ALA, 1981) and is as follows:

> REFERENCE TRANSACTION: An information contact which involves the use, recommendation, interpretation, or instruction in the use of one or more information sources, or knowledge of such sources, by a member of the reference/information staff.[2] Information sources include (1) print and nonprint materials; (2) machine-readable data bases, including bibliographic, full text, and numeric; (3) Library bibliographic records, excluding circulation records; (4) other libraries and institutions; and (5) persons both inside and outside the library. A question answered through utilization of information gained from previous consultation of such sources is considered a reference transaction even if the source is not consulted again. A contact which includes both reference and directional service is one reference transaction. Duration should not be an element in determining whether a transaction is reference or directional.

[2]"Reference/information staff" means librarians, other media professionals or technical staff who provide service.

5. Library/LRC Orientation Participation Rate. Library/LRC Orientation Participation Rate measures the number of students receiving orientation to the Library/LRC as a percentage of the student population.

Orientation is a planned activity whereby students receive an overview of either the full range of the collections and services available, or some aspect of the learning resources program at the college. Examples of such orientation experiences include group orientation lectures and/or tours of the Library; the LRC only; the media center only; group bibliographic instruction on how to research a writing or other assignment. Self-guiding audiotape tours or slide-tape presentations to a class (or similar AV program) are also counted.

One-to-one instruction that occurs during the reference interview is not counted here; it is counted in Output Measure 4: Reference Transactions per FTE User.

6. Library Skills Course Completion Rate. This output measure determines the number of students completing a Library/LRC skills/research course, either in-class or self-paced, in proportion to the FTE student population. The result is expressed as a percentage.

The number of units credit received or the level of the course (introductory or advanced) is not a factor here, only that a formal program of instruction was completed. Specialized Library/LRC technology, instructional media technology, or similar courses with a vocational objective are not counted.

7. Faculty Audiovisual Services (Hardware). This output measure determines the number of hardware items delivered or charged out to faculty by the Library/LRC for instructional purposes in proportion to the FTE faculty population.

8. Faculty Audiovisual Services (Software). The audiovisual software measure determines the number of items delivered or charged out to faculty for instructional purposes in proportion to the faculty population. Audiovisual software includes films and video programs owned and managed by the Library/LRC or rented from outside sources. Other examples include audiotapes, computer software, transparencies, and media programs transmitted from the Library/LRC to the classroom.

9. Media Production per FTE Faculty. This output measure provides an estimate of media production output in proportion to the faculty and administrative staff population. Examples of media production include a poster, a brochure, off-air audio or video taping, and a photograph or original illustration for a lab manual. Production time can vary from an hour or less to a month or more.

10. User Success/Satisfaction Rate: Description. User Success/Satisfaction Rate provides a useful indicator of how successful users think they are in finding the information or physical item they need. A Library/LRC survey has been developed to collect this information. These issues are addressed by question (1) which tells you what they were looking for and question (2) which tells you whether they found it.

Additional questions are asked in the survey to determine whether users are satisfied with what they find, why they are looking for the information, who the users are, and whether they ask for help in finding the needed information. These are also very important questions, but must be analyzed separately from the success rate, which is reflected by the total "Yes" responses to question 2 on Library/LRC survey form. You need not use questions 3–6 on the survey to collect data for this output measure unless desired. (See Further Analysis for details.)

11. Turnover Rate. The turnover rate output measure provides a useful indicator of the activity level of the Library/LRC's collection. Specifically, it determines the average number of uses per cataloged item in the collection. The significance of this measure is perhaps best understood by comparing the community college Library/LRC to the large research Library. Research libraries have relatively low turnover rates because of the larger proportion of less often used materials in their collections. However, community college Library/LRC collections, because they are designed to serve primarily the ongoing instructional program in the classroom, have smaller more active collections and therefore higher turnover rates.

12. Interlibrary Loan and Delayed Fill Rate. The interlibrary/LRC loan output measure is concerned with the extent to which the Library/LRC fills requests for items not immediately available within the facility. Specifically, Interlibrary Loan and Delayed Fill Rate measures the number of items the Library/LRC makes available to the user within two weeks of request, compared to the total number requested. These are items that were requested through a hold, recall, search, in-process expediting, or interlibrary/LRC loan procedure. All types of media are counted, except film and video tape rentals, which are counted elsewhere in Output Measure 8: Faculty Audiovisual Services (Software).

References

Accrediting Commission for Community and Junior Colleges, Western Association of Schools and Colleges (1987). *Handbook of Accreditation*. (ERIC Document Reproduction Service No. ED301298 JC880605).

Allen, Kenneth W., and Allen, Loren (1973). *Organization and Administration of the Learning Resources Center in the Community College*. Linnet, Hamden, Connecticut.

American Library Association, Association of College and Research Libraries (1979). Quantitative standards for two-year learning resources programs. *College and Research Libraries News* **40**(2A), 69–73.

American Library Association, Association of College and Research Libraries, American Association of Community and Junior Colleges, Association of Educational Communication and Technology (1972). Guidelines for two-year college learning resources programs. *College and Research Libraries News* **33**(7B), 305–315.

American Library Association, Association of College and Research Libraries, Association of Educational Communication and Technology (1982a). Guidelines for two-year learning resources programs: revised, part one. *College and Research Libraries News* **43**(1), 5–10.

American Library Association, Association of College and Research Libraries, Association of Educational communication and Technology (1982b). Guidelines for two-year college learning resources programs: revised, part two. *College and Research Libraries News* **43**(2), 45–49.

American Library Association, Association of College and Research Libraries, Association of Educational Communication and Technology (1990). Standards for two-year college learning resources programs. *College and Research Libraries News* **51**(8), 757–767.

Apple, Elizabeth (1978). Survey of a learning resources center: Facilities and use. In *Quantitative Measurement and Dynamic Library Service.* (Ching-chih Chen, ed.), pp. 185–199. Oryx Press, Phoenix, Arizona.

Bender, David R. (1980). *Learning Resources and the Instructional Program in Community Colleges.* Library Professional Publications, Hamden, Connecticut.

Bierbaum, Esther Green (1990). The two-year college LRC: Promise deferred? *College and Research Libraries* **51**(6), 531–537.

Bommer, Michael R. W., and Chorba, Ronald W. (1984). Planning, decision tasks and information needs. In *Issues in Library Management: A Reader for the Professional Librarian*, pp. 1–10. Knowledge Industry Publications, Inc., White Plains, New York.

California Community Colleges Board of Governors (1984). (Action No. 840331, March), 1107 9th Street, Sacramento, California 95814.

California Postsecondary Education Commission (1974). *Standards for Community College Library Facilities.* (Report 74-2). 1020 12th Street, Sacramento, California 95814.

Cronin, Mary J. (1985). "Performance Measurement for Public Services in Academic and Research Libraries." (Occasional Paper No. 9). Office of Management Studies, Association of Research Libraries, Washington, D.C.

Dale, Doris Cruger (1977). The community college library in the mid-1970's. *College and Research Libraries* **38**(5), 404–411.

Daniel, Evelyn H. (1976). Performance measures for school librarians; Complexities and potential. In *Advances in Librarianship* **76,** pp. 1–51. Academic Press, New York.

Dennison, Lynn C. (1978). The Organization of library and media services in community colleges. *College and Research Libraries* **39,**(2), 123–129.

DeProspo, Ernest R. (1975, Summer). Potential limits and abuses of evaluation. *School Media Quarterly*, 302–302.

DeProspo, Ernest, R., Altman, Ellen, Beasley, Kenneth E. (1973). *Performance Measures for Public Libraries.* Chicago: American Library Association.

DeProspo, Ernest, and Liesner, James W. (1975, Summer). Media program evaluation: A working framework. *School Media Quarterly*, 289–301.

Drucker, Peter F. (1973, Fall). Managing the public service institution. *The Public Interest* **33,** 43–60.

Feldman, Daniel S., Jr., Gagnon, Jim, Hofmann, Rich, and Simpson, Joe (1988). *StatView SE+ Graphics the Solution for Data Analysis and Presentation Graphics* (computer program). Abacus Concepts, Berkeley, California.

Feldman, Nancy C. (1974, January). Commentary. *Library Trends, Evaluation of Library Services* **22,**(3), 395–401.

Fisher, Russell (1986, April). California community college libraries: Spiraling downward. *Wilson Library Bulletin*, 15–19.

Fisher, Russell (1989, October). Libraries post gains in print budgets. *California Library Association, Community College Librarians Chapter, Newsletter*, 1–2.

Genung, Harriet, and Wallace, James (1972). The emergence of the community college library. In *Advances in Librarianship* **93**, pp. 70–75. Academic Press, New York.

Hamburg, Morris, Ramist, Leonard E., and Bommer, Michael R. W. (1972). Library objectives and performance measures and their use in decision making. *The Library Quarterly* **42**(1), 97–128.

Hicks, Warren B. (1984). *Survey on the Effects of State Budget Cuts on Community College Learning Resource Centers: A Narrative Survey.* (ERIC Document Reproduction Service No. ED244662 JC840244).

Homer, Eleanor M. (1930). A junior college measuring stick. *American Library Association Bulletin* **XXIV**, 296–297.

House, Ernest. (1978). Assumptions underlying evaluation models. *Educational Researcher*, **7**, 4–12.

Lancaster, F. W. (1977). *The Measurement and Evaluation of Library Services.* Information Resources Press, Washington, D.C.

Lancaster, F. W. (1988). *If You Want to Evaluate your Library . . ..* University of Illinois, Graduate School of Library and Information Science, Champaign, Illinois.

Learning Resources Association of the California Community Colleges (1978). *Facilities Guidelines for Learning Resources Center.* 4000 Suisun Valley Road, Suisun, California 94585.

Learning Resources Association of the California Community Colleges (1980). *Personnel and Materials Guidelines for Learning Resources Programs in Community Colleges.* 4000 Suisun Valley Road, Suisun, California, 94585.

Matthews, J., and Associates (1985). *A Review of Library Space Standards for the California Community Colleges.* A report presented to the Chancellor's Office, California Community Colleges. Chancellor's Office Library, 1107 9th Street, Sacramento, California 95814.

Peterson, Gary T. (1975). *The Learning Center: a Sphere for Non-Traditional Approaches to Education.* Linnet Books, Hamden, Connecticut.

Reeves, Pamela (1973). Junior college libraries enter the seventies. *College and Research Libraries* **34**, 7–15.

Sherwood and Associates (1987). *Performance Measurement in California Community College Libraries and Learning Resources Centers: A Report to the Chancellor's Office, California Community Colleges.* Chancellor's Office Library, 1107, 9th Street, Sacramento, California 95814.

Simas, Robert J. (1983). *Assessment System for the Evaluation of Learning Resources Programs in Community Colleges.* Learning Resources Association of the California Community Colleges, 4000 Suisun Valley road, Suisun, California 94585.

Terwilliger, Gloria (1983, Summer). Evaluating the role of the learning resources center. *Community and Junior College Libraries* **1**,(4), 23–25.

Title 5, California. *Code of Regulations*, Section 57030.

Van House, Nancy, Lynch, Mary Jo, McClure, Charles R., Zweizig, Douglas L., and Rodger, Eleanor Jo (1987). *Output Measures for Public Libraries: A Manual of Standardized Procedures.* American Library Association, Chicago, Illinois.

Van House, Nancy, Weil, Beth, and McClure, Charles R. (1990). *Measuring Academic Library Performance: A Practical Approach.* American Library Association, Chicago, Illinois.

Viet, Fritz (1975). *The Community College Library.* Greenwood Press, Westport, Connecticut.

Wallace, James O. (1972). The practical meaning of standards. In *Quantitative Methods in Librarianship: Standards, Research, Management, Contributions in Librarianship and Information Science* (Vol. 4) (Irene Braden Hoadley and Alice S. Clark, eds.), pp. 31–38. Greenwood Press, Westport, Connecticut.

Wallace, James O. (1976). Newcomer to the academic library scene: The two year library/learning center. *College and Research Libraries* **37**, 503–513.

Wilhelm, Mary Lou (Spring 1986). Evaluating the quality of learning resources programs in community colleges. *Community & Junior College Libraries* **4**,(3), 17–25.

New Patterns for Scholarly and Business Communication in Denmark

Helge Clausen
State and University Library
DK-8000 Århus
Århus, Denmark

I. Introduction

In the 1980s a convergence between computer science and communication research became visible in many fields of human enterprise. One of the main issues of the 1990s is the completion of integration in the computer/communication area, forming the infrastructure for the future information society. A common trend toward the year 2000 may be formulated in this way (Clausen, 1992):

> Computer *hardware* will continue to grow in capacity, efficiency and integration, while physical size and prices will continue to decrease.
>
> The *software* industry will continue to produce new types of tools for an increasing number of purposes since prices seem to have stabilized. Artificial intelligence, expert systems, groupware, multimedia systems, hypertext systems, etc., will become prevalent in many areas of human life in the '90s, from individual work in the home to automated production.
>
> *Telecommunication* costs are generally decreasing, which will encourage an increase in use (Anderla and Dunning, 1987). The growth of non-voice data transmission is app. 20–25% annually on average worldwide. It is reported that electronic mail may be sent fifty times more cheaply than ordinary mail. It is expected that when all offices are equipped with word processors, e-mail may replace all postal services in the business community. Tens of millions of public and private electronic mailboxes already exist worldwide; the number is expected to grow by 40% annually in the years to come. . . . Electronic Document Interchange (EDI) has recently experienced a breakthrough especially in business communication.

A technical precondition for this development is the undiminished implementation of networks, which is generally believed will take place in the years to come, at least in the western world. Technically, the ISDN (Integrated Services Digital Network) will be the "motorway" of digital communication in the 1990s. In this intelligent network integration between speech, data, text, and video services will be possible. According to the European Conference of Postal and Telecommunications Administration (CEPT) (1992), the year 1993 will see a great number of international ISDN connections mainly between countries in the western world. The largest electronic network in the world is the Internet, which has about 5–8 million users in the academic world. A recent trend is the opening of user-paid Internet services for commercial traffic, companies registering as commercial organizations on the Internet, and public e-mail services adding Internet gateways to their networks (Arnum, 1992). This development will, of course, be of great benefit to the academic and the business worlds.

Another precondition is further development in information science and communication studies, which may imply a paradigm shift from the predominant classic communication model by Shannon and Weaver to a nonlinear, holistic-dynamic concept, for example, the so-called *Convergence Model* by Kincaid and colleagues (Rogers and Kincaid, 1981). The most promising concept is CSCW (Computer-Supported Cooperative Work), which is believed will revolutionize most information work when implemented on a wide scale.

This development will be of fundamental importance for all information professionals (librarians, information specialists, information brokers, etc.). In the 1980s the library and information world saw many types of information technology being implemented. Work routines have changed. New jobs have been created. As it has been shown (Clausen, 1990a), a whole set of new professional challenges has arisen (new types of users, new subjects, new categories of information, new ways of work, information overload, etc.). Moreover, the question of quality in information work has been debated increasingly during the last few years. In Europe some efforts have been made in order to prepare for development and implementation of certified quality systems according to the ISO 9000 series in libraries and information services, as reported by Johannsen (1992a,b). When such systems are introduced, they will influence the content of traditional information work to an extent that only a few people will realize.

In particular, parts of the academic and business worlds have taken computerized information technology and telecommunication into use. Consequently, these two groups of advanced users (as seen from a library point of view) may put forward claims for advanced services not yet implemented or even developed. The traditions of different information professionals will take different steps to meet the expectations of advanced academics and business people. For a contemporary account of business information seen from a managerial perspective see, for example, Cashmore and Lyall (1991).

As an example of how to cope with these complex problems and how to prepare for the information profession's near future, we will focus on the situation in Denmark, a Scandinavian country influenced by its two larger neighbors, Germany to the south and England to the west.

II. The Library and Information Sector in Denmark

Being one of the small countries in Europe, Denmark occupies an important role as being the only Scandinavian country that at the moment is a member of the European Economic Community (EEC). Traditionally, Denmark has strong relations to the other Nordic countries (Norway, Sweden, Finland), all of which have decided to apply for EEC membership within the next few years. In this connection Denmark has an important role to play regarding the unification of Europe. A short view of the information market situation in the Nordic countries is given by Clausen (1990b).

Denmark may serve as an example of a highly developed country regarding the level of public service, living standards, use of advanced information technology, telecommunication, and professional education. Computer literacy is generally high. According to a recent Delphi study (Clausen, 1992), in 1996 90% of all Danish pupils who have completed ninth grade will have acquired a user's knowledge of PCs. Three years later they will have acquired the same degree of competence in electronic information retrieval. In spite of the fact that Denmark has a population of only 5 million, it has made substantial contributions in science, technology, literature, and art, as well as other disciplines.

Telecommunication networks are well developed in Denmark. For instance, according to the EEC Information Market Observatory (1992), Denmark will have the highest number of ISDN lines in 1994 (24.5 per 1000 inhabitants; EEC average: 15.7 per 1000 inhabitants). Recently, Denmark has invested in a series of activities and projects in eastern Europe, the Baltics, and the CIS (Harrington, 1992): "Denmark's geographical location and access to a large network of international telecommunications links makes Denmark a natural telecommunications hub for traffic between East and West."

The library and information sector in Denmark differs from what is known in many other countries such as England and the United States. The most important characteristic is the almost total absence of private information brokers. This fact may be seen as a consequence of a long tradition of having a strong publicly supported library system, which has deemed it a matter of honor to place free information at the public's disposal.

There are four sections in the Danish library system: (1) academic and special libraries; (2) public libraries; (3) school libraries; and (4) private (i.e., company) libraries. Academic and special libraries normally go under the common heading of "research libraries."

A. Research Libraries

The majority of the research libraries are parts of other institutions, mainly of institutions for higher education. Some of them constitute semiautonomous units within a larger setting, while a few are independent institutions. Among these we find some of the largest and most important in the country. As a general rule, the research libraries are funded directly by the State. From a legal point of view, however, a few of them are private institutions, most of which receive rather substantial subsidies from the State. This is connected with the fact that in Denmark there are no institutions of higher education that are entirely private.

All major Danish research libraries are open to the general public with no restrictions other than those imposed on students and academic staff. Some of these libraries provide more loans to users from outside their institutions than to internal users and a few have specialized in serving the industry. Thus, the National Technological Library of Denmark (DTB) for many years has been leading in this field. In 1989, an interesting attempt was made at developing a new service for research and business. In Aarhus, some of the research libraries took the initiative to open a new center aimed at serving local scientists and the trades and industries. This will be dealt with in detail in Section IV,B.

The staffing of the Danish university libraries and other major research libraries is comparable with that found in German academic libraries. This is so because the Danish academic tradition is heavily influenced by the continental, and particularly, German, tradition. There are two different kinds of librarians: (1) research librarians (who have a university degree and additionally a postgraduate course in librarianship), acting as subject specialists; and (2) librarians (graduates from the Royal School of Librarianship), attending to more general professional tasks. To these positions must be added clerical staff and other positions.

B. Public and School Libraries

The public libraries are all funded and governed by the local authorities. Among the statutory duties of Danish municipalities is the obligation to run a public library. The Danish public library system belongs to the most advanced in the world. The staff is well educated. All librarians must have completed four years of training at the Royal School of Librarianship or be in possession of a similar professional degree. Figures for lending and other activities generally are high, compared with the size of the population. Contrary to the research libraries the public libraries in Denmark have taken their inspiration mainly from the Anglo-Saxon countries.

In recent years some of the major public libraries have established special departments for business service. This indicates a considerable shift in objectives, as the public libraries in Denmark had not previously made any special efforts for business, trade, and industry. In most cases the local authorities took the initiative in order to support local business.

The Danish school libraries are also funded entirely by the local authorities, being integrated in the schools. They serve the purpose of being at the disposal of the young readers.

C. Private Libraries

Most of the private libraries in Denmark belong to the major private companies. Normally, Small and Medium-sized Enterprises (SME) do not have a library or documentation center of their own, and instead use the services of the research libraries or public libraries. Some SME use the services of information brokers or consultants, the number of which is small. The largest Danish information broker, the Danish Technical Information Service (DTO), is a well-established firm, which receives some public financial support.

D. Interlibrary Cooperation

There is a strong tradition for cooperation between the different types of libraries. Furthermore, it is an old practice that this cooperation is carried out without any financial arrangements apart from those that originate from third parties. Thus, the role of the research libraries is not restricted to serving research and higher education. They also provide the general public with scientific literature. Danish research libraries serve as a superstructure for the public library system. When an ordered book of other document is not in the collections of the public libraries, a request is sent to the National Loan Center at the State and University Library, and the item is found either in one of the Danish research libraries or in a foreign library. Normally, the material is forwarded free of charge to the person who needs it. Until a few years ago most of the procedures regarding ordering of documents and interlibrary loans were carried out manually.

E. Information Work Automation

As early as 1965 the first library in Denmark (The Library of the Copenhagen School of Economics and Business Administration) began to catalog its books with the aid of a computer. The first Danish OPAC (Online Public Access

Catalog) was introduced to the public in 1979, followed by most other research libraries in the eighties. Today, OPACs made in both Denmark and abroad are in operation.

A pooled database of Danish research library catalog records together with current records from the Library of Congress and the British National Bibliography was established in 1981. This database (ALBA/SAMKAT) is an essential element in shared cataloging among research libraries in Denmark. All libraries participating in the cataloging cooperation have online access to the common database, which is run by UNI-C, the Danish Universities Computer Center. The cataloging cooperation is guided by the National Library Authorities. Presently, the database contains about 5 million records, half of which have localization data from about 250 Danish research libraries. All major Danish OPACs may be accessed by anyone who has a PC and a modem via direct telephone call, the national packet switched network (DATAPAK), or other networks. This service is free of charge other than that due to telecommunication.

Some of the major research libraries have developed small systems for conversion of their card catalogs. Because of limited budgets, the extent of the task, and difficulties with handwritten catalogs, this project will take several years to complete.

The Danish public libraries run a similar system with a shared database. This database (BASIS) contains all records in the Danish national bibliography from 1972 onward. BASIS is administrated by the Danish Library Center which is a private company serving all public libraries. The number of public libraries that have automated their catalogs is increasing rapidly. A considerable number of different OPACs is being used, most of which are produced in Denmark. A recent review of the impact of automated systems in Danish public libraries is given by Evald (1991).

Unfortunately, the research libraries and the public libraries run different systems for their catalogs. Both systems, however, contain MARC records, which opens up new opportunities for integrating the two systems. Such plans have been discussed for a couple of years and will be described in Section IV,A.

F. The Danish DIANE Center

In 1981 a national center for information about online information retrieval, telecommunications networks, and databases was established in Copenhagen. In 1986 the Center became a permanent institution under the Ministry of Education. The Danish DIANE Center employs four information technology specialists, among these two librarians. DIANE is an acronym for DIrect

Access to Networks in Europe. There are similar centers in several other European countries.

The DIANE Center can be contacted by phone, telefax, or in person concerning information and advice regarding online searching, communication problems, network facilities, CD–ROM, or in-house databases. In order to fulfill its obligations, the Center publishes a newsletter, a directory of Danish databases, and other printed material. These services mainly are free of charge; there is a charge for publications, however. Moreover, the Center organizes courses and meetings about electronic information systems. Its facilities are being used by many database hosts who give courses and training sessions for users.

In order to extend its services further and modernize the possibilities for access, in 1990 the DIANE Center introduced a small but tailored bulletin board and e-mail system, DIANE ONLINE. This system offers free access to everyone. Thanks to the network owners even the X.25 telecommunication is free of charge. There is no formal registration of users. For that reason the number of users is not known, but the number of calls gives an indication of their number (Dansk DIANE Center, 1991). During its first year more than 23,000 attempts were made to access the system. The Center estimates that more than a thousand individual users have accessed DIANE ONLINE in its first year. Sixty-seven percent of the attempts were successful (70 per working day on average). Accessing a new system always causes some trouble for most users. DIANE ONLINE soon became popular among Danish online users and others able to use a computer and a modem. The use of the system has stabilized around 1000 successful calls a month.

After a successful log-in procedure, the main menu gives the following options:

1. Database searching
2. Information about the databases in DIANE ONLINE
3. A short course in database searching
4. Technical information about DIANE ONLINE
5. Bulletin boards, including messages from the Danish Online User Group
6. Publications from the DIANE Center
7. Messages to the DIANE Center
N. News/changes at the DIANE Center
9. What is the DIANE Center and how can it be useful to you?
0. Logging off from the system

The Center's most important task is to promote the use of online information. Special attention is given to domestic databases as a number of sample databases are presented in DIANE ONLINE for demonstration purposes. The novice—or anyone interested—may try out such databases when selecting option 1 at the main menu. Among the test databases the following are available:

1. Display (a full-text version of the DIANE Center's newsletter from 1986 onward)
2. DANSKE (descriptions of more than 130 Danish publicly available databases)
3. NORDISKE (descriptions in English of more than 430 Danish, Norwegian, Swedish, and Finnish publicly available databases)
4. NUA (network user addresses and other information about more than 300 database hosts worldwide)
5. BIBLIO (the online catalog of the Center's own library of literature on information technology; about 4000 references)
6. BROKER (short description of more than 100 Danish online information services, based at libraries and companies)

Many online users take the opportunity of trying some databases out in the free demonstration version in DIANE ONLINE, especially when there is no free (or inexpensive) version available elsewhere. The retrieval language used is a simplified version of CCL (Common Command Language), which is the language recommended by the EEC and being used by many European hosts. A new type of user of these demonstration databases has emerged recently. The educational sector in Denmark is showing an increasing interest in electronic information and communication systems. DIANE ONLINE therefore is used by many teachers for demonstration purposes because it is monetarily affordable. This means that many students in secondary schools, high schools, and colleges attend basic courses in the use of information systems, such as general computer courses and word processing courses.

The fifth option on the main menu gives access to seven different bulletin boards:

1. From user to user
2. General board on information retrieval—ideas and comments
3. Telecommunication
4. Retrieval languages and search technique
5. Business information
6. Technology, medicine, chemistry, etc.
7. DOUG, Danish Online User Group.

It is possible for the user to read any message on these boards and write his own as well as his comments to other users' messages. In this way, a simple form of computerized conferencing system has been created. The number of boards may vary according to needs and actual use.

One of the boards (option 7) contains the agenda and minutes of the Danish Online User Group, which meets three times per year. The objectives of the Group, its program and rules, and the list of members of its Executive Committee are also available. The Group has stopped sending out minutes, which earlier was a heavy financial burden. After 2–3 years, the members of the Group have become used to this form of communication, which—given the subject matter of interest—seems to be quite natural.

Option 7 on the main menu offers the opportunity of leaving a message to the staff of the DIANE Center. Replies are given through other communication media. During the first year this option was rarely used (about once a day on the average). This should be compared with the number of telephone calls to the Center (about 20–25 per working day) asking questions and requesting advice. The staff at the Center supposes that the mailbox facility is being used when the Center's telephone lines have been busy for a long time. In most cases, when the mailbox is used it is in matters of lower priority (e.g., ordering of publications). In such cases the mailbox may be considered a supplement to the telephone.

It is in the intention of the Danish DIANE Center to develop DIANE ONLINE further. The quite heavy use of the system for nearly three years may be interpreted as support from the users. According to the objectives of the Center, DIANE ONLINE is constructed as a system mainly for novices. More experienced users may, however, also benefit from it. The system is not unique, as similar systems are running in other countries, but mainly within geographically limited groups or as in-house systems. DIANE ONLINE seems to be the only national system of this kind. DIANE ONLINE is placed on five PCs in five identical versions and may thus be accessed by up to five users at a time through the Center's own PAD. The advantage of a modest system like the present one is that it is inexpensive to purchase and maintain and flexible to administer, in comparison with larger mini- or mainframe systems. A more thorough review of DIANE ONLINE may be found in Clausen (1992).

In spite of its technical simplicity, DIANE ONLINE is a relatively complex information system. It contains a number of databases, bulletin boards, and e-mail facilities. The collection of sample databases is exceptional. Training databases are normally found in large foreign database hosts only. It is easy to use even for the novice. One important side effect is that the online user becomes accustomed to a CMC system (Computer-Mediated Communication), which may consist of electronic mail, bulletin board systems, and computerized conferencing. This is a relevant and necessary introduction to the information system scenario of the present decade, where traditional online becomes too narrow a concept, as Gordon (1986) observed.

> Using the micro to search for information, while ignoring the electronic mail files so available to us, is missing an important aspect of online information communication.

Clausen (1991a, b, 1992) has given accounts of how CMC systems are being used and how they may become important tools for the future information professional.

III. A Delphi Study

A. Method

With reference to the topic of the present chapter, some forecasts concerning future developments in the use of information technology in everyday life, in science, and in business is relevant in order to discern some trends.

In connection with the author's doctoral studies in Computer-Mediated Communication (Clausen, 1992), a Delphi study was carried out. Empirical data were needed in order to examine the expectations concerning future development and use of specific CMC applications. The Delphi technique was selected because experts on CMC in Denmark were rare and difficult to identify. Designed to obtain opinions from an expert panel in a specific subject field, a Delphi study is carried out in a number of rounds, where opinions are resubmitted until a sufficient consensus is obtained. Anonymity is guaranteed during the study, which is carried out through the mail. The Delphi technique is described in detail by Linstone and Turoff (1975).

A panel of 38 members from Denmark was selected. The following criteria for selection were used: (1) at least five years in information work; (2) professional qualifications in Library and Information Science; (3) deep insight into Information Technology; and (4) a general view of the information sector. Furthermore, the panel members were selected in order to reflect total Danish information profession according to four occupational categories: (1) research libraries; (2) internal libraries and information centers in trade and industry; (3) private and semipublic information sectors; and (4) information science.

A preliminary list of 47 statements was compiled concerning future development within information technology in general, the library and information world, and CMC applications. The statements were formulated according to the rules described by Linstone and Turoff (1975, pp. 93, 232–233), Salancik, Wenger, and Helfer (1971), Martino (1972, pp. 54–58), and Martyn and Lancaster (1981, pp. 63–65) concerning, for example, length of questionnaire, length of statements, and precision. The list of preliminary statements was reviewed by the panel members who gave their comments. On this basis, 42 final statements were formulated and used in three rounds of estimation.

The Delphi study proved to be a success. Not only was the response rate satisfactory (between 100% and 84% in the four rounds) but the "Delphi Effect" was also unmistakable. In a successful Delphi study the estimates given by panel members should converge during the rounds. The degree of convergence may be measured by the standard deviation (*SD*) for all distributions of estimates. If the SD decreases from one round to the next the Delphi Effect is positive. This was the case in 37 out of 42 cases. An account of the major findings of the Delphi study are given below.

B. General Findings

A few general findings from the Delphi study will be presented below. The findings concern the use of information and communication technology in everyday life of the general population. This forms a background for the following presentation of findings concerning professional information work in the academic environment (Section IV,A) and in the business information environment (Section IV,B).

In Section II some forecasts concerning computer literacy among Danish students were mentioned (in 1996 90% of all Danish students who have completed ninth grade will have acquired a user's knowledge of personal computers, and in 1999 the same students will have a user's knowledge of electronic information research). Concerning distribution of computer equipment, Denmark apparently has one of the highest numbers of computers per capita (more than 800,000 PCs in a population of 5 million, according to Holmstad, 1993). The Delphi panel expects that in 1996 there will be as many PCs in private Danish households as there are typewriters today, provided that training and attitude change in a majority of the population will have taken place.

On the basis of this level of computer literacy and incidence of computer equipment and telecommunication networks, it is predicted that by the year 2002 10% of all Danes will use electronic mail for their private correspondence, mainly replacing traditional mail. In 2003 the number of private Danish households with a fax machine (including a telephone) will be equal to the number of households with a telephone only. A panel member maintains that the fax will be superseded by genuine e-mail. This finding may be compared with a finding from another Delphi study (Koskiala and Huhtanen, 1989): in Finland 51% of the population is expected to have their own fax machine in 1996 and 73% in 2010. Ungerer (1989) has some similar forecasts for the entire EEC: 9% in 1995 and 15% in 2005.

Ten percent of all private Danish households are expected to subscribe to at least one videotext system in the year 2000, and 50% in 2006. One panel member does not believe in videotext systems. He expects them to be replaced by (other) new information technology. For the entire EEC, Ungerer (1989) has the following forecasts: 20% in 1995 and 35% in 2005.

In 1992 the author saw an electronic "book" at a conference. In the present Delphi study an electronic "book" was referred to as follows: "The contents of the book are on a chip (not a diskette or CD–ROM), which can be placed in a reader unit with a screen, about the size of an average book. The graphic quality of the screen is equal to that of printed books " (Clausen, 1992). The panel members expect such a device to be technically feasible in 1994, economically feasible in 1999, and for sale in most places in 2004. A member of the panel has a comprehensible objection to this: "The book is good enough!"

As mentioned in Section II,E, many of the Danish public libraries already have their own OPACs. The panel members expect 1997 to be the year when 90% of all Danish public libraries have acquired online catalogs, containing references to (at least part of) their collection of books. One year later it will be possible for private users to place an online book order/reservation to a Danish public library from their own PC. This is not seen as a technical problem, but merely as a political one. An interesting commentary is that "Ordering from home terminals may compensate for the closing down of small libraries " (Clausen, 1992). This point of view corresponds well with what is expressed in one of the conclusions in the comprehensive forecast study "Information UK 2000" (Martyn, Vickers, and Feeney, 1990):

> Towards the end of the decade we may be able to browse electronically in a **remote library** offering electronic borrowing and tele-delivery . . . . This implies that a few regional libraries could service the whole of the country's needs for tele-borrowing, and the role of other libraries will become that of a switching centre rather than a resource . . . and a provider of documentation and training.

On the basis of economic difficulties in major parts of the western world the idea of the "remote library" is supposed to be realized in many places. This will be made possible by the latest developments in information and communication technology. But how will the "remote library" influence the use of libraries? King (1992) has a list of factors that affect library use: (1) completeness of library collection and services; (2) distance to the library; (3) awareness of services; and (4) performance of services.

It is true that in the case of "remote libraries" physical distances have increased. Nevertheless, the advanced user may experience a better and more efficient service being able to search in the library's OPAC from his home or working place, realizing, for example, that the book he is interested in is out on loan, but that he may reserve it. When the book is returned to the library it will be sent to him automatically. In such circumstances, an increased distance to the library is not always experienced as an obstacle to library use. A Danish research library is planning to offer such services in a year or two as an extension of its traditional services.

One statement in the Delphi study touched what normally is dealt with in science fiction. The year is 2012: an intelligent telephone is in use that automatically translates calls between Danish and the main languages (speech recognition, computerized translation, and artificial voice, that is, automated simultaneous translation). The panel members agreed unexpectedly that such a device will have been developed in the year 2012. Two comments deserve to be quoted: "Neural nets will make it possible both economically and technically"; "It will hardly be available in Danish " (Clausen, 1992).

IV. Information and Communication in Denmark in the 1990s

In this section, two main trends in the beginning of the 1990s in the library and information sector in Denmark and their implications will be treated: first, the development of a new joint automated library system for both research and public libraries (the DANBIB Project), and second, the creation of a formalized network for business information in Denmark. In order to illustrate the expected development in the next ten to fifteen years, relevant findings from the Danish Delphi study are used.

A. The DANBIB Project

In Section II,E it was mentioned that there exists two different systems in Denmark for cataloging cooperation and national loan service. One system (the ALBA/SAMKAT) is used by most research libraries, while the other (BASIS) has been developed for the use of the public libraries.

In order to create a joint database consisting of all Danish bibliographical records with localization data, a working committee appointed by the National Library Authorities has prepared a plan for this important renewal. A shared database, a shared network, and common standards will enable all Danish libraries to cooperate more closely concerning reuse of bibliographic data and interlibrary loan service. The vast majority of Danish libraries have great expectations for this system, which is made possible only by the following circumstances: (1) the existence of two advanced systems, based on the handling of MARC records; (2) high quality of telecommunication networks;

(3) a will to cooperate in all types of libraries; and (4) the small size of the country. The new system (the DANBIB System) is planned to be operative in 1993 and will offer facilities and functions such as:

1. Cataloging (reuse and transmission of records)
2. National bibliography (preparation of the Danish National Bibliography)
3. Localization data (adding localization data by all libraries)
4. Online searching and ordering
5. Legal deposit (administration and control)
6. Administration (e.g., compensation for public lending right)

Furthermore, some Computer-Mediated Communication facilities are planned, namely electronic bulletin boards like those created by the Danish DIANE Center, computerized conferences for certain form of professional discussion, and electronic mail for messaging between all participants. Among these, the already existing "mailbox" for interlibrary loans in Denmark will be integrated and extended. Links to international library systems will be established. According to Griffiths (1992) many OPACs (more than 300) can be accessed via the Internet. There is no doubt that the DANBIB System will become a major step forward in Danish library communication and services will take a quantum leap. It will be a visbile sign of the traditional cooperation between different types of libraries in Denmark.

What about the information professionals who are going to use the new system? Most of them already have used the two existing systems for years. Computer literacy among Danish librarians has increased dramatically during the last five years or so. Genuine CMC systems have been used in a small number of cases recently. At the Frederikshavn Public Library a project was carried out in 1989–1991 involving the PortaCOM electronic mail system as a means of communication between the library and the local technical college (Johannsen, 1991). The PortaCOM system has been used in a number of situations, for example, by the Danish Technical Information Centers. Especially in reference work electronic networking was tried out. Among the findings were that the use of e-mail implied an increased degree of precision and a faster feedback. The librarians also profited from this, as they got the opportunity of extending their professional competencies beyond the traditional role of the librarian. Add to this that the library acquired some basic experiences with quality management as the PortaCOM system collected all relevant information about the service performed.

The Danish Delphi study has some findings that are of interest in this connection. How will the role of the information professional develop in the near future? How will the roles of the librarian and the user change in the light of computerized information technology? Will the end user take over online searching? The Delphi study expects that in 1997 50% of all online searches performed in Denmark in external, publicly available information databases and banks and other similar electronic services will be carried out by end users (i.e., those who are using the retrieved information themselves). The same statement, maintaining that 90% of all online searches are made by end users, caused some differences of opinion among the panel members. The finding (the year 2005) was not reliable. Several panel members did not believe that more than 70% ever would be reached. This leaves a great deal of intermediary functions to future information professionals, especially when it is taken into consideration that the number of available online systems is supposed to increase.

In many other fields the librarian is expected to work with the electronic media. For instance, this is the case with periodicals. In 1998 the amount of information in electronic professional periodicals, including newsletters (not printed), is expected to be 10% of the amount of information in printed periodicals. Fifty percent is predicted to be reached in 2006.

Concerning full-text databases a dramatic increase is expected to take place. In the year 2001 50% of all new, publicly available technical and scientific periodical and report literature will be online-accessible full text in electronic form at database hosts. The 90% share is predicted in 2010. A 16-year-old prediction (Sauter, 1977) says that in 1997 paper will be replaced as a document storage medium by full-text digital media. Koskiala and Huhtanen (1989) found in the Finnish Delphi study that in 2010 between 70 and 90% of information will be published in electronic form.

The professional communication among information professionals is also going to change considerably, according to the Delphi panel. In the year 2000, measured by the amount of information transmitted, e-mail will be used as much, among information professionals in the western world, as is traditional mail, phone, fax, and telex in all. This communication will be supported by systems like the DIANE ONLINE (Section II,F) or a larger information and communication system tailored for Danish information professionals, including e-mail, professional newsletters, a calendar of arrangements, and a gateway to some database hosts.

An increasing part of Danish information professionals' work (in terms of time) is predicted to take place as telework at their private address from where they are electronically connected with their firm (10% in the year 2000). Below, similar findings for office workers as "telecommuters" are mentioned.

The supply of professional courses is predicted to increase and the methods used will change. In 2000 10% of all in-service training and courses within the library, documentation, and information field in Denmark will take place as distance learning, supported by electronic communication. Altogether, information technology will increasingly support more advanced studies (Open University model).

In Denmark, there is a realistic possibility of implementing such systems on a wide scale. Some systems for distance education have already been used for years for limited purposes. Recently a system for computerized distance education was developed in Denmark through joint efforts by IBM Denmark and the Royal Danish School of Educational Studies. The system (LEARN) makes use of IBM Network Services and may be described as an "electronic correspondence college," which may be used in most subjects and on many educational levels. The system has attracted attention in Denmark because it might be helpful in order to overcome some of the problems due to Denmark's geographical situation. Though a small country, it is characterized by the fact that the capital, Copenhagen (where 25% of the population is living), is situated on an island on the periphery of the country.

B. Cooperation in Business Information

In 1986, the first science park in Denmark opened up in Aarhus, the second largest town of Denmark. Of course, there had been research communities in connection with some of the institutions of higher education for many years. Research centers at some of Denmark's most advanced industries had also existed for a long time. Soon after, a few other science parks were established (in Copenhagen, Aalborg, and Odense).

In Aarhus, the State and University Library had been involved in the plans for a science park from the very beginning. The year after the start of the science park an Information and Documentation Center was placed at the science park (Clausen, 1987). This service was run as a collaboration between three local research and special libraries (The State and University Library, the Library of the Aarhus Business School, and the Aarhus Technical Library). This center was staffed only part-time, in a test period aimed at serving the internal needs for scientific and other information of the staff at the science park. In fact, it acted as an interface to the three libraries. On the basis of the experience gained in the test period it was decided to increase the activities of the Information Center. An independent center (the Business Information Center) was established in 1989 (Clausen, 1990c). This center still serves as the information and documentation center of the science park. Moreover, it got the assignment of developing new tailored services for local business, trade, and industry, making the resources of the three local research and special libraries more visible to them. Research and development activities in information technology for Library and Information Science purposes were also carried out. The Business Information Center thus became the first

Danish center of its kind, offering value-added information services, ranging from online searching to information system construction. The staff consists of 3–4 persons who are all competent in library and information work. In addition, a number of external consultants are attatched.

The Business Information Center cooperates closely with the local research and special libraries. A link to the business service of the Aarhus Public Library has also been established. Like these libraries, the Business Information Center has access to the national and international network of libraries and information centers. On the international level the Center is a member of GAVEL, which is a European consortium of individual information consultants, based in 15 countries in western Europe. All the members specialize in information and communication systems, and in providing solutions to information management problems. On the information broker level the Center is a member of the European Information Researchers Network (EIRENE), which for the time being has about 60 members representing 16 different countries, including some of the eastern European states (EIRENE, 1992).

Participating in international networking on two levels, the Business Information Center has some efficient relations to colleagues abroad, but what about the domestic situation? In this case inspiration was taken from England. In February 1991, the Business Information Network was officially launched, having already been operational for a year or so. The Network is a group of more than sixty public, academic, and national libraries and other information providers who have joined forces to promote business information, with members in England, Scotland, Wales, and Northern Ireland. The objective of the Network is to "improve the performance and competitiveness of British enterprise through the better use of business information" (The Business Information Network and Europe, 1992). Membership brings a range of benefits, including a monthly newsletter and a Directory of Members with accurate and detailed information about each member's resources and competence.

In October 1991, the Danish Business Information Center carried out a survey in order to get some facts about the supposed interest among public and private institutions in Denmark working with communication of business information. A questionnaire was sent to a sample of 117 out of about 350 institutions. The response rate was 39, of which more than 70% expressed a positive interest in joining a similar Danish network for business information. On this background the Danish Business Information Network was formed in the spring of 1992. Presently, the Network has about 60 members. It is funded entirely by members' subscriptions (currently DKK 1400 per year [about U.S. $225]) and by income from sale of publications to nonmembers. Among the members are public and research libraries, private information brokers, information consultancies, information producers, database hosts, and publishers. At the present, the Business Information Center is managing the Network, performing the following tasks according to Danish Business Information Network (1992):

1. Acting as secretariat
2. Publishing a quarterly newsletter
3. Publishing special reports about business information matters, providing Danish business information professionals with relevant news about business information work in foreign countries
4. Editing a Danish Business Information Directory, which describes all the members' services
5. Encouraging cooperation between members
6. Marketing of the resources of the Network aimed at users/customers in industry, finance and public administration
7. Arranging an annual conference on business information, which is open to the public
8. Cooperating with similar networks and other relevant bodies in other countries

So far, the Danish Network has only started its operations. No doubt, the initiative came at the critical moment when a number of specialized Danish business information services had emerged and operated for a few years. Being well established, they had resources for taking up external relations, both on a national and on an international level. In addition, a similar situation was present in other European countries, even though they differ considerably with respect to business information. This similar situation has eventually emerged from the policy of the European Community trying to unite European efforts concerning business, trade, and industry. Plans for a Europe-wide integrated system of information provision are being developed, for example, under the Library Action Plan, which is a program initiated by the Commission of the European Community. The Action Plan is designed to stimulate the growth of library services in Europe and to make the library stocks of Europe more accessible within the Community.

Being the two most developed networks for business information in Europe the British and Danish networks cooperate closely. Based on the situation at present, they may constitute an important starting point in a future European network.

The Danish Delphi study gives some forecasts about the communication and, hence, working situation in the near future, for information professionals working with business information as well as for office workers in general. In the year 2003 e-mail in Denmark in business and trade will be used as much as traditional mail, phone, fax, and telex (measured by the amount of information transmitted). In recent years, EDI (Electronic Document Interchange) has been implemented in many lines of business. A total redesign of European business is expected by many experts. The panel members predict that in 2000 in Denmark, the number of transmitted structured documents (e.g., invoices, customs, and shipping documents) by means of EDI will be equal to the number transmitted in the traditional way (paper and the mail services). The panel members expect an increase in efficiency in general information working routines. The application of e-mail and EDI in connection with implementation of the electronic office ("paperless" administrative work) will enable the development of new and more efficient working routines. If the present level of ambition is maintained with regard to the quality of service and the proportion of tasks, these new routines in the Danish private sector will result in an increase in efficiency of 10% of the economic resources invested in 1996 (25% in 2003, and 50% in 2011). This is, of course, a complex issue, which caused many comments from the panel members, for example, "Development will notoriously bring new services and economic effectiveness"; "Most of the activities in the private service sector are about problem solving, and this type of activity cannot be automated." (Clausen, 1992)

The so-called electronic office already has been introduced in some firms, also in Denmark. The Delphi study revealed a difference in date of implementation for Danish firms and Danish public administration. In the year 2001 the electronic office ("paperless," computer-based administrative work) will be introduced in 90% of Danish firms of more than 10 employees. This condition will have been achieved when the amount of incoming e-mail exceeds the amount of traditional mail (not advertising material). The same condition is expected in 2003 for Danish public administration. One panel member does not agree in this delay: "Changes will occur sooner in public administration because of better possibilities of standardization and fewer relations. Very large amounts of administrative work are already computerized." (Clausen, 1992)

Many resources are spent on internal meetings. In Danish firms, meetings with participants from several geographically separate departments are expected to take place as teleconferences (sound and picture) as frequently as in the traditional way when the year 2004 is reached. Teleworking is also seen as a realistic possibility in business and trade. According to a survey of 497 businesses throughout the United Kingdom in 1991–1992, more than one in eight British firms now use some form of teleworking (Teleworking popularity, 1992). The main benefit is increased productivity and the second largest benefit is retention of IT-related specialist staff. In 2002 10% (in 2012 25%) of Danish office workers' work (in terms of time) will be taking place at their private addresses from where they are electronically connected with their firms. Some comments from the panel members: "The trade unions will be against it!"; "It will never become a success, because the social environment is a necessity for company identification, which in its turn is a precondition for quality work"; "Maybe for employees with a higher education, not for clerks";

"Flexible distance work at home, in trains and planes, etc., in combination with traditional office work, is a reality today " (Clausen, 1992). A British report on information technology (IT Futures, 1987) expects 20% of the British workforce to be working from their private homes in 2010.

In many cases information professionals are disappointed with the business managers' attitude toward information. In this connection, the information professionals often feel underestimated. According to the predictions of the Delphi panel, in the year 2000 the attitude to information use in Danish business and trade will have changed so that information professionals (employees in the library, documentation, and information sector) will be recognized on a par with lawyers, economists, and engineers. Comments: "These jobs will be taken over by end users"; "Rubbish! There will be a need for real professionals."

V. Conclusion

According to Iljon (1991) there are more than 75,000 libraries and information centers of many different types in the European Community. The total stock is about 1.2 billion books plus other types of materials. On the basis of the diversity of library types in the EEC Member States, libraries on the whole must be judged as ill prepared and inadequately equipped to perform the crucial role of being an intermediary between the producer and the user of information. The Commission of the EEC has realized that a "mobilization" of the library sector is necessary if the information chain is to work in a satisfactory way. Appropriate skills and experience must be developed in the library and information sector. In order to stimulate this process the Commission has drawn up the Library Program, which aims promoting: (1) the availability and accessibility of modern library services throughout the Community; (2) more rapid penetration of new information technologies in libraries in a cost-effective way; (3) the standardization required for resource sharing; and (4) harmonization and convergence of national policies (Iljon, 1991).

In short, the four Action Lines of the Library Program indicate what the Commission would like to support:

Action Line 1: Computerized bibliographies
Action Line 2: International interconnection of systems and related international standards
Action Line 3: Provision of new library services using information and communication technologies
Action Line 4: Stimulation of European market in telematic products and services specific to libraries

Iljon (1991) expects the Library Programme to initiate significant changes in the European libraries. In the 1990s they will accommodate the needs of the entire Community in a comprehensive and efficient way, serving the academic, business, and general user.

As a Member of the EEC, Denmark is expected to take part in the "mobilization" of European libraries. Being one of the technically advanced countries, Denmark will be able to contribute to the development of other countries' library systems. There is a proportionately large amount of competence in Danish information professionals, which is available on the European information scene. Several projects are already in progress.

References

Anderla, G., and Dunning, A. (1987). *Computer Strategies 1990–9. Technologies - Costs - Markets.* Wiley, Chichester, England.

Arnum, E. (1992). The Internet goes commercial. *EEMA Briefing* **5**, no. 4, 16.

The Business Information Network and Europe. (Press release, March 1992). The Business Information Network, London.

Cashmore, C., and Lyall, R. (1991). *Business Information. Systems and Strategies.* Prentice Hall, Hemel Hempstead, England.

Clausen, H. (1987). Informationsformidling i forskerparker (Information services in science parks). *DF-revy* **10**, 170–172.

Clausen, H.(1990a). The future information professional: Old wine in new bottles? Part One. *Libri* **40**, 265–277.

Clausen, H. (1990b). Information and innovation in the Nordic countries. *International Forum for Information and Documentation* **15**, 34–37.

Clausen, H. (1990c). Ehrvers-Info / Business Information Centre—et nyt dansk BDI-center (The Business Information Centre—a new Danish Centre for Information and Documentation). *DF-revy* **13**, 179–182.

Clausen, H. (1991a). Electronic mail as a tool for the information professional. *The Electronic Library* **9**, 73–84.

Clausen, H. (1991b). Scenarios for electronic mail as a tool in the information profession. In *Preprint of Workshop, 13th International Teletraffic Congress, Copenhagen, Denmark, 1991* (Th. Herborg Nielsen, ed.), pp. 21–28. North-Holland, Amsterdam.

Clausen, H. (1992). Electronic mail and the information professional: A study of computer-mediated communication and its future prospects in the information field. Doctoral Thesis, Department of Information Science, The Aarhus School of Business Administration, Economics and Modern Languages, Aarhus, Denmark.

Danish Business Information Network (1992). *European Business Intelligence Briefing*, June, 219–220.

Dansk DIANE Center (1991). DIANE Online blev populær (DIANE Online became popular). *Display* **10**, no. 5, 12–13.

EIRENE (1992). *Directory of Members.* First Contact Ltd., London.

European Conference of Postal and Telecommunications Administrations (1992). *User Handbook ISDN.* CEPT, Bern, Switzerland.

Evald, P. (1991). Computer supported library work, system development and strategic vision—The impact of information technology on Danish public libraries. *International Journal of Information and Library Research* **3**, 87–110.

Gordon, H. A. (1986). Electronic mail . . . an underutilized area of the online experience. *Database*, August, 6–7.

Griffiths, J. M. (1992). "Quality in Libraries." Paper presented at the 50th Anniversary Conference at the National Technological Library of Denmark, Lyngby, Denmark, September 9, 1992.

Harrington, M., ed. (1992). *Europa 1992 Telecommunications*. Atalink Ltd, London.

Holmstad, D. (1993). Dansk verdensrekord i kaerlighed til pc'en (Danish world record for love of the PC). *Computerworld* **13**, no. 1, 1.

Iljon, A. (1991). Bookshelves and megabytes. *XIII Magazine*, No. 4, 8–9.

Information Market Observatory (1992). *Report on main events and developments in the electronic information services market 1992*. IMO, Luxembourg.

IT Futures (1987). *IT Futures . . . IT Can Work. An Optimistic View of the Long-Term Potential of Information Technology for Britain*. National Economic Development Office, London, England.

Johannsen, C. G. (1991). *Erhvervsinformation og undervisning i Frederikshavn Kommune. Slutrapport* (Business Information and Education in Frederikshavn Municipality. Final report). Royal School of Librarianship, Aalborg, Denmark.

Johannsen, C. G. (1992a). The use of quality control principles and methods in library and information science theory and practice. *Libri* **42**, 283–295.

Johannsen, C. G. (1992b). Danish experiences of TQM in the library world. *New Library World* **93**, no. 1104, 4–9.

King, D. W. (1992). "Value of Information." Paper presented at the 50th Anniversary Conference at the National Technological Library of Denmark, Lyngby, Denmark, September 9, 1992.

Koskiala, S., and Huhtanen, A. (1989). The Finnish Delphi Study: Forecasting the extent of information technology use in libraries in 1996 and 2010. *The Electronic Library* **7**, 170–175.

Linstone, H. A., and Turoff, M., eds. (1975). *The Delphi Method: Techniques and Applications*. Addison-Wesley, London.

Martyn, J., and Lancaster, F. W. (1981). *Investigative Methods in Library and Information Science: An Introduction*. Information Resources Press, Arlington, Virgina.

Martyn, J., Vickers, P., and Feeney, M. (1990). *Information UK 2000*. Bowker-Saur, London.

Rogers, E. M., and Kincaid, D. L. (1981). *Communication Networks. Towards a New Paradigm for*

Rogers, E. M., and Kincaid, D. L. (1981). *Communication Networks. Towards a New Paradigm for Research*. Free Press, New York.

Salancik, J. R., Wenger, W., and Helfer, E. (1971). The construction of Delphi event statements. *Technological Forecasting and Social Changes* **3**, 65–73.

Sauter, H. E. (1977). Assessments of defense information and documentation needs. In *AGARD Conference Proceedings No. 225*. Papers presented at the Technical Information Panel Specialists' Meeting held in Lysebu, Oslo, Norway, 22–23 June 1977, pp. 10-1–10-8.

Teleworking popularity grows. (1992). *Online Review* **16**, No. 1, 32–33.

Ungerer, H. (1989). *Telecommunication in Europe*. Office of the Official Publications of the European Communities, Luxembourg.

The International Federation of Library Associations and the United States: What Happens Next?

Nancy R. John
University Library
University of Illinois at Chicago
Chicago, Illinois 60680

I. Introduction

International relations were once viewed as the sphere of the rich and famous and the government. This is not the case any more. Newspaper headlines speak to the international scene. The nightly news is beamed to us from around the world. We watch governments tumble live before our very eyes. International conditions affect the availability of particular foods at the local grocery store. Educational leaders call for us to educate the "citizen of the world" (Rhodes, 1991). We can no longer live solely within our borders.

As librarians, we understand very well the universal power of information. We have much to contribute to today's world if we recognize our opportunities. In the United States, librarians are used to interpreting library interests broadly. As a result, U.S. library associations and their members are active in the political issues of our day. We are quick to speak out against abridgment of fundamental freedoms. We value, in particular, the First Amendment to the U.S. Constitution. On the international scene, human rights issues spark our concern and passion. However, the precepts of democracy, as we know them, are not necessarily operating beyond our borders. This complicates our role when we are moved to action by the political plight of our international brothers and sisters. There is a fundamental challenge to respond to these causes we hold dear while at the same time respecting cultural and political differences. It is time for us to address the international professional questions with the same vigor we have brought to issues of fundamental freedoms, but with a care and respect for the professional traditions of others.

In order to understand how librarians in the United States might expand

225

and improve our effectiveness within the International Federation of Library Associations and Institutions (IFLA), we need first to have a good understanding of what IFLA is and how it works. In later sections of this article, I discuss U.S. involvement in IFLA, IFLA's influence in the international scene, and the future of exchange and twinning programs.

II. What is IFLA?[1]

Founded in 1927, IFLA was created to provide librarians throughout the world with a forum for exchanging ideas, promoting international cooperation, unifying library practices, and advancing the cause of librarianship. It is an independent, international nongovernmental association with headquarters in the Royal Library of the Netherlands located in The Hague. IFLA has been given Consultative Status A (the highest classification) with the United Nations Educational, Social and Cultural Organization (UNESCO), which means that IFLA is expected to contribute to and shape UNESCO programs within IFLA's area of expertise. In particular, IFLA participates in UNESCO's General Information Programme (PGI). IFLA also consults with other nongovernmental organizations with interests in information; two organizations are worthy of special mention, the Federation for Information and Documentation (FID) and the International Congress of Archives (ICA). IFLA also holds special status with the International Standards Organization (ISO), the International Council of Scientific Unions (ICSU), and the World Intellectual Property Organization (WIPO).

In 1927, IFLA members numbered 15 countries. Presently IFLA has members from 135 countries; of these, 85 are countries in the developing world. Membership is open to associations; affiliation is open to institutions and individuals. Institutional affiliates make up about 75% of IFLA's membership of 1284 (as of December 1991), whereas the remaining quarter are just about equally split between association members and personal affiliates.

The main objectives of IFLA are to initiate and coordinate research and studies; publish and disseminate information; organize meetings, conferences, and seminars; and collaborate with other international organizations in the field of information, documentation, and archives. IFLA works through its professional groups (32 sections and 12 round tables), which are organized into eight divisions. Three divisions address types of libraries (general research, special, and libraries serving the general public) and four divisions are

---

[1] Information for this section has been taken from IFLA's publications, particularly "Facts & Features about IFLA: The World of Library and Information Services," IFLA, 1992.

for types of activities (bibliographic control, collections and services, management and technology, and education and research). The eighth, the Division of Regional Activities, covers the developing world; it has three sections: Africa; Asia and Oceania; and Latin America and the Caribbean. Table I is a graphic representation of IFLA's Divisions and Sections.

Table I   IFLA Divisions, Sections, and Round Tables

Division	Sections	Round Tables
I. General research libraries	National libraries Parliamentary libraries University libraries and other general research libraries	
II. Special libraries	Art libraries Biological and medical sciences Geography and map libraries Government libraries Science and technology libraries Social science libraries	
III. Libraries serving the general public	Children's libraries Libraries for the blind Libraries serving disadvantaged persons Library services to multicultural populations Public libraries School libraries	Children's literature documentation centers International Association of Metropolitan City Libraries (INTAMEL) Mobile libraries National Centers for Library Services (ROTNAC)
IV. Bibliographic control	Bibliography Cataloging Classification and indexing	
V. Collection and services	Acquisitions and exchange Government information and official publications Interlending and document delivery Rare books and manuscripts Serial publications	Newspapers
VI. Management and technology	Conservation Information technology Library buildings and equipment Statistics	Audiovisual media Management Management of library associations
VII. Education and research	Education and training Library theory and research	Continuing professional education Editors of library journals Library history Research in reading
VIII. Regional activities	Africa Asia and Oceania Latin America and the Caribbean	

Membership in a section or round table is open to any person or organization interested in supporting its activities. Each section is governed by an elected standing committee, composed of up to twenty national experts in the field; standing committee members are nominated and elected by the membership of the sections for four-year terms and are eligible for reelection once. The elected members elect, in turn, the officers—generally, the Chair and Secretary/Financial Officer—of each Standing Committee. These Section officers form the Coordinating Board that governs each Division. The Coordinating Board chooses its own Chair and Secretary. The Chair of the Division, or a designee, serves on IFLA's Professional Board.

The Professional Board is the group delegated with the responsibility to manage the professional component of IFLA's programs, including conferences, publications, and fellowship programs, as well as sectional, divisional, and core program activities. Management is achieved through control of two things: the programmatic funds and the IFLA imprimatur on projects. The Professional Board elects its own chair from among its outgoing members. The Board is responsible to the IFLA Executive Board. The chair of the Professional Board is an ex officio member of the IFLA Executive Board. A member of the Executive Board is also designated to sit in on the meetings of the Professional Board.

The Executive Board is the highest elected body in IFLA. Its full membership consists of the President and the Treasurer and six other members; all are elected at a meeting of the IFLA Council. The Council is the highest organ of the Federation, the general assembly of members. The Council meets regularly in odd-numbered years in conjunction with the annual conference. The Executive Board has full powers of administration for the Federation except as limited by the powers of the Council.

The newest unit in IFLA's structure is the discussion group. Discussion groups are being tested in a four-year-long pilot program to examine whether such groups can provide an effective way for IFLA to react to short-lived topics and to provide a forum for members to discuss issues in librarianship informally. Until this pilot project, begun in 1992, the only informal group structures were the Working Group and Task Force structures. Both these groups are to be assigned particular projects to accomplish on a strict timetable. At the end of a project the Working Group or Task Force is either dissolved or must become a committee, section, or round table. The discussion group concept may provide another route to keep IFLA responsive to current topics.

The other arm of IFLA's program structure is IFLA's Core Programmes. Five IFLA Core Programmes undertake activities that intersect the interests and concerns of all libraries and their users. IFLA's Core Programmes provide ongoing focus on these major issues of importance to the world's libraries: UBCIM, Universal Bibliographic Control and International MARC (Germany); UAP, Universal Availability of Publications (United Kingdom); PAC, Preservation and Conservation (France); UDT, Universal Data Transmission (Canada); and ALP, Advancing Librarianship in the Third World (Sweden). All the programs except ALP are hosted by national libraries; ALP is located in the University Library in Uppsala, Sweden. Each Core Programme has a Director, usually a member of the host institution's staff, and program support staff who usually work solely in the Core Programme's headquarters. Core Programmes issue newsletters and journals, plan conferences and seminars, prepare standards and other works for publication, and assure that IFLA is active in the important issues relating to the particular area. They may play a significant role in raising the funds to support these activities, as IFLA relies heavily on grant funds and other outside project money (e.g., special contracts for projects). Each Core Programme works closely with the member-based activities and with the IFLA Headquarters staff.

The final group of individuals, with whom IFLA's survival and vitality ultimately rest, is the IFLA Headquarters staff. Eight staff, three professionals and five support staff, keep the IFLA program moving forward. In 1992, Leo Voogt became IFLA's newest Secretary General. Voogt is assisted by Winston Roberts, Coordinator of Professional Activities, and Carol Henry, Executive Officer. IFLA's regional offices also keep the IFLA program visible in the developing world. The three regional offices are located in Dakar, Senegal, Bangkok, Thailand, and Saõ Paolo, Brazil.

The annual conference is one of the major ways in which IFLA promotes librarianship around the world. The location of the annual conference is determined by IFLA's Executive Board. Member associations invite IFLA to consider holding a conference in their home countries. The 59th conference was held in Barcelona, Spain in 1993. Future conferences have been scheduled: 1994, Havana, Cuba; 1995, Istanbul, Turkey; 1996, Beijing, China. Since the annual conference reaches only 2000 librarians, IFLA's program of regional conferences extends the reach of IFLA activity significantly. Each year, the IFLA units sponsor a dozen or more conferences, seminars, and workshops in conjunction with national and regional associations on topics of importance to IFLA members. From a seminar on public libraries held in Cuba to a workshop on UNIMARC held in Hungary, these seminars reach many more librarians than the annual conference.

IFLA's program also reaches many librarians through its publishing efforts. IFLA issues a number of titles for its members: *IFLA Journal* (quarterly); *IFLA Annual; IFLA Trends* (biennial report); *IFLA Medium-Term Programme* (current edition is 1992–1997); *IFLA Statutes and Rules of Procedure;* and *IFLA Communications: A Bibliography of IFLA Conference Papers* (annually). In addition, various sections and divisions, as well as the Core Programmes, produce newsletters and journals for their members and subscribers. IFLA has two general monographic series: *IFLA Publications* (four per year) and *IFLA Professional Reports* (irregular). Most major publications of IFLA are published for IFLA by K. G. Saur (Munich) through a contractual relationship. A brochure listing all currently available publications is distributed by Headquarters each year.

Finally, IFLA assists librarians through an active program of grants and awards. The Robert Vosper IFLA Fellows Programme, sponsored by the Council on Library Resources as a tribute to Robert Vosper, Honorary IFLA Fellow, is given to individuals to undertake work in areas of interest to IFLA Core Programmes. The Gustav Hoffmann Study Grant, the successor award to their Martinus Nijhoff Study Grant, offered by K. G. Saur (Munich) allows a librarian in a country where librarianship is a newly developing profession to study an issue in one or more countries of western Europe. The Hans-Peter Geh Grant for Conference Participation supports a librarian from the former Soviet Union attending a conference in Germany or elsewhere. The Guust van Wesemael Literacy Prize was established in 1991 to commemorate the significant contributions of IFLA's Professional Coordinator (1979–1990) and Deputy Secretary General (1979–1991). The prize is to be used by a library to expand its holdings of materials on literacy. The Dr. Shawky Salem Training Grant, managed jointly by IFLA and FID, allows a national from an Arab country to spend one to three weeks studying library or information science in western Europe. The Margreet Wijnstroom Fund for Regional Library Development supports work by IFLA's regional offices to involve librarians from the regions in IFLA's projects and programs.

With this brief overview of IFLA, we now turn to a review of American involvement in IFLA, and, more generally, in the international sphere.

III. U.S. Involvement in IFLA

In his inaugural address, given at the 58th general conference of IFLA in New Delhi, India, Robert Wedgeworth, the current President of IFLA, summarized the beginnings of U.S. involvement internationally and, especially, in IFLA. Wedgeworth is the second president of IFLA from the United States. The first American President, elected in 1931, was William Warner Bishop, university librarian at the University of Michigan from 1915 to 1941. Bishop's international interests were highlighted in the United States in 1993 with the opening of the exhibit "Rome Reborn" at the Library of Congress. A press release (Library of Congress, 1992) issued on the occasion of the exhibit described Bishop's contributions to the establishment of the Vatican Library.

The loan of rare materials for "Rome Reborn" is, in the words of Father Leonard Boyle, "an attempt on the part of the Vatican Library, at a distance of over sixty years, to express its gratitude to all those from North America who contributed so forcefully to 'the common convenience of the learned' which is at the heart of the Vatican Library."

The direct association between the Vatican Library and the Library of Congress began in the fall of 1927, when two employees of the Vatican Library were sent to the Library of Congress to work in the cataloging department. The visit was part of an overall project funded by the Carnegie Endowment for International Peace to improve the cataloging and organization of the Vatican Library.

In the spring of 1928, the chief cataloger of the Library of Congress, Charles Martel, led a group of American librarians who were sent to the Vatican to catalog a sample portions [sic] of the collections as a guide for the Vatican to follow in the future. Working with Mr. Martel were C. M. Hanson of the University of Chicago; William Warner Bishop, director of libraries at the University of Michigan; William C. Randall, also of the University of Michigan; and the Norwegian John Ansteinsson of Trondheim, who later became director of cataloging [sic] for the Vatican Library.

On the foundations laid by this group, the reference collection was classified according to the Library of Congress system, as were all new books. The reading rooms were renovated and the level of lighting improved and a new entrance was opened. Fourteen miles of steel shelving were added, and new catalog cards were added to a complete set of printed cards from the Library of Congress."

Bishop clearly saw opportunities to share American know-how internationally and acted on them. Wedgeworth (1992) pointed out in his remarks that "Bishop was one of the first U.S. librarians to promote an international approach to the field." He then highlighted some of the major accomplishments internationally for librarians and libraries during 1991–1992, and concluded, "One of the major priorities for my tenure as IFLA President will be to develop a stronger capability for making your activities visible and understandable to the public." In his close, he cited the success that the work of major figures, including Bishop and S. R. Ranganathan, has had on creating today's opportunities and challenges.

While Wedgeworth and Bishop are the only two Americans to have become president of IFLA, hundreds of American librarians have been and are contributing to the role the United States plays in IFLA. In fact, U.S. librarianship has been involved in the international scene for more than a century. IFLA participation is only one way to this role and although this article concentrates on that route, it by no means intends to suggest that other avenues are less important, less significant, or less worthwhile. The opportunities to contribute to an improved international citizenry are many, and the more U.S. librarians who take up the challenge, the more the United States will learn from and offer to librarians in other countries.

Among the major international activities were efforts to rebuild libraries in Yokohama and Tokyo after the earthquake in 1923. In 1920, the United States supported the establishment of the American Library in Paris. In 1941, the Biblioteca Benjamin Franklin was founded in Mexico with American support. It was followed in 1942–1943 by the creation of other American library outposts in Managua, Nicaragua; Montevideo, Uruguay; Kinshasa, Zaire; Calcutta and New Delhi, India; London, England; and Madrid, Spain. The American Library Association foreign exchange program began as early as 1929. In 1993, two dozen librarians will participate in the ALA USIA Library Fellows program. Throughout the history of international book fairs, the United States has been a strong and active supporter. United States publishers have regularly displayed their stocks at these fairs, and American librarians, especially those involved in collection building, have been regular attendees to the major book fairs, most notably the fair held in Frankfurt each year.

Dedicated American librarians have been serving on IFLA committees and boards since IFLA's establishment. Several American colleagues have been recognized formally for their contributions to IFLA. Among them are Robert Vosper and Henriette Avram, both Honorary Fellows of IFLA. A recent attempt at quantifying U.S. participation in IFLA yields interesting results (*IFLA Handbook*, 1993). In 1985, IFLA's two major boards—the Executive and Professional Boards—had three Americans serving on them. In 1991, there were five Americans out of the seventeen positions. The same trend is reflected in major IFLA offices: in 1985, two U.S. librarians were officers of divisions, and in 1991, five Americans held offices. In Sections, U.S. librarians now comprise 87 of 610 potential section member positions, up from 45 positions in 1985. Of 240 Round Table positions, U.S. librarians hold 23, up from 1 position held in 1985. Since 1985, U.S. participation has nearly doubled from 63 to 120.

Why is this? A number of factors are clearly at work. First, the 1985 IFLA General Conference was held in Chicago, Illinois. Thus, many more American librarians became aware of the opportunities that IFLA service might offer when they attended that conference. Of the 1765 attendees of the 1985 conference, more than 1000 of them were from the United States. Second, the conference venues from 1986 to 1991 (Tokyo, Brighton, Sydney, Paris, Stockholm, Moscow) no doubt contributed to the increased interest. Table II shows data drawn from the *IFLA Handbook* (1993). Many American librarians must pay their own expenses to participate in IFLA so that the attractiveness of a venue and the availability of cheap airfares will influence American participation.

There is clearly an increased interest on the part of Americans in participating in the global community. In recent years, Americans have shown greater curiosity about their ancestors, especially those from foreign shores (The Genealogy Craze, 1987). This curiosity has manifested itself in the enormous popularity of Alex Haley's works as well as the interest in Ellis Island records, which were prominently featured at the anniversary of the

Table II   U.S. Participation in Recent IFLA Conferences

Year	Location	Total participants	U.S. participants	Percentage
1985	Chicago	1765	1000+	56
1986	Tokyo	1900	NA	
1987	Brighton	1351	200+	15
1988	Sydney	1650	135	8
1989	Paris	1541	215	14
1990	Stockholm	1660	280	17
1991	Moscow	1492	123	8
1992	New Delhi	1173	105	9

Statue of Liberty in 1986 (Zeidel, 1992). Recent political changes have resulted in funding agencies providing increased support for librarians to travel from foreign countries so that more foreign librarians have visited the United States. This has lead to more U.S. librarians visiting foreign countries. Indeed, the world is shrinking. Political upheavals have opened tourist routes. That librarians, as a group, are curious to visit newly opened countries is not surprising (Roman, 1989).

Finally, it is clear that technology has leveled the international professional playing field. The quality of international phone calls has improved exponentially in the past decade; it is easier with direct dialing and the cost has decreased. Telefacsimile transmission and electronic mail can virtually eliminate time differences, allowing American librarians to have more effective communication with the European headquarters of international organizations despite a 6- or 7-hour time difference. Also, English has become so widely used that Americans, whose lack of foreign language ability is known around the world, can communicate more effectively face-to-face with many more foreigners than they could just a few years ago. While all these factors are significant in increasing U.S. involvement internationally, it is important to note that there has also been an increasing interest in the U.S. library association leadership—on the part of both elected and hired leaders—which has resulted in greater awareness of IFLA among U.S. librarians.

The U.S. IFLA association members have met as a group for more than twenty years; this group is referred to as the U.S. IFLA Committee. The group consists of the executive directors of the U.S. association members of IFLA. A primary function has been to divide up the annual assessment for IFLA dues among the association members and to apportion the U.S. organizational vote allotment (35) for the IFLA Council meetings. The member organizations are the American Association of Law Libraries, the American Library Association, the Art Libraries Society of North America, the Association for Library and Information Science Education, the Association for Research Libraries, the Medical Library Association, and the Special Libraries Association. This group organizes an annual meeting, called the U.S. Caucus, of all U.S. librarians attending the IFLA conference.

Most recently, the group has begun to work to leverage U.S. participation in IFLA. This group produced a draft statement of "U.S. Objectives for Participation within IFLA," which has been reviewed and endorsed by most of the boards of the member organizations. The current ALA-endorsed version of that statement is included in its entirety in the Appendix. These objectives are meant to provide a framework for the U.S. member associations to make their own strategies to further librarianship internationally through participation in IFLA. The statement addresses five broad areas: the leadership role of librarians in support of learning, open exchange of information, international standards, internationalization of librarians and library programs, and increased involvement of members in IFLA. Objectives are listed under each area of concern. The participating organizations expect to foster greater cooperation among U.S. associations and increased coordination of activity through the application of this document. A detailed discussion of this document appears later in this article.

It is clear that U.S. librarianship has made some outstanding contributions to the international community (Wedgeworth, 1993; Morsch, 1957). Among them is the development of the MARC format to promote electronic exchange of bibliographic records. The United States is a leader in adapting technology to libraries. United States librarians have championed the need for IFLA to be responsive to librarians in developing countries. United States associations have put forth resolutions to IFLA on important topics: acid free paper, South African abridgments of intellectual freedom, and promoting the holding of IFLA conferences in the developing world. We are justly proud of these contributions.

All of these accomplishments suggest that the U.S. library community is already assuming major leadership roles internationally. To some extent, this is true. However, all the assessments of U.S. international library activity made in the past half century agree that our approach to international library issues is reactive, passive, lacking coordination and consensus, underfunded, episodic, and short-term (Doyle, 1988; Shaw, 1947; Sullivan, 1972). Just as the library profession is not yet well enough valued throughout society, the value of international activities is not widely embraced or supported from within the profession. In fact, most international accomplishments can be attributed to the vision of a single librarian, or to the presence of external funding for a particular project. While this is not reprehensible, it does speak to the fact that U.S. international library programs are not well developed. What can U.S. librarians do to change this?

IV. The International Scene Today

IFLA and other nongovernmental organizations (NGOs) are going through difficult times. The financial base on which they have relied for their program is eroding. Long-time supporters of IFLA are barely able to pay their dues let alone offer even small added support. New countries have little ability to pay dues, and librarians are often not powerful enough to influence the government at a high enough level to make IFLA membership a priority. Because of reduced dues income, UNESCO, a major supporter of IFLA activities, is itself tightening its belt. Other sources of funding are scarce and no longer reliable. At the same time, IFLA has an enormous opportunity to contribute to the advancement of learning and knowledge. Colleagues in emerging democracies need the support of IFLA to create strong libraries, foster vital programs of library education, promulgate national standards, develop strong professional associations, and promote international cooperation. Standards, preservation, document delivery, and technology are important long-standing issues for every library around the world. The environment in which librarianship has been practiced is changing rapidly. Pricing of library materials, format of library materials, and ownership and access issues are a few of the significant added pressures. IFLA needs all the volunteer support it can gather to address these newer challenges.

More than half of the world does not have basic library service. Materials are not available, and the lack of information prevents the citizens of many countries from improving their status. As countries try to establish democratic institutions, they are hampered by the lack of information about the functioning of such structures. For example, the library of the newly established Russian parliament receives no American newspapers. A library school in Africa is fortunate if it has one or two subscriptions to American library journals. American libraries worry about whether we have enough computers; in Romania, until three years ago, all typewriters were registered with the government and few libraries have typewriters.

Many countries would like to adopt national and international standards. Unfortunately, they cannot afford to buy copies of the existing standards. If they do get a copy and translate it into the local language, it is unlikely that the translation will be able to be published because there is no publishing infrastructure. Librarians in such countries often learn on the job. There is little opportunity for formal library education. Library educators, who may well know how important training is, may be unable to provide training because of lack of teaching materials and books. Finally, the image of the profession is an important one. At a recent IFLA conference, a librarian from the developing world observed that for all our hard work and accomplishments, several major national libraries in the West are not headed by professional librarians.

Specific professional issues need to be addressed: UNIMARC, preservation, electronic data flow, the cost of publications, and copyright. Approaches that seem clear in one country become much less clear in another. For example, intellectual property rights for published materials are widely recognized in the United States as is the right of libraries to lend freely. Libraries follow agreed guidelines for copying. In the developing world, where the cost of a publication, if it were able to be purchased at all, may exceed the cost of making a photocopy of it by a factor of ten or twenty, the pressure to ignore laws becomes enormous. Preservation issues are important worldwide, but acid paper may be the last concern of a librarian whose library exists in 85% humidity and 120° heat. How can U.S. librarians bridge the gap?

V. The Future

A. Exchanges

It is clear that American librarians have much to offer to foreign librarians. And we have much to learn from them (Swank, 1964). The most effective proven way to share information and experiences is through exchanges. Exchanges last from a few days to a year or more. The exchange provides a chance to understand the similarities as well as the differences in the setting where librarianship is practiced. When the participant comes from a country that is significantly different from the country being visited, the exchange format will allow the individual to get a far better understanding of daily activities. Too often, learning by lecture or reading articles is not successful because lectures and articles cannot communicate the context of a process. If the reader cannot imagine what a catalog department in a major American research library looks like, it may be impossible to understand articles describing authority control or cooperative cataloging projects. Exchanges are effective, but they have limited impact in that usually only one host library and one foreign librarian participate.

B. Twinning

Another program used to improve foreign relations is to match cities in one area of the world with cities in another. This matching, which is referred to as twinning or linkages, results not only in ceremonial recognition, but also in joint projects, student exchanges, visits by groups of businessmen, and special programs for tourism. Such programs can be an effective way for a library to learn about information issues in other parts of the world and to increase the value of the experience. Libraries may be able to piggyback onto existing twinning programs to further library cooperation. For example, librarians whose libraries are part of organizations that already have an established twin can seek a role for the libraries in the twinning relationship. Many individual American libraries have established effective linkages. Cooperation can consist of exchange of materials, hosting visiting scholars, students, and librarians, and sponsoring seminars.

Why twin? Matching libraries in one part of the world with libraries in other parts of the world can accomplish the following (John, 1991; Weber, 1992):

1. Improved exchange of information about the issues facing libraries irrespective of location. All libraries, regardless of location, share common problems—not enough money, conflicting priorities, difficulties in locating materials for the collections, problems of cataloging and preservation, the need to improve the library's physical plant, and increasing pressures to employ technology to the traditional roles of the library.

2. Improved access to information. Publications emanating from developing countries are the most difficult to identify and to locate because many of these countries do not have national bibliographies or well-developed distribution mechanisms. This leaves libraries elsewhere to rely on expensive, often inadequate, services to locate the desired materials. Indigenous libraries have local sources and are in a better position to locate materials quickly. In a close, library-to-library relationship, the libraries can agree to share the resources that each library can locate easily. For libraries with large constituencies from foreign countries, such a relationship can provide copies of badly needed items such as daily newspapers and popular reading. Likewise, libraries in developing countries have difficulty identifying and locating materials from the developed world because they may not have access to national bibliographies or well-developed distribution mechanisms. They lack negotiable currency.

3. Increased information about new techniques for library management and new technologies for library programs. There is a great need for information on how to improve the practice of librarianship using new technologies and techniques. Much of the information on how librarians practice librarianship is shared at national library conferences. Few of these conferences have published proceedings, and for those that do, obtaining them can be expensive and difficult. Librarians in developing countries do not have access to information about technology, let alone to the technology itself. Advancements in

library management techniques must be learned from journals that are received many, many months after publication.

4. Greater awareness of the issues facing libraries in developing countries. Through twinning relationships with libraries in the developing world, U.S. librarians can learn what are the important issues facing libraries in developing countries. Libraries in the developing world will learn that libraries elsewhere also face difficult and expensive problems. While the differences may readily appear, a close relationship between the libraries will allow similarities to become apparent as well.

5. International sharing of problems at the operational level. Twinning allows sharing all year long, not just for a few hours at a conference.

6. Involvement of all levels of library staff. In addition to changing the sharing of professional expertise from just an annual activity, a twinning program will match staff at all levels. The staff who check in the journals can discuss problems in that arena, catalogers can share the processing tips, and reference librarians can trade information about meeting the needs of special users.

7. Librarians gain a broader view of the profession. Participation in librarianship outside of one's home country helps to develop an international outlook. Whether the librarian has international professional contacts, is involved in twinning or other partnership programs, or participates in an exchange program, the librarian gains considerably from the exposure to different professional viewpoints.

Libraries in North America might expect to provide information in the form of unneeded duplicate publications and discards, professional literature, publicity concerning needs of the library with which it is twinned, and professional advice and counsel. Libraries might provide one copy of all publications by their parent body (e.g., a town, university, company) and a selection of local materials about a subject in which the twin is interested. Arrangements based on exchange of material goods cannot be expected to ensure equity. Given the difficulty that some librarians in developing countries have in obtaining publications put out in their locality for themselves, it may not be possible to obtain such materials for the twinned library. However, the developing country library may contribute their own expertise; exchange of children's stories (oral tradition) and everyday artifacts from the developing country to make its twin more aware of the culture.

Book donation programs are another way to further libraries. A library may well want copies of relatively current reference books (e.g., last year's reference directories) regardless of the condition, but will not be interested in twenty-year-old textbooks. The final decision regarding the shipment of titles remains with the receiving library. If materials are to be sent, the responsibility for postage costs needs to be established.

The most successful twinning programs begin with small levels of support and easily attained, clear, focused outcomes. For example, a librarian from one of the libraries may plan a personal trip to the other's country and this trip can be the basis of a first miniexchange. Shipments of books can be small and occasional. In fact, it is useful to start out small until the fastest, safest, affordable method of shipment is clear. These activities are small involvements which, in the aggregate, move libraries forward. The remainder of this article addresses the larger more coordinated approach to internationalism and support of IFLA.

C. U.S. Participation in IFLA

The U.S. objectives in IFLA (U.S. Objectives, 1992) state that they were written "to encourage discussion on active U.S. involvement and participation" in IFLA. The drafters hope that the objectives "will focus deliberations on what the U.S. objectives for participation within IFLA should be so that we can define appropriate strategies." The preamble addresses international librarianship in the following perspective: "Our collective values and commitments—access to information, intellectual freedom, public awareness— all have global implications, and likewise, what happens globally affects U.S. libraries. Furthermore, many concerns of U.S. libraries are universal—the scope of our collections, the needs of our patrons, adequate funding, technical standards, education of the profession. Historically, the library associations have been vigorous in their support of human rights and intellectual freedom. If these concerns are viewed only in a national context, they are diminished, and the fullest accomplishment of our goals becomes impossible."

The first policy objective is "To advance the leadership role of librarians throughout the world to put knowledge for the benefit of the general public and decision-makers in industry, government, and the profession and to promote education and the role of libraries in support of basic learning." Some of the strategies enumerated that U.S. librarians can undertake to support this objective include: educating the profession about the importance of its role in the creation of national information policies, lobbying for improved infrastructure in support of the provision of information services, improving the status of the library profession, promoting library education, and championing human rights and intellectual freedom. All of these are activities that our national associations currently address, albeit some are addressed more effectively than others. This leaves us the challenge to improve our national strategies while expanding them beyond our borders. Studying information policies from a global perspective is one approach that could result in a publication, a conference program, or a seminar. Library education can be enhanced by increasing opportunities for foreign librarians to study in U.S. library schools and for U.S. library educators to teach abroad. We can support the availability of current U.S. professional literature in foreign countries and collect foreign professional literature in U.S. libraries. Finally, the recent explosive growth of the Internet points out one way to consider infrastructure changes to increase information flow. Whereas access to the Internet is widely available in university settings in the United States, other sectors of the United States have much less access. We need to not only help American public libraries get reliable, inexpensive access to the network, but provide the support for foreign librarians to gain open, easy access as well.

The second policy area is the "open exchange and dissemination of information, and access to information, in all formats." Strategies suggested include removing restrictions to access, supporting the recovery of libraries affected by disasters, encouraging awareness of preservation techniques, and improving the availability of materials through improved support for interlibrary lending. This is an area in which the United States has achieved a lot; and we have shared our wealth of experience in information exchange and dissemination willingly, but not yet widely. We need to help foreign libraries more often. We need to share our technical expertise. We need to assist foreign librarians in establishing resource sharing networks.

The third area is international standards. United States librarians have been active in the development and implementation of national standards. We have also participated in the international standards process. But national pride has kept us from adopting international standards locally, and instead we too often adhere to our own national version, replete with exceptions. United States librarians must either do the work to earn the respect of international colleagues and thereby carry our version of standards into international adoption, or learn to accept that our method may not be the best one.

The final two areas address increased involvement in IFLA. Strategies to realize this include enhancing IFLA's financial base, encouraging participation in IFLA programs, increasing U.S. participation while recognizing the need to keep regional balance in IFLA committees, encouraging new members of IFLA, and supporting IFLA's Core Programmes. Indeed increased involvement in IFLA is problematic. United States librarians learn many useful leadership skills through national association activities. These skills are needed by IFLA. At the same time, IFLA's vitality comes from the diversity of views represented by its committees. A preponderance of any one area can limit the overall effectiveness. But U.S. librarians flock to only ten or so high-profile sections and round tables, potentially overburdening one section and ignoring another. United States involvement should be broadly based.

However, few institutions or organizations belong to more than one or two sections. The U.S. members should join more sections and support IFLA's program through section membership. However, aside from the traditional involvement through sections and round tables, U.S. librarians could benefit IFLA through planning regional conferences, authoring articles, and preparing draft grant proposals. All of these are skills we have to share with IFLA. Few articles in IFLA's journals are authored by American librarians. American library associations organize only an occasional regional seminar. The ALA-initiated seminar jointly sponsored by South Asian librarians preceding the IFLA conference in New Delhi is an example of how U.S. librarians can enhance the U.S. role in international librarianship.

Another opportunity to contribute to IFLA's productivity and influence is through participation in the projects and plans described in the *Medium Term Programme 1992–1997* and in the "Action plans" developed by each section. These documents lay out the road map for IFLA's major programmatic objectives in the coming five years. There will be many opportunities in the next few years to expand the focus of a national or regional program to become an international program, or to take an international program and adapt it to the national or regional level. This symbiotic relationship of IFLA and national programs is at the root of the successful international programs run by many other countries.

We are poised at a unique time in history where new countries have emerged each year. The precepts of democracy have been adopted if not implemented by many of these new countries. The librarians of the United States understand well what the roles of libraries are in a democracy. There are thousands of librarians who need to learn from us what the libraries in their countries can mean to their citizens. While U.S. librarians are not the only professionals who can articulate this, we are a country with a long tradition of free, widely accessible public libraries. We have an opportunity to influence how accessible information is in eastern Europe. Will we take up the challenge, or will we let librarians in countries where public libraries are few and far between, with short hours and limited services, be responsible for the role model adopted? Will the U.S. library community's efforts in support of national laws that ensure the right of individuals to borrow copyrighted materials freely and to make copies for certain specified noncommercial uses become an international model, or will the lending right with fees prevail? We have a chance to make a difference.

Finally, we must consider the most important aspect of our internationalism—what we can learn from foreign librarians. From these librarians, we learn not only to value the best of American librarianship, but to see where we can do better. A few obvious examples include the multilingual catalogs that many foreign libraries provide, the rich exhibit programs of the great foreign libraries, and the benefits derived from the leadership of a national library producing a national bibliography. We can be reminded by our colleagues in less industrialized areas what it means for a library to concentrate on the basics because it has no technology to distract it.

VI. Conclusion

U.S. librarians offer much to the international community, but we have much more to offer. Through greater participation in international activities, the United States can exert a leadership role. To do this, the United States must foster the participation of more American librarians in international programs and projects; international activities are for everyone and not just the old, respected members of the profession. We must also involve librarians representing a broader spectrum of library expertise. United States librarians must set clear goals and work toward them. The librarians of Scandinavia are an excellent example of what happens when a region decides that one aspect— the developing world— will receive its concerted efforts. The librarians in Scandinavia have made the developing world a priority in their professional association activities as well as in the funding programs of their governments. Libraries make a commitment in currency and in staff to pursue assisting the developing world to have better, stronger library service. They sponsor groups of experts to provide advice to developing countries, prepare and disseminate reports, and sponsor attendance of librarians at conferences. The government provides strong support to activities that foster cooperation with the developing world. The Scandinavians have a strong history of international cooperation. It was a Norwegian librarian who accompanied William Warner Bishop on his visit to the Vatican, and who would later become director of cataloging of the Vatican Library.

If we set goals and work toward them, trying not to let external opportunities change our direction, we will achieve more. We must work to gain support of the grass-roots level, to develop a consensus in the profession on the value of and approach to international activities. We must embrace the concept of a world-class citizenry and become world-class librarians promulgating resolutions, influencing policy decisions, fostering development and application of standards and protocols for interlibrary cooperation, and working toward a free and open market for the trade of information and information services. Our own heritage will lend itself to our support of the democratic approach. Through such practical programs as exchanges and twinning arrangements, and through the provision of information services accessible around the world, we will stop looking inward for all our answers and will realize the long-term goal of sharing the best American librarianship has to offer with our colleagues across the globe.

Appendix: U.S. Objectives for Participation within IFLA [2]

The following objectives were written by the U.S. Association Members of IFLA to encourage discussion on active U.S. involvement and participation in the International Federation of Library Associations and Institutions (IFLA). The semiannual meetings of the seven U.S. association members of IFLA have provided a forum for discussing topics such as IFLA elections, U.S. representation on IFLA committees, and social activities. It is hoped that this paper will focus deliberations on what the U.S. objectives for participation within IFLA should be so that we can define appropriate strategies and actions.

Any objectives established for U.S. participation and involvement in IFLA must reflect the overall objectives and strategic plans of each of the member associations. Each association participates within IFLA to advance the goals and objectives determined by its membership. Our collective values and commitments—access to information, intellectual freedom, public awareness—all have global implications, and likewise, what happens globally affects U.S. libraries.

Furthermore, many concerns of U.S. libraries are universal—the scope of our collections, the needs of our patrons, adequate fundings, technical standards, education for the profession. Historically, the library associations have been vigorous in their support of human rights and intellectual freedom. If these concerns are viewed only in a national context, they are diminished, and the fullest accomplishment of our goals becomes impossible.

The U.S. association members of IFLA have as their mission to provide leadership for developing, promoting, and improving library and information services and the profession of librarianship toward the broader goal of enhancing learning and ensuring access to information for all. However, participation in the international arena occurs not only to achieve the individual association's goals, but also because libraries are important economic assets, libraries are the carriers of civilization, and libraries enhance learning and

[2] This statement appears as approved by the ALA Council in June 1992. The statement, as approved by each of the Associations, varies slightly in its text. Furthermore, the ALA International Relations Committee is expanding the text to explain more completely ALA's intentions in terms of its participation in IFLA. Reprinted with permission from the American Library Association.

understanding. Libraries can be agencies for change based on knowledge, reason, and experience.

Policy Objectives

1. To advance the leadership of librarians throughout the world to put knowledge for the benefit of the general public and decision-makers in industry, government, and the profession and to promote education and the role of libraries in support of basic learning.

Strategies
    A. Influence the formulation, change, and dissemination of national and international information policies.
    B. Promote the means that will strengthen library, information, and telecommunications services worldwide.
    C. Enhance the knowledge, integrity, status and roles of librarians and information specialists in all disciplines of library science.
    D. Promote professional and continuing education for all library and information services personnel.
    E. Promote and support human rights and intellectual freedom everywhere.

2. To encourage the open exchange and dissemination of information, and access to information, in all formats.

Strategies
    A. Collectively address abuses and restrictions to information access and library services.
    B. Cooperate in efforts to provide resources, financial and technical assistance to libraries devastated by disasters.
    C. Encourage international awareness in and participation in preservation and conservation programs.
    D. Encourage the formation and growth of international networks and interlibrary loan agreements and procedures.

3. To foster international standards.

Strategies
    A. Participate in the development of standards relating to library and information services, including standards of professional practice.
    B. Participate in the development and use of standards for the electronic transfer of information.

    C. Participate in the development and use of standards for bibliographic control and research.

4. To encourage the involvement of librarians, information specialists, and other library personnel in international library activities and in the development of solutions to library service and information issues that cross national boundaries.

Strategies
    A. Create opportunities for exchange with colleagues in areas of expertise in order to establish an international dialogue (e.g., exchange programs,. teaching opportunities, work-study projects, and conferences).
    B. Support IFLA's Round Table for Management of Library Associations and other mechanisms by which associations can share experience and expertise.
    C. Participate in the IFLA exhibits to market internationally library association products and services.
    D. Increase awareness of IFLA products and services.

5. To increase associations' and institutions' involvement in IFLA.

Strategies
    A. Cooperate with other associations to enhance IFLA's fiscal stability.
    B. Encourage individuals to participate in IFLA conferences and programs.
    C. Work to increase U.S. participation in IFLA programs and committees while maintaining sensitivity to the international community.
    D. Encourage increased membership in IFLA.
    E. Support the IFLA Core Programmes.

References

Doyle, Robert P. (1988). *The American Library Association and International Relations: Accomplishments, Current Activities, Observations, Strategies, and Plan of Action.* Chicago American Library Association.

The genealogy craze. (1987). *World Press Review* **34**, 30–31.

IFLA Handbook (1993). Prepared for the U.S. Association Members of IFLA by Robert P. Doyle.

John, N. R. (1991). IFLA projects on twinning of libraries. *IFLA Journal* **17**, 315–325.

Library of Congress (1992). *The Vatican Library and the Library of Congress: Background, December 7, 1992.* (PR92-147; 12-07-92; ISSN #0371-3527).

Morsch, L. M. (1957). Promoting library interests throughout the world. *ALA Bulletin* **51**, 579–584.

Rhodes, F. H. T. (1991). Shaping the future: Science and technology 2030. *Physics Today* **44,** 42–49.

Roman, S. (1989). U.S.–USSR bonding. *American Libraries* **20,** 1000–1002.

Shaw, R. R. (1947). International activities of the American Library Association: A policy statement of the A.L.A. International Relations Board and a report to the board. *ALA Bulletin* **41,** 197–230.

Sullivan, P. (1972). The International Relations Program of the American Library Association. *Library Trends,* **1972,** 577–591.

Swank, R. C. (1964). As much to learn as to teach, the ALA International Relations Office. *Library Journal* **89,** 4465–4468.

U.S. Objectives for Participation in IFLA (1992). As adopted by the American Library Association Council and Executive Board.

Weber, D. C. (1992). "Sister Libraries." Poster session, IFLA Annual Conference, New Delhi, India.

Wedgeworth, R. (1992). "New Beginnings." Paper presented at the IFLA General Conference, New Delhi (88. Opening 1 E).

Wedgeworth, R. (1993). *Statement to the U.S. National Commission on Libraries and Information Science.* Denver, Colorado, January 22, 1993 (unpublished document).

Zeidel, R. F. (1992). Ellis Island and the American immigration experience. *USA Today* **121,** 24–33.

Index

Academic libraries
  collaboration across department barriers,
    21–26
  electronic journals and, 150–152
  end user bibliographic instruction, 22,
    24–25
  integration of information systems, 22,
    25–26, 100
  networked information systems, 22–24
Access to Electronic Journals in Libraries,
  167
Acquisition
  budget growth and cost control, 37–38,
    49–53
  cooperative, 53–54
  electronic journals, 160–161
ACRL, *see* Association for College and
    Research Libraries
ADONIS, 49, 64
AEDNET (Adult Education Network), 157,
  163
ALA, *see* American Library Association
ALBA/SAMKAT, 208, 215
Alexandrian Library, 83–84
  bibliographic organization of
    material, 84
American Library Association, 86
  USIA Library Fellows Program, 232
American Physical Society Task Force on
    Electronic Information, 168–169
Apple Computer, 17
ARL, *see* Association of Research Libraries
ArticleFirst, 49
Association for College and Research
    Libraries, 52
Association of Research Libraries, 23, 37,
    43, 52, 82
Associative indexing, 153

BASIS, 208, 215
Bellcore (Bell Communications Research
    Laboratory), 50
Bibliographic instruction, 24–25
BIBSYS, 130, 133
BITNET, and electronic journals, 152,
    156–157
BLEND project, 151, 154–155
Boolean operators, 114, 120, 123–124,
    128–129
British Library Research and Development,
    BLEND, 151, 154–155
BRS, 61, 65, 90
Business Information Center, Denmark,
    218–222
Business Information Network
  Denmark, 219–220
  Great Britain, 219
Business Periodicals Ondisc system,
    University of Michigan, 49

CARL, *see* Colorado Alliance of Research
    Libraries
Cataloging
  CONSER guidelines for electronic
    journals, 159, 161–162
  in Denmark, 208
  OCLC guidelines for electronic files,
    161–162
CAUSE, 23
Center for Knowledge Management, 26
Center for Research Libraries, 40, 54
CEP, *see* Consortium for Electronic
    Publishing
CEPT, *see* European Conference of Postal
    and Telecommunications
    Administration

Chalkboards, electronic, 6
Cheshire, 123, 126–127, 132
Chief information officer, 21
CitaDel, 49, 65
CNI, *see* Coalition for Network Information
Coalition for Networked Information, 17,
    23–24, 46, 150
Colaboratories, 6
Collaboration
    electronic communities, 8–9
    emerging technologies and, 3, 5–7
        electronic mail services, 6
        Internet, 6, 14, 22–23
        local area network information
            dissemination, 8
        remote interactive search systems, 7–8,
            15–17, 26
    group work technology and information
        literacy, 9
    reference teamwork, 4–5, 15
    relationship management, 5
    and university as scholarly community, 41
Collection development, 33
    acquisition budget growth and cost
        control, 37–38, 49–53
        differential pricing, 51
    balance between access and purchase,
        50–51
    comprehensive, 36
    cooperative acquisition, 53–54
    cooperative selection, 40
    electronic information and, 96–97
    information repositories and, 34
    library automation and, 38–40
    meeting institutional objectives, 34
    policy, 39–40
Collection management, *see* Collection
    development
Colorado Alliance of Research Libraries,
    49, 65
Commission on Preservation and
    Access, 92
Common Command Language, 76
Community college learning resources
    programs, 175–200
    California, 179–197
        adoption of space standards, 181–182
        Library Services Coordinator, 183–185
        output measures, 184–200, 185, 187,
            190, 191

Proposition 13 and funding, 183–184,
    196–197
development, 176–177, 179–184
evaluation guidelines and standards,
    175–176, 178–184, 193–197
input and output measures, 175–176, 182,
    184–200
usage, 192, 193–197
Learning Resources Center Guidelines
    Committee, 180
library as major component, 178–179
Community college libraries, *see* Community
    college learning resources programs
Computer Human Factors, 154
Computer-Mediated Communication system,
    211–212, 216
Computer networks, 63, 203
Computers, and libraries, 88–89
Computer-Supported Cooperative Work, 204
Computer systems, 63
    processing power, 62–63
Comserve, 156, 163
Consortium for Electronic Publishing, 43–44
CONTU (National Commission on New
    Technological Uses of Copyrighted
    Works), 44–45
Copyright, 33
    data originality and, 45
    electronic access issues and, 45
    national site license model, 46–47
    software, 45
Copyright Act of 1976, 44
Copyright Clearance Center, 47
Copyright law, 36, 44
    electronic, 44–45
Copyright Royalty Tribunal, 46
Council on Library Resources, 23, 26
CSCW, *see* Computer-Supported
    Cooperative Work
Cybrarians, 4

Danish Technical Information Service, 207
Database industry
    full-text, 42, 49
    growth of, 42
Denmark
    business information cooperation, 218–222
    computer literacy, 205, 213, 216
    DANBIB project, 215–218

Delphi study, 212–218, 220–222
DIANE (DIrect Access for Networks in
    Europe), 208–212
electronic correspondence college, 218
Electronic Document Interchange (EDI),
    220–221
electronic information, 216–218
electronic mail, 213–214, 216–217,
    220–221
information technology, 212–218
libraries, 205–222
    automation, 207–208
    cataloging, 208
    cooperation, 207
    online public access catalog, 208, 214
telecommunications networks, 205, 213
Departmental barriers, to communication
    and information access, 8
Dialog Information Services, 17, 25, 39, 90
    electronic databases, access to, 61, 65, 68
DIANE (DIrect Access for Networks in
    Europe), 208–212
    Common Command Language, 210
    Computer-Mediated Communication
        system, 211–212
Document delivery, 49
    in Denmark, 220–221
    usage, 51
DTB, see National Technological Library of
    Denmark
DTO, see Danish Technical Information
    Service

EDUCOM, 23
EIES project, 151, 153–155
EIRENE, see European Information
    Researchers Network
Electronic databases, 61–76
    access criteria
        hardware cost, 67–68
        license agreement, 68
        political sharing, 70
        remote users, 69
        resource sharing, 69
        search functionality, 68–69
        usage, 67
    access to
        bibliographic utilities, 65

commercial online vendors, 65
library consortia, 65
local mounting
    on LAN, 66
    on mainframe computer, 66
    stand-alone CD-ROM, 66
CD-ROM stored, 62–63, 66
full-text, 64
indexing and abstracting services, 63–64
online searching, 61–62
time-sharing systems, 61–62
user interfaces, 75–76
Electronic information age, 23
Electronic journals, 42–43, 50, 149–170
    acceptance, 165–166
    access to, 150, 152, 156–158, 162–164,
        168–169
    acquisition, 160–161
    advantages, 149–150
    archiving, 164–165
    author participation in, 154–157, 165–166
    bibliographic control, 158–162
    cataloging, 159, 161–162
    definition, 150–152
    distribution, 151, 156–158
    experimental publications, 156–158
    indexing and abstracting services, 152,
        162–164
    interactive computer conferences and, 154,
        167–168
    memex proposal, 152–153, 169
    published by scholarly societies, 166–167
Electronic mail services
    copyright and, 45
    in Denmark, 213–214, 216–217, 220–221
    dialogues and conferences, 6, 13
Electronic publishing, definitions, 150–153
Empowerment, individuals, 12
ERIC, 162–163
ESA-IRS, see European Space Agency's
    Information Retrieval Service
European Conference of Postal and
    Telecommunications
    Administration, 204
European Economic Community, 205
European Information Researchers Network,
    219
European Space Agency's Information
    Retrieval Service, 129
Expanded Academic Index, 64–65, 72

Facilities Guidelines for Learning Resources Center, 181
Farmington Plan (1947), 54
Faxon Research Services, 49
Faxon Xpress, 49
Feist Publications vs. Rural Telephone Service Co., 44–45

GALIN, *see* Georgia Academic Library and Information Network
GAVEL, 219
Georgia Academic Library and Information Network, 70–76
   Current Contents, 72–73
   Expanded Academic Index, 72
Global Online Information Project, 167
Gutenberg Project, 16

HEIRA, *see* Higher Education Information Resources Alliance
Higher Education Information Resources Alliance, 17, 23–24
Hypertext, 169

IFLA, *see* International Federation of Library Associations and Institutions
Indexing, associative, 153
Indexing and abstracting services
   databases, 63–64
   electronic journals, 152, 162–164
Information
   access technology, 42
   access to, 41, 48, 86, 88, 100
   availability of, 84–85
   bibliographic access versus document delivery, 38
   CD-ROM stored, 8, 19, 38–39
      databases, 62–63, 66
      full-text, 49
      reference works, 64
   as commodity, 36
   conversion to electronic format, 92–93
   electronic, 19, 33, 42
      access to, 61–77, 97
      collection and preservation, 96–97
      communication and, 41
      in Denmark, 216–218

fragmented, 2, 11
   invention of printing press, 84–85
   islands, 10–11
   networked, 2, 14, 22–24, 42, 48
   networking technology and, 24
   nonlinear access to, 42
   obtaining by interpersonal communication, 11, 76
   parallel processing of, 12
   resource sharing, 53–54
   storage, 92–93, 100
   technology-dependent, 95–96
   universal power of, 225
Information Access Corporation, 64–65, 72
Information age, 47
Information explosion
   journals and, 35, 37
   research libraries and, 98–99
Information Lens, 135
Information literacy programs, 9
   productivity and, 13
Information resources, collaborative management, 26
Information searching, 6, 51
   Boolean operators, 114, 120, 123–124, 128–129
   Common Command Language, 76
   keyword, 42
   online public access catalog, 112–132
   remote interactive search, 7–8, 15–17, 26
   search strategy, 3–4, 114–115
   user interfaces, 16, 22, 75–76
Information services
   certified quality systems, 204
   productivity and, 4, 10, 12
Information systems
   integration of, 3, 22, 25–26
   networked, 2, 16–17, 22–24
Information technologists, librarians and, 9–10, 14, 24
Information technology, 33, 39
   communication and, 41
   in Denmark, 212–218
   photographic copying systems, 88
   productivity and, 1
   research libraries and, 87–93, 90–91, 99–100
Institute for Scientific Information, 51, 74
Integrated academic information management systems, 25

Integrated Information Center, 26
Integrated Services Digital Network,
    203–205
Interlibrary loan, 52
    as essential service, 37
    expansion of services, 49, 53
    increased use, 37
    research libraries and, 98–99
    resource sharing, 53–54
    user fees, 53
International Federation of Library
        Associations and Institutions, 225–245
    conferences, 229
        U.S. participation, 233
    core programs, 228–229
    divisions, sections, and roundtables, 227
    funding, 235
    grants and awards, 230
    Internet, 240
    management structure, 228–229
    objectives, 226
    standards, 235–236, 240
    twinning, 236–239
    and UNESCO, 226
    U.S. involvement, 230–235, 239–245
Internet, 6, 14, 22–23
    commercial traffic, 204
    document delivery services, 49
    electronic journals and, 42–43, 152, 157,
        160–161
    and International Federation of Library
        Associations and Institutions, 240
    national telecommunication network, 63
    online public access catalog, 98, 112, 138
ISDN, see Integrated Services Digital
    Network
ISO 9000, 204

Journals, see also Electronic journals
    full-text online, 64
    information explosion and, 35
    just-in-time acquisition, 64
    published
        by commercial houses, 36–38
        by scholarly societies, 35–36, 43–44

KISIR, see Knowledge-based Intermediary
    System for Information Retrieval

Knowledge, and networked information, 2
    Internet, 6
Knowledge-based Intermediary System for
        Information Retrieval, 124–125, 133

Law librarians
    legal research training, 19
    librarian–lawyer collaboration, 18–21
Law libraries
    full-text online resources, 18–20
    information sharing and, 21
    internal data bases, 20
    organizational flexibility, 18, 20–21
    value of information, 18–19
Learning Resources Association of the
        California Community Colleges,
        180–182
LEXIS/NEXIS, 18–19, 49, 65, 71
LIBRA, University of Georgia, 71–76
    MEDLINE, 74
Librarians
    as consultants, 16, 23, 150
    as gatekeepers, 24, 50
    information technologists and, 9–10, 14, 24
    interactive reference technology and,
        15–16
    new technologies and, 87–88
    as virtual agents, 7, 14, 16
Libraries
    access budget, 52
    collaborative alliances, 1–3
    computers and, 88–89
    consortia, 54, 65
    electronic environment, 47–56
    electronic journals and, 170
    indicators of quality, 52
    integration of services, 55
    just-in-time philosophy, 47
    nationally networked collections, 40
    organizational structures, 55
    as repositories, 34–35
    resource ownership versus access, 33–57
    resource sharing, 53–54, 69
    user access fees, 52–53
    user-centered perspective, 47, 55
        user expectations, 48, 50
    as virtual communities, 7, 15, 57
Library automation
    collection development and, 38–40

customized information access, 24
  in Denmark, 207–208
  organizational change and, 55–56
Library Bureau, 87
Library Information Technology
  Association, 6, 23
Library of Congress, 83, 88, 92–93
  American Memory Project, 93
  Networking Advisory Committee, 45
Library Research Consultancy Project, 23
Library skill
  organizational processes and, 15
  promotion of, 4, 14–15, 17–18
  shared skills alliances, 14–15
  transferrable across departments, 12, 15
LITA, *see* Library Information Technology
  Association
LiveBoard, 6–7, 9
Local Area Networks, 63

Management information systems, 3
  and interpersonal communication, 5, 11
  lack of effectiveness, 11
Management research, teamwork, 2, 10
MARC format, 38–39, 89
  electronic journals, 159, 161–162
Massachusetts Institute of Technology, 90
  Electronic Journals Task Force, 160–161
Mead Data Central, 17
Measuring Academic Library Performance, 52
MELVYL, 22, 26, 114, 117–118
  OASIS user interface, 124, 130, 132–133
Memex proposal, 152–153, 169
Mental Workload, 153–154
Microcomputers, 62–63
Microfilm, 88, 92
Midwest Inter-Library Center, 54
Monographs, electronic, 50
Music industry, and copyright, 46–47

NAPA, *see* National Academy of Public
  Administration
NASA, 16
  Far West Regional Technology Transfer
    Center, 7
National Academy of Public Administration,
  164–165

National Endowment of the Humanities, 92
National Research and Education
    Network, 63
National Science Foundation, EIES, 151,
    153–155
National Technological Library of Denmark,
    206
NOTIS, 69

Office of Technology Assessment, 45
Online Computer Library Center, 17, 49,
    65, 89
  Duplicate Detection Project, 130
  electronic journals and, 158, 161–162
Online public access catalog, 22, 38–39
  data deficiencies in, 118, 130–131
  definition of, 111
  in Denmark, 208, 214
  experimental systems, 132–136
    BIBSYS, 130, 133
    Cheshire, 123, 126–127, 132
    Information Lens, 135
    Information Visualizer, 133
    KISIR, 124–125, 133
    OASIS, 132–133
    Okapi, 132
    Project Janus, 134
    RightPages, 135
    Rosebud, 134–135
    Scisor, 135
    third generation, 136
    Tipster, 135
    Topic, 135
    Wide Area Information Server, 134
  integrated information services, 137
  search failure, 115
  search functionality, 112–132
  search results, 117–118, 129–130
  search strategy, 114–115
    advanced features, 116–117, 120–121,
      126–129
    keyword versus subject heading,
      119–120, 131–132
    user interfaces and aids, 124–128
  usage, 112–113, 120–121
    models of users, 122–123
Open Systems Interconnection standard
    Z39.50, 16, 22, 76

Patents, software, 46
Periodical Abstracts, 64, 72
*Personnel and Materials Guidelines for California
    Learning Resources Programs*, 181
Photocopy machine, 89
Preservation of Historical Records, 96
Productivity
    collaborative technological alliances, 24
    information alliances, 14
    information literacy training, 13
    information services, 4, 10, 12
    information technology, 1
Project Intrex, 90, 92
Project Janus, 134

Reader's Guide, 46
Reengineering
    business organizations, 11–12
    with library skill, 17–18
    reorganization for flexibility, 12
Reference
    building shared understandings, 3
    emphasis on human interaction, 9
    expertise in electronic workplace, 9
    fragmented information, 2
    improves productivity, 2
    as information alliance, 2–5
    interviewing, 2–3
        by nonlibrary professionals, 18
    legal, 18–21
    in networked communities, 6
    as part of teamwork, 15
    real-time, 7, 22
    as strategic resource, 4
    virtual relationships, 14
Remote interactive search system, 7–8,
    15–17, 26
Research libraries
    from acquisition to access, 86–87
    CD-ROM products, 89–90
    collection and preservation of materials,
        83, 92–95
    comprehensiveness and access, 85–87
    conversion to electronic format, 92–93
    definition, 80, 82–83
    in Denmark, 206
    electronic information and, 105–106
    funding, 99, 102
    future, 79–82, 94–107

history, 79, 83–91
    impact of technology on, 80–81, 87–93
    information explosion and, 98–99
    information technology and, 90–91,
        99–100
    interlibrary loan and, 98–99
    needs of scholars, 82, 95, 104
    online services, 89–90
    origins of, 84–85
    photographic copying systems, 88
    resistance to change, 102–103
    resources, allocation, 91, 104
    resource sharing and, 86
    size of, 83
    specialized collections, 105
Research Libraries Group, 49, 54, 65
    Conoco study, 54
Resource sharing, 53–54
    electronic databases, 69
    research libraries, 86
RightPages, 135
Rosebud, 134–135
Royal Society of London, 35

SABR (Selected Articles By Request), 51
SAFIR, 124
Scisor (System for Conceptual Information
    Summarization, Organization and
    Retrieval), 135
Serials, *see* Journals
*Shared Minds: The New Technologies of
    Collaboration*, 6, 41
Simultaneous remote search system, 7
Software
    copyright, 45
    patents, 46
Special libraries, 82–83
Special Libraries Association, 1
State University of New York, Oswego,
    55–56
Superbook, 50

Teams
    autonomous, 13
    electronic mail services and, 13
    virtual overlay groups, 13–14
*Technical Processing in Large Research
    Libraries*, 89

Teltech, 7–8, 13, 15, 16
Tipster, 135
Topic, 135
Total quality management
    absence of library collaborators, 11
    teamwork, 12
TULIP (The University Licensing
    Program), 43

UMLibText system, University of
    Michigan, 49
UnCover, 65
UnCover2, 49
United States IFLA committee, 233–234
University Microfilms, 64, 72
University of Georgia, 61, 70–76
    electronic databases, 70–76

Virginia Polytechnic Institute and State
    University, and electronic journals,
    159–160
Virtual communities, and interactive
    reference, 15
Virtual libraries, staff, 101

Westlaw, 18–19
Wide Area Information Server, 23, 76, 134

Xerox Corporation, 6

Z39.50, see Open Systems Interconnection
    standard Z39.50

ISBN 0-12-024617-1

9 780120 246175

90040